Secure UNIX

Secure UNIX

Samuel Samalin

McGraw-Hill
New York San Francisco Washington, D.C. Auckland Bogotá
Caracas Lisbon London Madrid Mexico City Milan
Montreal New Delhi San Juan Singapore
Sydney Tokyo Toronto

McGraw-Hill

A Division of The ***McGraw-Hill*** *Companies*

Library of Congress Cataloging-in-Publication Data applied for

ISBN 0-07-054554-5

1 2 3 4 5 6 7 8 9 0 DOC/DOC 9 0 0 9 8 7 6

The production supervisor for this book was Pat Caruso. This book was set in ITC Century Light. It was composed by McGraw-Hill's Desktop Publishing Unit.

Printed and bound by R. R. Donnelley.

To Mom

Contents

Preface

Presently, organizations are under attack by computer fraud, theft, and abuse, most often from trusted inside people. Computerization has brought great benefits, including enormous new profits; however, without keeping track of what's really going on and making sure it's authorized, the profit can quickly turn into overwhelming liability. Above all, that means protecting yourselves from the inside person of power, privileges, and access who's bent on ripping you off. Also, global industrial espionage is rife, and it's time for widespread application of confidentiality enhanced technology.

Secure UNIX is a different breed of UNIX system software that not only has corrected all of the flaws that allowed previous security problems to happen but also has added powerful new security features that make Secure UNIX the most secure general purpose computers there are. *Security is one of the major strengths of UNIX.*

Secure UNIX is based on information systems security guidelines, such as the Orange Book, Federal Criteria, CMW, and ITSEC. The newest, the Federal Criteria, is comprehensive, commercially oriented, and practical. These guidelines are the U.S. government's and its foreign counterparts' response to the need to plug the security holes in systems such as UNIX, and they are the leading industry-wide security standards.

Manufacturers followed by building a new breed of Secure UNIX machines based on the guidelines: SUN's Trusted Solaris, CMNs of the major workstation vendors, Secureware's CMW+, etc. There also are certification programs whereby manufacturers could submit their products for evaluation as to whether their products meet the guidelines. It's a highpoint of government-industry cooperation and the vitality of UNIX.

The standards that this book follows as a base are the most secure levels of the Federal Criteria but also includes CMW-type features, such as networking and X Window. I have sought to derive the basic functionality described in those guidelines and envision how this functionality will be used to solve the problem of organizational security. To do that, I also lay out the basic concepts and the organizational policies needed to use Secure UNIX so that you can have an assurance of security.

I use the term *Secure UNIX* to refer to machines that are based on the previous guidelines and *pre-Secure* to refer to those that aren't. Along with the conceptual and functional tour of Secure UNIX, I give a vision of an advanced security architecture using Secure UNIX with every available security technology and required organizational method, called the Trusted Information Base (or TIB).

The basic information herein is required background for those who will buy, manage, administer, or use Secure UNIX systems and for anyone who is concerned with organizational information security. This book is about UNIX environments, although mainframe or PC connectivity is covered from the UNIX perspective.

Secure UNIX is a new system software version of UNIX that is certified to be free from bugs and security holes and that has many new features that automatically provide, or can be used to provide, information system security. It runs on ordinary hardware (i.e., anything that runs UNIX, including micro PCs, SPARC workstations, mini or super computers, etc.).

Secure UNIX provides the security features found on mainframes and moves them into distributed environments. Mainframe experts will find the methods used here familiar.

When Secure UNIX is used properly, you are "assured" that it is providing security (you can "trust" it to be secure) up to a certain level described in the guidelines. The vendor-supplied machines and system software are the new Secure UNIX. Only when you use them properly by adhering to the principles and policies described herein can they be said to be trusted systems in trusted environments. Trusted systems have achieved a level of assurance that they manage information securely.

A good machine provides security tools, but security is achieved only if you thoughtfully use these tools. Security has to be an integral part of not just your computers but also your organization. I'll start with a computer with a core that is built on security, like Secure UNIX, and show you how to develop a Secure UNIX Organization.

Secure UNIX is Business UNIX. It doesn't allow everyone to be able to do what they want. To avoid the horrendous security problems of that life style, you need to take a realistic, self-protective look at your users and give them only as much power as they need to do their jobs.

Secure UNIX goes far beyond keeping out hackers and viruses. It's a new era of information confidentiality, system reliability, and information protection.

Like the Wild West, the early days of UNIX were free. However, let's not forget that those days also were anarchy where bad guys were free to come and shoot up the town. Now it's time to send for the lawman.

Better yet, you should call the social worker. Bad security habits are real bad habits. The first step is to acknowledge the problem. Come join the SDA

(Sitting Ducks Anonymous). Here are the clear worthwhile steps that you can take.

Many people have stayed on mainframes where security has been assured. I'm not advocating mainframes; but UNIX has to achieve the same level of security as on mainframes. The good news, and the subject of this book, is that Secure UNIX has done just that.

Secure UNIX provides even more security than mainframes in areas such as confidentiality protections. This is the age of global industrial espionage, and it's time for widespread application of confidentiality enhanced technology.

The functionality that has arisen on Secure UNIX that is comparable to mainframes and more includes:

- Auditing of transactions and activities such as login, access to critical data, use of privilege, etc.
- Replacing the superuser with administrative privileges and administrative roles that balance and reconcile each others actions.
- Providing strong authentication and precise identification. All user activity is tied to and audited by a unique user identifier, including administrators and remote users.
- Guaranteeing the authenticity of the system infrastructure, including servers and logins, through the use of trusted paths and public-key certification.
- Establishing a system of user credentials whereby users present their level of access to system resources.
- Tying access rights to authentication strength and other access-level factors.

I'd like to summarize for advanced readers where this book is headed and what it will advocate as far as enterprise security.

The combination of strong authentication, MAC (mandatory access control) labels, and ACLs (access control lists) are the backbone of advanced security architectures that I will set forth using Secure UNIX. (MAC labels are covered in detail in chapter 5, and ACLs are discussed in chapter 2.)

Strong authentication using public key technology, etc. will be embedded into login, network login, and smart cards. Public-key authentication also will be applied to the system infrastructure itself so that processes and servers will be authenticated.

Major applications, such as databases, will have very precisely controlled ACL. The ACLs of their files will be guarded against unauthorized changes.

ACLs will be combined with strong authentication and MAC labels to provide precise access for major applications, such as databases. The user identifier and an indication of the authentication strength reflected in the label will be conveyed to the database, which will use these factors to make a check of its ACL to determine precise user access.

Sam Samalin
Secure Computers Inc.
1317 Third Avenue
Suite 100
New York, New York 10021
(212) 484-9728

Acknowledgments

Thanks to Sun Microsystems, RSA, and Haystack Laboratories for illustrations used in the book. Special thanks to Marc Brown, IBM, SecureWare, Dockmaster, Posix, NCSC, and John Baker, editorial miracle worker.

Chapter

1

Goals, Threats, and Policies

From the perspective of a UNIX user, users own their files. In reality, however, people work for organizations, and it's ultimately the organization that really owns the files. As such, it is the organization that should have control over what can be done with users' files. Through laws and policies, the organization imposes its needs on users of its information. Users or their impostors—by mistake, disgruntlement, larceny, or mischief—can't ignore that any more.

There is good news and bad news. The bad news is that security takes user and management training, administrator staffing, work on a constant basis, as well as a permanent commitment of resources. However, the good news is that your systems will be *more* open, networkable, easily administered and operated, and really under control for the first time. I hope to dispel the notion that security means interfering restrictions, clogging red tape, and unacceptable overhead.

However, to ensure that users act securely, organizations must propagate policies. It helps if we keep in mind how vulnerable we are as organizations and as a society to computer abuse. It's time to do something about it.

Policies are mandatory rules put in place by an organization to meet its needs. They can be as strict as each organization requires. They are communicated to users, whose adherence to them is monitored.

I am going to describe four security policies (precise access, confirmed authorization, confirmed integrity, and precise usage), which are general guidelines that you can use to make specific policies for your organization. For each policy, I'll describe the goals that it achieves and the threats that it fends off.

Before I introduce the policies, however, I first will summarize the goals of security and the threats to meeting the goals. See the next chapters for more detailed information on the new Secure UNIX features that are used to implement these policies.

Goals

There are three goals of computer security: information confidentiality (the prevention of user information disclosure or theft), system integrity (the prevention of system corruption), and system availability (the prevention of attacks on systems that would deny their services to users).

The three goals—confidentiality, integrity, and availability—are overlapping in that they are somewhat mutually dependent, but they are conceptually useful in this book especially because I assign fairly distinct types of security methods to practice to achieve each of them.

Separate methods of achieving each goal give a higher degree of "double checking" or "failsafe" system redundancy in the security architecture that is described. De-emphasizing their overlapping effects makes the objectives clearer without creating omission.

Integrity is ensured by a distinct set of administrator-run programs and procedures. The other goals are ensured by protections and features that form the basis of the overall user environments and are provided "automatically" by the system. Confidentiality is provided by the security mechanisms of the system itself rather than by administrator-run programs, as integrity is.

As for the mutual dependency, for example: A lapse in system integrity that results in the corruption of a system file can affect both confidentiality and availability. Further, because confidentiality is ensured in part by access control, a breach of confidentiality might indicate that an integrity violation also occurred.

Confidentiality

The *confidentiality goal* is defined as the assurance of authorized use of an organization's information, including the need to keep unauthorized people from being able to access it, and the prevention of its theft or disclosure either by eye contact, printout, storage media, or network by unauthorized *or authorized* users.

The foremost fact that you must recognize is that the major threat to your organization's information security is from *within* the organization. The people who are doing the big computer crimes are the insiders—the people whom organizations gave their trust to and gave access, privileges, responsibilities, and power to. Countering the inside threat is emphasized in this book.

So confidentiality doesn't apply to outsiders only. However, organizations also routinely require levels of confidentiality among their members on a need-to-know basis. The capacity of a computer system to meet group and individual users' requirements for it is essential.

The goal of an advanced system is to transparently provide strong and flexible levels of confidentiality in a way that's easy to administer and creates minimal overhead. We want to be able to work side-by-side and share terminals, file systems, and network services with the people in the next corral or in the branch offices. Yet we as individuals and as groups within organizations might not need or want to share our information or parts of it with others.

It is essential that, if you don't need to share your information, *your organization must ensure that it can't be shared.* It turns out that this is your first and dearest organizational security policy. When access rights are kept allocated on strict as-needed basis, you reap essential benefits:

- If an impersonator or embezzler is on the system, they can steal only as much as they have access to, which is as much as you allocated them.
- You are better able to keep track of and respond to the access that normally is taking place when you have precisely decided what access you are permitting.

Organizations ensure that the unshared isn't shared in two ways: by making it a policy that users shouldn't share even if they can and checking that the users don't and also by preventing them from sharing using new Secure UNIX access control features that define what activity is allowed.

In either case, I view the problem of keeping the "not needed to be shared" unsharable as one of what I call *access precision.* That is, if you don't need access, you don't get it.

In the first case, users have the power to change the access control on their files by using the familiar UNIX access control features (or some new but similar ones). However, organizations make it policy that they only allow those individuals that need access to have it. You also monitor the system to make sure that the policy is being carried out.

In the second case, you construct your user environments to implement the maintenance of your confidentiality requirements by automatic system screening of all user activity and disallowing unauthorized actions.

Confidentiality is maintained by a related chain of function: the Identification, Authentication, Access Control, and Accountability chain. All of the elements must be fully present if the chain is to be of any strength.

Secure UNIX has fully implemented all links of the chain. All users on the system have a unique user identifier name, they are strongly authenticated to be who their identifiers claim that they are, their access control is done according to their identifiers, and they are held accountable by it.

If any one of those elements is deficient, organizations won't be able to control or know what activity is taking place on their systems. First, system access is controlled by authenticating user identifiers. Then, users' access to resources is controlled by the identifier and is accounted for via the auditing system or application logging.

The new precision is always to the user identity. If the users' identities are uncertain, their access is kept restricted.

Building walls to provide confidentiality doesn't work for computers any more than it does for national defense in the age of the smart missile. You need protections that are built into your systems and are transparent powers of normal functioning.

Therefore, the trend towards specialized, dedicated security front ends, firewall machines, and hardware is only part of the answer. They're difficult to build and maintain and won't be effective unless they're based on Secure UNIX.

Confidentiality protection must not be gained at the expense of the openness and connectivity that made UNIX desirable. With Secure UNIX, those openness traits are much stronger than ever.

It is like a house with many rooms with secrets in them. If the only protection is a locked front door, then only people who can know all the rooms' secrets can be allowed in. Therefore, it is less open. However, if each room in the house is locked, users will know only the secrets of the rooms that they have the keys to. Therefore, the house is more open. That way, information can be shared in unlocked rooms but still be protected in locked rooms.

The goal of Secure UNIX confidentiality is to ensure that the organization's requirements regarding confidentiality are met by both outsiders and insiders.

These requirements must be given by the organization as policies and be imposed on the users of its information systems. Users then must be constrained by the information systems in conjunction with the organizational security policies to meet the confidentiality requirements.

Organizations then must have the monitoring and feedback systems in place to know if confidentiality has been lost.

Secure UNIX provides confidentiality by means of access control to determine which users can access files. The familiar UNIX mechanisms have been made more precise, and entirely new ones were added that are checked automatically by the system and can't be overruled by a user.

Secure UNIX also logs information access so that organizations can detect when confidentiality is lost.

Given these new tools, what confidentiality goals can you reasonably expect from Secure UNIX, and how are they attained? The improved access control offers more precision, including the ability to specify precisely which users and groups are authorized to use information. Because the main method of assuring confidentiality is access control, confidentiality can be made more precise.

This new precision makes a critical difference for UNIX because it means the difference between impractical control and precise access control. So, with it, you can flexibly combine groups of users, omitting individual users from groups in some cases and including them in others. Object access can be specified for individuals rather than groups.

The greater power to specify individual users' access rights to objects is exported system- and network-wide in a Trusted Information Base (TIB). Combined with strong authentication for users, it becomes a trustable, distributed security architecture.

Confidentiality is the need to keep information private and safe from disclosure or theft. A major advantage of UNIX is its inclusion of many users that share resources (i.e., its diverse connectivity). On pre-Secure UNIX, however, this meant a threat to confidentiality.

Given the far higher degree of access precision provided by Secure UNIX, confidentiality is increased even while openness is increased. It makes it easier to share information and still maintain the desired confidentiality. Under UNIX, this is essential to the goal, because Secure UNIX is UNIX: multiuser, networked, and sharing resources.

For confidentiality protection, regular UNIX access control isn't enough, even with added precision. What is needed is a way to control what users can do with information *after* they've been allowed access to it. This means something that users can't get around, something that's specified by the *organization*, rather than by the file owner.

This is needed for confidentiality because it protects the organization against the inside person in whom it misplaced its trust. It is built into the system and is checked automatically for all user activity by the system. It should operate system-wide, covering all devices, services, networks, and facilities. It should work by a fixed, unalterable property of all information and system objects so that all system activity can be checked against the property to see if it is allowed.

This new confidentiality protection includes typical access control, where a user is checked for access permission before he or she can open a file, but it also goes far beyond that. Once the user has access to the file, it controls what the user can do with the file and performs access checks on all system activity attempted with the file. For example, users might be able to access a file, but then they might not be able to transmit the file to the e-mail system if the organization forbids it.

This would stop the misuse of information to which the organization has granted authorized access to a trusted user. For example, RUA (Robot User "A"—an "it") is a big deal maker at the SHAFTCO Corp. RUA wants to shaft SHAFTCO back because it was shafted by SHAFTCO on its bonus. It tries to send the company's customer list to SHAFTCO's competitor.

Because the list was deemed by SHAFTCO to be highly confidential, it was marked as such by the company, even though RUA created, is the file owner of, and has access to it. When RUA attempts to send it out the network, the system automatically stops it by comparing the fixed properties of the file and the network. The system determines that the file isn't allowed on that network. When RUA attempts to change the access on the file so that RUB (Robot User "B") at the competitor can login and take it, it again is stopped by the system because RUA can't change the confidentiality property of the customer list and RUB isn't allowed to have access to it.

The type of confidentiality provided in this example system is provided in Secure UNIX. Secure UNIX provides:

- Access properties for all information that the organization, and not the file owner, defines
- Access properties throughout the system
- Automatic and nondefeatable checking of all attempted access between different users or between users and the system.

The advantage is that the organization can determine what users can do with information and who they can give it to. The control includes what, where, when, and how users, data, and the system interact.

The goal of confidentiality requires more than allowing file owners to precisely specify who can access their files. That still gives users, rather than the organization, the power to decide the fate of their files. If file owners can change the files' permissions and give it to anyone that they want, they can transmit, copy, and move it any where they want. This is not very confidential.

The problem is that, if the organization gives its trust to people and gives them access to or ownership of its files, it then is vulnerable if those people are bad or even have accidents. The other problem is that, if a trusted user is being impersonated, the impersonator gets to do what it wants with everything that the user had access to.

Somehow the organization has to get more control over what its users can do. The goal is to have the system automatically check whether user activity is authorized by the organization. The organization has to be able to specify to the system what its relative confidentiality requirements are for each file. The system should know how to translate those requirements into system-wide, automatic orders about whether users have authorization to do anything with the files.

Given that functioning, SHAFTCO might have given RUA authorized, legitimate access to a file, but that doesn't mean RUA can do anything it wants to it. SHAFTCO might allow RUA to read and write the file but not to let RUA let RUB have access to it or not let RUA copy the file to a tape, send it out a network, etc.

Secure UNIX implements that type of confidentiality functionality in the following way: It allows an organization to assign a confidentiality rating, called a *label*, that the organization (rather than the file owner) permanently places on all files. No matter which users have access to the file, they can't change its label. (See chapter 4 for more information about labels.)

I've discussed how confidentiality requires greater precision and also greater organizational control over activity, but there is a final part of the goal. Organizations also must know when the file is accessed and by whom. With this information, organizations must be ready to respond when confidentiality is threatened.

One of the benefits of access precision is that you are better able to monitor what is going on. If what's going on is clarified—such as identifying a particular user accessing a file rather than just the group that the user is a member of—and if what is going on is easily verified because you've specifically decided in advance whether the user can access the file, you can spot problems more easily. Compare that to a file that has imprecise access control and lets every one in a huge group in, many of whom don't really need to have access.

To protect confidentiality, you have to know if it has been lost so that the problem can be contained and remedies can be taken.

By being precise and eliminating the unnecessary access, you narrow the activity to what is needed.

A secure system has to have a logging mechanism of some kind to capture and record all system activity for analysis to detect problems and respond to them. Secure UNIX systems use a logging system called *audit*, which can generate large amounts of data. By keeping the recorded activity to a minimum by precision, you make the job of collecting and analyzing these records possible and more efficient.

There has to be a way to monitor all essential system activity, such as which users log on, the files that are accessed, or the commands that are issued. This information then has to be collected and analyzed for undesirable occurrences, and if any are found, responses have to be made.

If a client list is being accessed and copied by RUA, shouldn't you know it? If you are wondering why it is doing that, you can ask it. If you are sure it shouldn't be doing that, you can disable its user account. You can change the file's access permissions and correct your problems.

However, if you don't know what's going on, it might be too long before you discover that you even have a problem. By then, it might be too late to do anything about it. Besides, there's the nip-it-in-the-bud aspect: Problems might start small and get worse unless stopped early. If you know confidentiality has been violated, you also can engage in damage control, rather than get broadsided.

Integrity

If you depend on your systems to provide security protections such as access control for you, you have to be assured that the systems are functioning properly. That includes having guarantees from your system providers that there aren't any security bugs in the system to begin with, setting up the system properly for your use of it, and continual assurances that nothing has gone bad while you are using it.

As for the assurance that the provided system is free from bugs, there is a huge U.S. government/industry program to do system testing and make official U.S. certifications that systems are bug-free and tested up to security levels specified in standards. You therefore can have a high degree of certainty that the systems that you buy will be secure.

Next, you have to install and configure according to the provided instructions, programs, and administrator interfaces. These also are certified to be correct. Also, you should install only shrinkwrapped and version-controlled products.

Having done that and come up securely, the trick is stay that way. You do that through what I call *administrative security*. Administrators run programs that always are verifying that system files haven't been altered, that system data files are internally consistent, etc.

Finally, systems must be in place that assure that any upgrades or backup restorations are verified.

Integrity-checking administrative software is available based on versions developed at Universities, such as Tripwire, COPS, and Crack.

Integrity checking ensures that no attacks have been made on the system-provided security mechanisms. They sometimes are redundant to the security provided by other systems. For example, the audit mechanism should detect most of the errors that would be detected by administrative security programs such as a modification of system space.

As is often the case in systems engineering, judicious redundancy is a prime method for system reliability.

Availability

Availability refers to machine readiness. It is a separate goal because there exists a class of computer abuse known as a *denial of service attack* that's purpose is to bring down or cut off a system from its users.

The goal is to prevent users from having the capability to inhibit the system's ability to provide multiuser service. If any one user can tie up excessive system resources, it would tend to threaten availability, either by accident, carelessness, or on purpose.

Administrative security programs, as well as the audit system, analyze the system for these types of problems.

To prevent resource-availability problems from becoming system-availability issues, a resource quota must be in place, and resources statistics must be a part of the administrative security monitoring programs.

Other availability issues involve access to the system such as communication lines.

Threats to the Goals

The three goals are the antithesis of the many threats that information systems face. For each goal, I'll discuss some threats that pre-Secure UNIX was vulnerable to and how Secure UNIX eliminates them.

Confidentiality

The threats to confidentiality are that an unauthorized user will gain access to the system or access to resources, that users might attain roles and privileges that they aren't authorized to, and that users won't be accountable for all of their security activity.

There are many flavors of unauthorized users. The most notorious is the hacker who guesses a password and impersonates an authorized user. That scenario implies the outside, network stranger.

Another unauthorized user might be the person inside the organization who might have spied on others hands while they typed in their passwords.

Either type might have used a *Trojan horse*, which is a program that has a secret purpose. It might steal information, such as a password, or masquerade as the compromised user to cover misdeeds, which might be done by hijacking the user's access rights and privileges.

Trojan horses can either impersonate other users' programs or well-known system programs, such as servers, that provide services, such as networking. A server spoofer would be a massive security threat because many or all users would be compromised. Of course, I'll discuss how to prevent this.

In the past (pre-Secure UNIX), the UNIX networking infrastructure has had a security vulnerability. Due to bugs in networking services, poorly automated administrative procedures, etc., there were gaps in the normal login mechanisms, resulting in unauthorized system access.

As bad as unauthorized system access is, it is important to note that the damage is limited to what can be done or seen once it occurs. An unauthorized privileged administrator access is worse than an unprivileged one. The less each user has access to, the less the threat.

The threat that an unauthorized user will gain access to resources is the most direct threat to confidentiality. Unfortunately, this happens too often as a result of the poor use of the basic defenses provided by UNIX: user-specified access control. Access to directories, files, devices, etc., must be carefully controlled.

On pre-Secure UNIX, the control mechanism was cumbersome, and even careful use was inadequate. Now, users can use the new controls to be more precise and to limit access to authorized users. Secure versions of major applications, such as database management systems, have integrated the new access-control powers of Secure UNIX to the system Identification, Authentication, Access Control, and Accountability chain.

Compounding the pre-Secure problems was a lack of fundamental Identification and Authentication. Not enough emphasis was put on making sure that every user that could gain system access was uniquely and positively identified.

Identification is the assignment of a unique user name to each user. Authentication is proving that a user is identified by that name, usually by entering a password. Once identified, the user is subject to access control by that name.

Pre-Secure Identification and Authentication had many problems, including sloppy password systems. Also, there were accepted practices that allowed root or network logins without unique identifications.

Secure UNIX ensures that all users undergo full Identification and Authentication.

Unauthorized access also took place when authorized users gave access to unauthorized users. New Secure UNIX access controls (called labels) that are specified by the organization prevent this.

Another threat to confidentiality by unauthorized access on pre-Secure systems was that, if an abused password was root or if the abuser managed to take advantage of the bugs that were too common in pre-Secure UNIX within root-owned programs and get a root shell, they had access to everyone's information on the system.

The threat that users might attain roles and privileges that they aren't authorized to have was caused by poor Identification and Authentication on administrative accounts, as well as by Trojan horses. Many programs ran with root privileges, and bugs allowed them to be exploited by intruders.

Secure UNIX has eliminated root access by the use of privileges.

Integrity

The threats to integrity are that the system might be generated or installed insecurely, it might be insecurely used, or it might be insecure due to defects or weaknesses in its design. Unauthorized root access could result in corruption of system file space and the implantation of Trojan horses.

Availability

The threats to system availability are excessive use of disk and CPU resources, improper system crash recovery, an inability to monitor and restrict system resource usage, and a lack of a backup, restore, start-up, and maintenance mode.

Policies

To meet the goals of information security, I'll describe the basic organizational policies that serve as guidelines for every organization. Think of the policies stated here as guidelines or concepts that your organization uses to implement concrete policies for its unique needs.

Specific organizational policies would proceed from these abstract policies to extensive details of all aspects of the system, resources, and data, including authorizations for all users, user and administrative responsibilities, rules of usage, data handling, etc.

There are four policies that can counter the threats when implemented by your organization. They are precise access, confirmed authorization, precise usage, and confirmed integrity. Each policy can meet one or more goals.

I'll describe the Secure UNIX policies and each of the goals and threats that it affects. Many of the same protections that maintain information confidentiality, such as precise access control, also maintain its own integrity and that of the system, too. It often is the case that, if unauthorized users can't spy on your information, they can't vandalize it or the system integrity or availability either.

Secure UNIX has a new and powerful armada of features. I'll briefly mention them here but leave their indepth description to later, more technical chapters.

The principles and policies determine how you use the new tools of Secure UNIX. Carrying them out requires working together.

Precise access policy

The precise access policy states that access to all system resources is granted to users precisely according to their authorized requirements of them. Resource access includes all resources including:

- System—Granting users access onto systems
- Information—Granting users access to files
- Privilege—Granting administrative privilege to users
- Service—Granting use of system services such as communications or printers

The goals that the precise access policy meets are confidentiality and, in some cases, integrity and availability. It protects confidentiality by being an essential part of maintaining an assurance that access to resources is being done by authorized users. It also acts as protection against unintentional or overly costly losses in the case where a problem has occurred, such as a stolen password. If users have no more than the access that they need, the losses in that case will be minimized. This latter effect is an example of what I call an *access firewall*, and there are others that I'll describe later.

Pre-Secure UNIX was not precise enough, which was another major flaw. It couldn't specify multiple groups, or users in those groups, for granting or denying access. The result was the use of mass groups that were formed with little discrimination regarding who really needed to be in or out. Without detection, any user that managed to steal a password could examine the victim's files and probably a lot more.

There has to be more of an access firewall in place. It's not enough to think that password or other system-entry authentication is the sum total of a system's defenses because, once they are in, the system is wide open to users, authorized or not.

The precise access policy protects integrity and availability by keeping access to system files restricted to authorized administrators. Corruption of system files could lead to integrity, availability, or confidentiality problems.

The precise access policy is that all access to system resources is given by the organization only to those who require it. This is a wide ranging principle that extends to many features of Secure UNIX access control: file access control, labeling, administrative privilege, and access to communications, databases, and peripherals such as terminals or tape.

To keep access precise, you make policies on what access users can allow to their files. Beyond that policy, you use labeling to restrict the access that users allow to their files.

We divide the powers of the pre-Secure superuser into Secure UNIX administrative privileges. Multiple users get these powers in a way that provides a system of checks and balances. They get no more than the powers that they need to do their jobs.

Access to the system itself also is kept precise. Secure UNIX has improved the security of password authentication by enforcing password effectiveness. It allows the organization to specify when users can login, which terminals they can use, and whether they can login by networking services. It has new anti-Trojan horse protection called *trusted path.*

Precise access management ensures that access is given out strictly to those that need it. There are practices that you can use to encourage this. You can set forth a policy of it to users, and you can check that its being followed.

It is essential to your need to know what's going on. If you know who uses the system and what they do with it, you can tell when something is wrong. There's a crucial corollary to that: Unnecessary access of any kind is a security hole often sought out by trespassers.

To avoid unnecessary access, you have to make a habit of not leaving unneeded access around. You need to have a policy that makes the importance of that clear. The policy is meant for all users (general or administrative), and auditors have the responsibility to ensure that users conform to it.

These Secure system measures will maintain confidentiality on data, even in the case where a user password is stolen because you keep the access precise. Impostors no longer can count on ineffective access control to give them unnecessarily wide access.

However, confidentiality concern doesn't have to refer only to anonymous "thems" out there. On UNIX, file systems are shared. An organization might have many departments and staff. As a matter of course, people might not want their coworkers, coworker's secretaries, or those above, below, or beside them to be privilege to their files.

Labeling can be used to provide improved confidentiality to user information in that respect, too.

Another threat to the goal of confidentiality is that users might attain privileges that they aren't authorized to.

The use of privilege is assigned by the concepts of the precise access policy. It is assigned in precise amounts only to those who require it. As you shall see, it also is assigned similarly to programs as well. This deters the threat that unauthorized users or programs will attain privileges and hurt information confidentiality.

Confirmed authorization policy

The confirmed authorization policy is that all resource access affecting security is confirmed to be authorized after it occurs. This uses Secure UNIX audit, an activity logger that logs events such as resource accesses after they occur. Confirmed authorization states that organizations must process the records of activity in order to verify that the user had the authorization of the organization.

In order to effectively carry that out, it requires that the organization has a precise access policy in force. Otherwise the amount of activity records would be excessive, and you'd have no way to confirm what activity was authorized if you weren't managing who was authorized to do it.

The goals that the confirmed authorization policy meets are confidentiality and, in some cases, integrity and availability. It confirms authorization of the use of administrative privilege and access to an organization's most important data, and it detects abusive use of the system. It therefore would allow the correction of unauthorized activity or attempted misdeeds that would cause threats to the goals.

The confirmed authorization policy also fights unauthorized system access.

Much of the activity related to the use of these features also is logged by the system audit facility. Logins are audited, and the record includes related data such as the terminal or network. The record is used to confirm the authorization of system access, which fights unauthorized access and the threat to confidentiality.

The confirmed authorization policy states that all activity that takes place on the system must be confirmed authorized by the organization. To confirm authorization, all activity must be accountable to a specific user and known to be legitimate. If it's not legitimate, action can be taken. All users—including users who are administrative, remote, database, or application users—are identified and accountable for all system use whether it's of system services, applications, or user information.

Security administrators and users coordinate and reconcile activities so that normalcy is maintained and suspicious activity is conspicuous.

You must always observe system activity and be ready to respond to trouble. You can observe activity using a Secure UNIX continuous activity logger called Secure Audit. You can observe the most significant loggings and be ready to act if there's trouble.

The confirmed authorization policy also counters the threat of unauthorized file access. Important file access is audited, and unauthorized access would be detected and stopped. All system file access and especially important user file access are audited.

The confirmed authorization policy prevents misuse of privilege because all use of privilege is audited and because secure organizations confirm that its use is authorized. Any attempt to alter the system data files that list which users are assigned privileges would be detected and corrected.

The final threat to confidentiality is that security-relevant actions might not be accountable to an individual user. Knowing who is accessing your files is essential to preserving confidentiality.

Two major advantages of UNIX are its multitasking and its emphasis on the sharing of resources. On pre-Secure UNIX, that meant a threat to confidentiality because identification and authentication was sometimes weak. There also was an absence of a facility to record activity after it occurred.

Secure UNIX has ended that problem with a vengeance. First, it incurs stronger authentication in most contexts. In any case, (as I will explain later) authentication strength is considered via labels when access decisions are made. Second, the identities of the users are linked to all their activity—such as file access, commands, or privilege use—with the system auditing facility.

Those basic functions—identification, authentication, and auditing—are the two major aspects of the confirmed authorization policy. The threat to confidentiality from a lack of accountability is eliminated by authenticating that users are legitimately assuming their identities, then auditing their security relevant activities by it.

Enhanced accountability is crucial to making Secure UNIX secure. Users, including even remote users or administrators, have unique user identifiers that they must use when they login. Once they are authenticated and are in a login session with a shell, all their activity is associated with the identifier, including the commands that they issue, the file access that they do, the system services that they request, etc.

When users are proven to be who they say they are, the authentication procedures result in all of the security attributes of the users, their labels, role authorizations, system-entry information, as well as the pre-Secure attributes, such as their groups, being associated with the identifier.

Access decisions then are mediated by the system based on the attributes of the users and the files, such as users' identifiers, role membership, labels, owner of the file, whether it requires privilege to access, and its label.

Confirmed integrity policy

The confirmed integrity policy is that the authenticity, integrity, and internal consistency of the operating system be maintained and verified during all phases of system implementation, operation, and maintenance.

Confirmed integrity indirectly affects all threats as it is basic to the function of the system protections.

It meets the integrity goal and indirectly confidentiality and availability. It assures integrity by verifying that the system is delivered, installed, configured, and maintained in its correct and authorized state. It detects system corruption either by tampering, administrative error, or system failure. Secure environments have confirmed integrity procedures for all system phases and run programs that comb the system for inconsistencies.

The confirmed integrity policy protects the unpinning of the system's ability to defend itself from any threat: the system software and files, which include the authentication mechanism, the password data files, and the basic security functionality of the system.

It can detect unauthorized file access and can be accomplished by programs that check files for inconsistencies.

The goal of integrity refers to the need to prevent system abusers or their programs from invading in order to vandalize information, corrupt or delete files, defeat backup systems, or introduce bugs into programs that would cause data loss or corrupt file systems.

The threats to system integrity are improper system distribution, installation, usage, recovery, start, file system check, hardware test, defective systems, and systems that have bypassable access controls.

You counter the threat with the confirmed integrity policy. You ensure that, at every stage of the systems life-cycle, the consistency of the system software and configuration is checked against a certified description of the correct makeup. You constantly run programs that maintain descriptions and characteristics of the system software that they verify consistency with.

To counter the threat to system integrity from insecure system installation, systems must be delivered "shrinkwrapped" from the manufacturer with all their security features turned on by default.

Installation procedure should turn on the minimum security features by default. The documentation should emphasize how security defaults are installed.

Manufacturers should include checksums or cryptographic checksums so that users can ensure that the delivered software is authentic. Administrative tools should automatically verify that the software is delivered and installed without defect or adulteration.

The threat that security features will be improperly used is countered by documentation for all administrators and security management interfaces with ease of use.

Security management interfaces allow the configuring and displaying of system security attributes and configuration parameters, such as passwords, user accounts, system-entry requirements, labeling, ACLs, privileges, auditing, and resource quotas for the system and users.

The threat to system integrity from the system software or files being corruptible or circumvented is countered by assurances from the manufacturer that their products have been fully tested for weaknesses.

Another threat to system integrity is that there might be a way that users can get around the security of the system. This is countered by access control (which is the access separation between system and user resources, including memory, processes, files, and devices), assurances from the system developers (including specifications), and tests that prove the product conforms to them.

Other threats to system integrity are prevented by system start and recovery methods, automatic copy and verifying of the audit records, hardware tests, and checks of file system and storage integrity.

Precise usage policy

The precise usage policy states that, for system resources that affect availability, the resources that users are authorized to use are to be restricted by a quantity limit. Resources—such as processes, file space, and login terminals—can affect system availability if these resources are tied up.

This policy counters threats to the goal of system availability. Combating that threat requires monitoring disk and CPU usage, the capacity to disable accounts, quotas on users resource consumption (such as processes and disk), a process-kill capability, backup systems, and maintenance-mode capability.

The precise usage policy prescribes limits on resource usage that might affect system availability such as disk usage.

Summary

If you've gone as far as is reasonably possible towards persistently realizing your security policies by fully utilizing the security tools offered by Secure UNIX, you achieve the safest computing environment that you can practically have: a Trusted Information Base, TIB.

Chapter 2

System Access Control

To improve system access control, Secure UNIX:

- Has a new password authentication system.
- Supports other authentication systems (such as smart cards and public-key cryptography).
- Has a new security mechanism to combat Trojan horses (called the trusted path).
- Has time and method-of-entry restrictions on system use (called system-entry requirements).
- Has automatic inactive interactive session locks.
- Has more precise authentication on distributed operations and servers.
- Relates system access to an access control mechanism (called labels).
- Has the ability to verify users' system access after the fact with an audit system logger.

Passwords and other authentication methods are used effectively to ensure that authentication keeps out intruders and allow in only those who are authorized. Authentication is enhanced on Secure UNIX networking so that all users of networking services, such as remote mounts, are explicitly authenticated as opposed to allowing calls from virtually anonymous servers.

System-entry requirements keep system access limited to appropriate factors, such as time of day, networked or local, or terminal location. To prevent unauthorized users from hijacking interactive sessions, terminals are locked at the command of the user or if the session is inactive. Logins are recorded and confirmed for authorization by the system auditor, and improper ones can be terminated.

Identification and Authentication

Secure UNIX session management has many new features that strengthens authentication and more precisely manages user accounts and sessions, which brings important new safeguards to user sessions. The new built-in features include: password-formatted checks, periodic password changing, anti-Trojan horse systems, login scheduling, etc.

The prerequisite of sessions is that user accounts be established for users. Account creation is how users are authorized to use the system. Accounts' data files keep vital data about users such as their user identifier and home directory. Users that have accounts on systems can get login sessions on them by authenticating themselves.

It is essential that the identity of users be verified before they are allowed access to a system. The identity is the means of determining the users' access rights and also is the basis by which their activity is monitored and recorded.

The basic credential of a computer user's identify is a *user name*, which is a unique name. It is presented by the user during login, and the system then must authenticate the user's identity by checking the user's password, which is paired with the identifier. (See Figure 2.1.)

Authentication, proving the identity of users to allow their access to a system or its resources, is a key step in the establishment of a login session, which is an authorized period of use of a system by a user. Authentication is the single most critical security act. It typically is done during login by a password check.

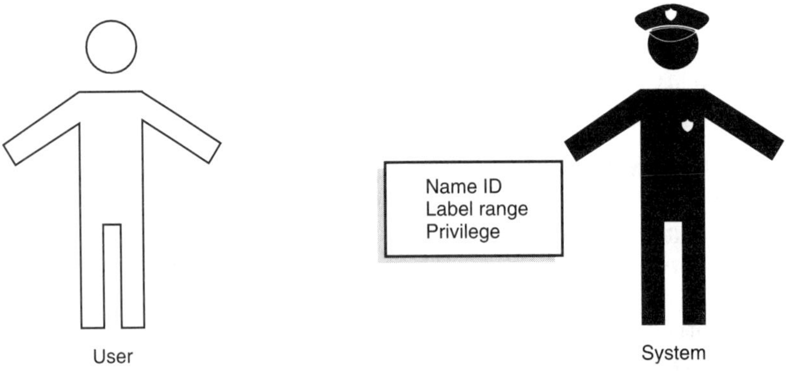

Figure 2.1 The user shell execs programs and commands with a user identifier.

By it, users not only obtain access to the system, but also assume their access permissions and privileges on it. If the procedure can't verify that the users are who they claim, then the wrong people get access to other users' information, or possibly more.

Once authenticated, users assume their user identities to the system. User identity is a major security aspect. The system access control to all system resources—such as files, privileged command use, or system services, such as networking—is done on the basis of it.

The identifier is not only the basis of access control, but all user activity is logged by user identifier in the Secure UNIX auditing system. Thus, identification and authentication are key steps in accountability and in carrying out the precise access and confirmed authorization policies.

Passwords

Secure UNIX has beefed up its authentication system, which is the system access gatekeeper. It disallows null passwords, does minimum complexity checks on proposed passwords, maintains lists of prohibited passwords, has successive login failure limits, requires periodic password changes, and disallows password reuse but allows the same password to be used by multiple users. It also can generate pronounceable (easy to remember) passwords, giving users a couple of choices. After a minimum time, users can change their passwords, which aren't displayed.

Identifiers are kept in the security database files. Secure systems have removed the encrypted password from the user-readable password file. The password is kept in a version of the password file that is available only to administrative users. That way, UNIX can use the password file as in pre-Secure UNIX, except for login that looks at the secure version of the password file with the passwords in it. (See Figure 2.2.)

However, the password file isn't changed. It still contains all of the user information, such as their names, in a database file.

Always have a password on all user accounts. The password is checked by administrative security programs. The system will provide the user's initial password. Users then can change their password when they first login, but they will have to wait a while between further changes.

Secure UNIX will make certain that all passwords are of the highest effectiveness. It offers two basic strategies for creating passwords: let the system create it for you or select one that you like or create one yourself that conforms to good format rules and the system will check it before it accepts it.

Passwords are never echoed during the login procedures, or in any other circumstances, nor are text passwords kept on the system in any instance.

System-created passwords are certain to have good format and be free from guessable parts but can be somewhat harder to remember. User-created

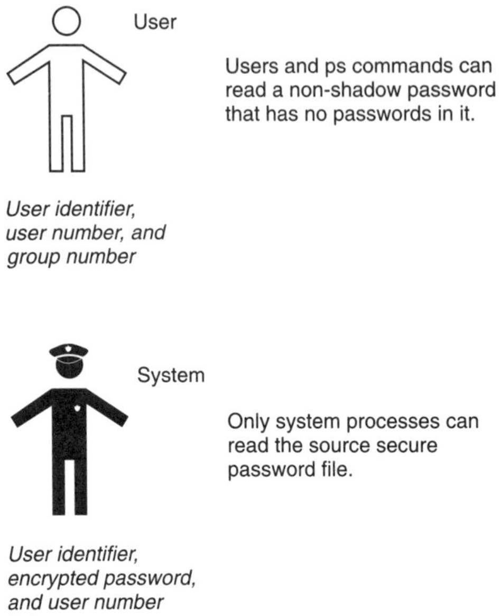

Figure 2.2 Shadow password.

passwords can be easier to remember but can be more guessable in that they, for example, contain personal information.

I'll be honest about passwords. Their effectiveness is a function of human psychology and not something that can be controlled tightly. Users are in private when they receive or make their passwords. The fact is that some people will jot them down somewhere and refer to them or will put guessable parts into their passwords that might pass the system format checks, both of which are unsafe.

User-made passwords are more rememberable, which is a key criteria. Secure systems offer the option of allowing the users to create their own passwords and also to ensure that they meet password-guessability rules. If their password is rejected, users get a review of these rules and can have a few tries.

Secure systems will generate passwords that don't suffer from the pitfalls of user created ones: they don't include any English words, names, or personal information about the user. They are harder to remember, though.

Ideally, passwords are impossible to guess, are kept memorized (not written down), and are never divulged. On a per-user basis, come as close to that as possible.

It's all a vast improvement over accounts with guessable user-made passwords or with no password. It eliminates a threat that ranked number one as the major security flaw of pre-Secure UNIX.

Although you ultimately must rely on users making the effort, what you can do is educate, motivate, cajole, and, above all, make it easy for users to have good password habits. You can stress its importance. You can train users in what constitutes good format and in techniques to improve their ability to remember.

Some users like inventing good passwords and remember them easily. They should have that option. Others might find it hard to invent passwords or to remember them. They should be given training on how to do it; however, if that doesn't help, they should use the system-generated passwords. Finally, there'll be users who don't care all that much and will just write their passwords down anywhere. These people are why you need all of the other protections of Secure UNIX.

Here's a good strategy. The best passwords can't be guessed and are rememberable. Users should be allowed to make up their own passwords according to the rules that I'll be laying out because such passwords are more rememberable. Those users that can remember system-supplied passwords and prefer them can use them. Those that have trouble remembering passwords in any case should be given training in creating passwords or in memory-building methods and be allowed to make their own passwords. If that doesn't help, they should use the system generated ones with a lockbox.

The users that don't treat their passwords safely probably will not admit to having trouble remembering their passwords (because they probably wrote them down).

Ideal passwords are unguessable, kept secret, and remembered by the users so that the passwords are not written anywhere. The general rule is that a password is not composed of guessable English words or personal information such as your name. Numbers and letters both must be used for a minimum of eight characters. You can throw in punctuation and miscellaneous symbolic characters, too. Good formatting and some common sense rules makes them unguessable, but keeping them secret might take some extra effort for some users.

Good password-creation strategies

I'll discuss some strategies for making good passwords. Many people remember words, but words are guessable. So start with words and encode or otherwise misspell them in a quirky way that you can recall. Leave out the vowels and throw in an odd character instead of a space:

- `chclt1mlk` (chocolate milk)
- `nclr#fmly` (nuclear family)

Use the first letters of a phrase, with uppercase and punctuation:

- `Ic,Is,Ic` (I came, I saw, I conquered)
- `Nt!Ioad` (No thanks! I'm on a diet)

Mutated words can be made by leaving out vowels, using phonetic spelling, substituting sound-alike consonants, using symbolic word parts, abbreviations, etc. Invent your own pidgin English of characters, numbers, symbols, mutated word spellings, and syllables and make up encoded sentences. Try to find sounds that have familiar meanings especially to you. Here are some examples:

8 = ate	m = am
r = are	+ = and
t = tea	& = and
2 = too	0 for o
y = why	1 for l
u = you	8 for a

Here are a couple example passwords:

- `i82nght` (I ate tonight)
- `rug0ing` (are you going)

Use slang, colloquialisms, or anything that you are familiar with, like, or will remember. The more tricks that you use on the password the better.

Make up your own kooky codes to use—like an order switch or substitution:

the = teh

the = da

this = dis

don = don't

Here are a couple example passwords:

- `dis+dawg` (this dog)
- `don(kno` (don't know)

However, the password must be remembered and not written down, so it must be easy to remember.

Practice techniques and a personal, unique, made-up "line alphabet" of baby talk, phonetic syllables, etc., then practice using them to make phrases that you'll remember easily. If you must write something down, try to write a hint of your phrase, rather than the phrase itself.

Practice until you have your own secret "password speak" language that you can construct phrases out of.

Password policy should stress avoidance of selecting guessable passwords, such as using a user or organization name. Some systems have a prohibited password list of well-known organization, user words, or information. Consistency-checking programs run password-guessing programs.

Systems automatically generate passwords. They should be random in that they show no cyclical pattern and aren't derivable from each other. They give the user a choice of a few. If the passwords are generated from syllables rather than characters, the syllables shouldn't be assumed secret.

Changing a password

Passwords are stored only in a one-way encrypted form that is stored in an administrative password file. Secure systems keep encrypted passwords in a separate, protected password file, which sometimes is called a *shadow password file*, rather than in the pre-Secure password file. Passwords are changeable by the user. The password-changing procedures include re-entry of the old password. The same password can't be reused for about six months.

If a user chooses a password that has already been chosen, it is allowed. What is not allowed is a user-selectable option for two users to share the same password.

Passwords must be changed on a regular basis, but not too frequently. After a minimum time, about two months (one month for administrators), a period begins in which the password must be changed. This period lasts about a month. If users don't do the change by the end of the time limit, their accounts are disabled and administrators must intervene.

Secure systems warn users for about a week that their password is expiring. Some systems allow a few more logins (with a warning) after expiration.

Even today, good passwords remain the most practical, inexpensive, and reliable authentication technique. No high-tech gizmo will ever supersede passwords. They are by far the most important security feature that any organization can have, and that will always be true.

Secure UNIX never keeps the text of the password on the system, either in the password file or in the system activity (audit) records. It also keeps the encrypted passwords in a private version of the password file, which is inaccessible to users except the system administrators. /etc/password no longer has passwords in it.

On pre-Secure systems, if abusers could login in any manner, they had access to the password file that contained encrypted passwords. With that, it was simple to run a program, on that system or by copying it over a network, that would guess passwords. (Guessing programs guess passwords from dictionaries, encrypt them, and compare them to the password file.)

Secure UNIX avoids this threat by keeping encrypted passwords in a file that is available only to privileged administrators.

Other authentication techniques

The other authentication techniques all have their pros and cons. I'll review some of those, but these other techniques should be used in addition to good passwords, not as substitute.

Challenge-and-response devices manipulate a system-supplied value (challenge) that is sent to the user during login and derive a response value that authenticates the owner of the device. The obvious problem is that the device can be "borrowed." Other devices such as smart cards are similarly used, but they also might require a secret number or password to be included.

One-time passwords are a variation of challenge-and-response. A random value or timestamp is sent to users. The users' login program or smart card mathematically "combines" their password and returns it. The system then can verify that users knew their password by doing the same combination on the random value. They give the advantage to ordinary passwords in that the password isn't transmitted.

The danger of these techniques is that they might lull you into forgetting the most important defense that you have: good passwords.

Biometrics involves using a physical characteristic of users to authenticate them. Voice, fingerprint, retina pattern, and video image can conceivably be used. These systems might be foolable by a reproduction of the characteristic, and they are expensive. It is better to invest in password education.

In the arena of network authentication, Secure distributed network authentication is now feasible with the use of digital signatures (see chapter 7). A digital signature uses a public-key cryptography method to provide authentication very practically and reliably. Look for the worldwide availability of it soon on the world's major public networks.

Digital signatures are computer generated, so they are used among networked hosts and users and among server processes that authenticate during system start.

Additional authentication procedures also can be used to protect system resources—such as files, applications, terminals, or services—after login. To ensure that these mechanisms conform to the same rigor that system passwords do, they should utilize the same system authentication used at login. Also, the proliferation of passwords is cumbersome and, thus, dangerous. If resource authentication, such as a password on a database, isn't integrated with the system authentication, don't use it. Only the system is "fit" to authenticate users.

There are some events that occur on a system that require extra identification assurances beyond what the computer's login procedures and passwords can provide. When it comes to identifying a person, there is one system that will never have a mechanical peer, and that is another person. We can know each other by looking at each other, hearing each other's voice on the phone (called at each other's number), seeing each other on a video monitor (or the long-promised picture phone), etc.

User Accounts

In order to be authorized to have a login session on a system, users first must have user accounts created for them. Only system administrators can add, remove, or change user accounts. Accounts contain records of users' passwords, their home directories, and other security information, which is all kept by the users' identifiers.

On Secure UNIX, user accounts contain additional security information. Users have label lists (see chapter 4) that determine what labels their login sessions can be at.

The label list also can determine how users can enter the system, because system devices also are labeled and users must have labels that allow them to use the devices for a login session. For example, dial-up terminals might have a special label that only certain users have.

Users' activity is logged by the system audit system (see chapter 6). Users' accounts include the information on what activity will be audited for that user. Some Secure systems also can include information in the users' accounts about what privileges users can invoke.

Session-management information, called *system-entry requirements*, also can be included on the user accounts on a Secure system. These requirements specify schedules for login for the user, as well as allowed modes of login such as networked or dial-up login.

The system keeps the users' security attributes, such as their label list, by the user identifier in the account. Within the login session, all user shells and processes spun off the shell are tagged with the identifier and by some of the attributes. All actions of the user have accountability by the identifier and can be clearly traced in the audit records by it.

Administrative accounts—such as adm, root, and sys—no longer have logins. However, administrators have privilege to access files owned by them.

All user accounts must have passwords. The system requires the user to select a password when they first login. They must change it regularly.

Accounts that aren't used for a time should be locked so that logins are disabled. User identifiers should be deleted or disabled if they aren't used for a few weeks. Disabling can be re-enabled, possibly automatically.

(Automatic re-enabling might be used in the case of a temporary user absence.) The status of user identifiers is displayable with the system administrator interface.

User absences should be reported to the system administrators. This requires care by the system administrators to work with users and personnel departments in other instances, such as terminations.

Verification that accounts are active takes place for all users as part of routine checking. You can automatically detect accounts that are idle and lock them. Secure UNIX can perform this task in the consistency-checking programs run by the system administrator. Idle interactive sessions would be detected there too, and the terminal could be locked, requiring another user login.

A "no-trespass" warning is displayed prior to login. It's something to at least deter the honest and to make it clear to any others that they will be caught and punished if they try to break in.

Attempts to break into systems by trial-and-error password guessing are inhibited by secure systems, but they can't be disallowed because it would effect system availability by locking up the terminal. However, if such an attempt is made, the system administrator will know it by the system auditing. They can investigate by going to the terminal, shutting it down, hanging up if its over a network, etc.

A login attempt will terminate if a user has about three failed login attempts. Login on that terminal then will be delayed for about a minute. This stops attempts to break-in by repeated trial-and-error. The delay can be increased slightly after subsequent cases. Using too long of a delay might allow an attacker to deliberately impair logins.

After failing to login, the user isn't barred from logging in, but the identifier is audited, and the administrator should be contacted because he or she will want to investigate. Like too long of a delay, barring the user would create another way to attack by disabling logins.

Once a login attempt is begun, the entire procedure must be gone through before any messages are displayed. This prevents any clues about the identifier or password from being given to a hacker. In the case of a login failure, the user isn't told why he or she failed. (See Figure 2.3.)

System-Entry Requirements

Beyond authentication, there are Secure system-entry requirements. They are schedules for login and limits on terminal and networking services use such as dial-up. On Secure systems, systems-entry restrictions can be implemented within the login, audit analysis, or consistency programs.

Users are permitted to login only at scheduled times. If they login at times other than that, their sessions can be terminated and their accounts locked.

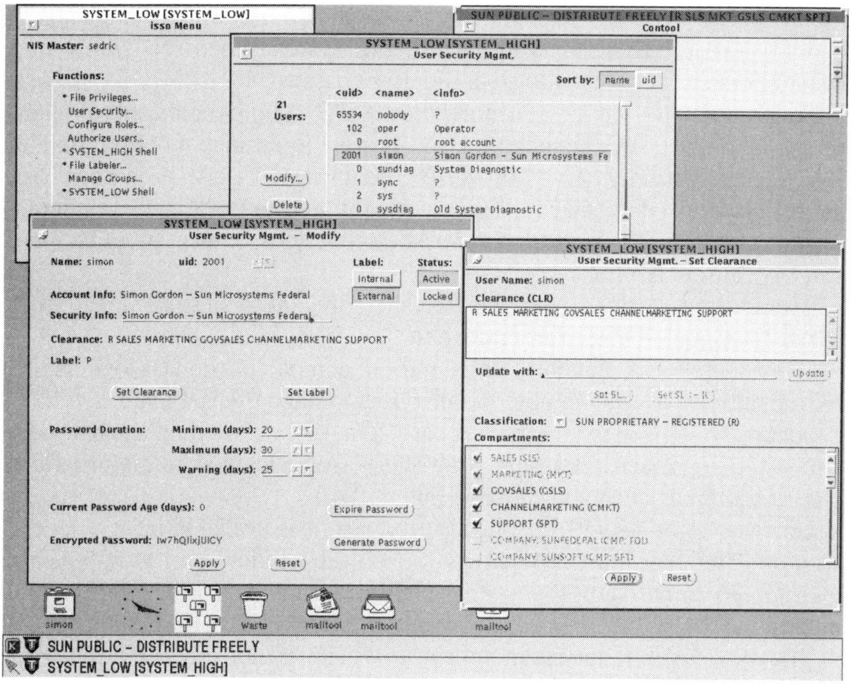

Figure 2.3 The security administrator sets up a user account.

Login can be restricted for particular users according to time of day, the day, or the date. This is very significant because it might be the times when there isn't an auditor scheduled to cover the activity. Also, it would make a login by the user during a restricted period very conspicuous.

Login authorizations also can be discriminated by local and remote network or dial-up. Secure systems can do this by keeping account information that specifies the login authorizations. The login program would access this information, checking that the user's label list includes the device labels of, for example, dial-up devices; otherwise, login would fail. The consistency program also could kill an unauthorized session just after it occurs.

Similarly, login authorization controls which terminals local users can login on. The terminals are allocated according to their level of physical security, such as restricting administrator login to the system console or high-labeled users to physically protected terminals monitored by a video camera.

This use of the labeling facility of Secure UNIX to implement system-entry requirements on login mode—such as terminal location, dial-up, or networking service—is another major reason to have labeling on your Secure system.

Secure UNIX provides an important new facility called the trusted path. It ensures that communications are direct and private between the user and the system. It is used before starting the login and password-changing procedure to ensure that they are the authentic system processes. That way, a Trojan horse can't be used to steal the users password.

Trojan horse protection goes further in a TIB. All processes, either client or server process, are checked for and protected against spoofing. Public-key authentication is used to verify the infrastructural processes. Resources, such as database servers, are guaranteed to be genuine to clients. Hosts that attempt to perform networked operations, such as mounts, must similarly authenticate.

Users have security credentials that they present to all system resources to verify or qualify their authentication.

Once users login, the date, time, and entry mode of the last login is displayed, along with the number of failed logins since the last login.

Secure systems have the trusted path, a major new weapon against password-stealing attacks. It assures that there are no login-spoofing programs left on terminals during login. (See Figure 2.4.)

On some systems with graphical terminals, it is available from a special window. The user must request login from the window, and they thus are guaranteed to be using the system login program for authentication, and not using a fake. It's the only available way to login.

The systems administrator interface, which grants privileges to users, also must be started from within the special trusted path window.

On character-based terminals, trusted path is available via a special character sequence. Administrators should make it quite publicly known and encourage its use. Although it should be the policy that trusted path be used by all users at login time and that is verifiable by the auditor, there's no way to guarantee that all users will remember to do it when they login.

Because the terminal driver will receive the character sequence before any application program, it is possible to guarantee that the users are accessing the authentic trusted path program by entering the sequence. The trusted path handling code can be part of the login sequence or the administrative interface.

Trusted path ensures that all other processes that receive input from the terminal are killed off before the login begins.

Login sessions are limited to one per identifier. This restriction might be implemented by the login using values from the account or implemented after login by the audit analysis or consistency programs.

Secure login restricts some users to login read-only.

Before and upon logins, secure systems display an advisory warning against unauthorized access, notifying that it's illegal. The message can be customizable, but it's important to be clear, because its a legal requirement in the case of prosecuting attempted break-ins and a deterrent.

There is a reauthentication procedure for terminals. This procedure is known as *keyboard lock* and requires a user to repeat the login procedure

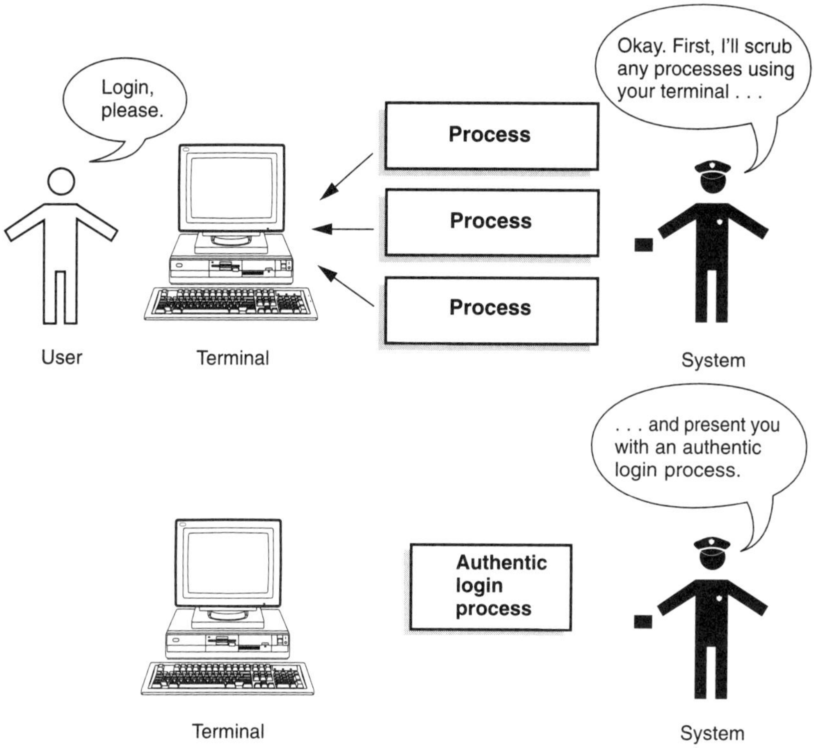

Figure 2.4 The trusted path.

when their terminal is idle for a while. Keyboard lock should be enforced on all terminals to prevent an unattended login session from being hijacked. Users can invoke keyboard lock to keep others out when they must leave their terminals. Keyboard lock can be implemented by X Window or by consistency-checking programs.

Upon login, the date, time, and location of the last login, an unsuccessful login attempt count, and the time until password expiration is displayed.

The SU command, wherein a user effectively changes their identifier to a privileged user during a login session, requires that the user be an administrator, or it is disallowed altogether. Setuid to unprivileged users also can be disallowed by default.

Default, anonymous, or guest logins are gone. They violate the accountability principle.

A major aspect of Secure UNIX is that all users are authenticated individually. There were many instances in pre-Secure environments when they weren't, such as superuser logins or networking services and remote mounts.

Another new Secure UNIX system access mechanism is login by user label. Labels are assigned to users and terminals, and the labels of each must be related in a certain way to allow access. This is an important new feature that has wide-ranging effects. I'll be exploring it fully in chapter 4.

Secure UNIX's audit system is used as a post authentication verification of the users login and system-entry authorization.

Policy can define how you use the system access control tools and also can guide your organizational coordination (e.g., mandating the communication between the personnel department and system administrators on unused user accounts upon absences or termination).

It does no good to have well-formatted passwords if the system has a built-in pressure for users to divulge them. Pre-Secure UNIX had unwieldy access control, which often led to users revealing their passwords as a means of sharing resources.

Chapter

3

Discretionary Access Control

First, I'll explain *discretionary*. It means that file owners can change the access permissions of their files in any way that they want (i.e., "at their discretion"). UNIX users are quite familiar with function via the access modes and `chmod`.

In the Secure UNIX context, the term *discretionary access control* is used to distinguish it from another form of access control, *mandatory access control*, the access characteristics of which aren't determinable by the owner (see chapter 4).

Generally, in the typical UNIX environment, there are a few categories of files: system space that is owned and accessed only by the system, files that are important to the organization and might be owned by application administrators or users (such as database management files), and files that are owned by and are private to users.

The organization cannot stop file owners from making their file access permissions any way that they want. In some cases, that isn't a problem, as it might not matter what users do with all of their files. Still, it is advisable to make it a matter of organizational security policy for users not to share their files unless there's a reason, and you can be aware if they do so by using system auditing. However, discretionary access control can be performed by the file owner. Owners can share their files, so it is crucial who owns files.

The kinds of discretionary access control that you really want to keep track of are changes to system space and organizationally important shared resources, such as a database or business information.

For the system, system file space is all owned by a small group of administrative users, and the permissions rarely change. That makes it relatively simple to make access precise and to monitor changes to it. A few owners and groups suffice (with setuid used on pre-Secure systems for user access to executables).

Where things have gotten complicated is the last category: shared organizationally important files, such as database files. That is where users and files proliferate and also where they are in a state of flux.

Files of this type can be owned by application administrators, who manage the group memberships and permissions for the files that they own.

The pre-Secure manner of coping with access control to these important files was either the setuid mechanism or the use of groups: Create a group for the database and give the group access to it. However, it was not really possible to deal with large numbers of large groups on a precise basis. What was needed was a way to add and subtract users from groups and to combine groups using a flexible and friendly interface.

Pre-Secure UNIX used an access control that was based on permission bits (or mode) that could be changed by the file's owner or by a superuser-privileged administrator. They specified read, write, or execute access for the file's owner, group, or all others. Other mode bits—the setuid, setgid, and sticky bit—were used on some files and directories (see Figure 3.1).

Pre-Secure UNIX didn't allow access to be specified for groups other than that of the file's group or to disallow it to particular users within groups. These serious limitations caused a tendency to lump users into huge, unwieldy groups and eroded access precision.

If you could not combine lists of small groups and exclude users in those groups, your alternative was to create large new groups for each file. What often happened was that mass groups were reused. These groups included a lot of users that you really didn't want to have access. That defies the precise access policy, which states that access only be given to users that require it.

ACL Formats and Interface

Pre-Secure UNIX had no way to impose the access requirements of the organization on users. Users that had access to files were pretty much free to do what they wanted with them. Secure UNIX has improved the access-mode mechanism. From now on, you can use a flexible mechanism to give access only to those who really need it.

Secure UNIX has extended the pre-Secure UNIX access permission bits with Access Control Lists (ACLs). ACLs extend, but also include, the pre-Secure method. Rather than refer to only the owning user and group, ACLs consist of a list of groups and users. Each entry has its own access mode for read, write, and execute. ACLs not only can specifically allow access to any of these, but also can specifically disallow access to any of them.

Access Type	Owner	Group	Other
Permission	*rwx*	*rwx*	*rwx*
Mode	*s*	*s*	*t*
	S	*S*	*T*

s = Setuid owner, setgid group, and execute
S = Setuid owner, setgid group, and not execute
t = Sticky and execute
T = Sticky only

Figure 3.1 Pre-Secure access control.

You use this new access control feature for precise access, whereby access is allotted only to those who need it. It can be used to combine small, precise groups. The access can be further specified to exclude particular users in those groups or to include individual users besides the owner.

ACLs are initialized whenever files are created. Files are created with `creat`, `open with the create argument`, `mkdir`, `mkfifo`, `copy`, etc. ACLs sometimes can be initialized by a command or routine argument. Otherwise, umask and default directory ACLs determine ACL initialization. Create modes can't be less restrictive than the default. (See Figure 3.2.)

ACLs are for files and directories. Directories have ACL defaults that refer to the files or directories created in them. Defaults are somewhat superseded by the umask mechanism (the Unix default permissions), but umask only affects a part of what the ACL is composed of: the "regular" owner/group/other modes. Default ACLs can be used to refer to the additional groups and users on the ACL list.

Files and directories created in directories with the default ACLs receive the default ACL, too.

The system accepts standard UNIX permission modes and command interface, but users also can take advantage of the new ACL functionality to keep access precise. ACLs are a practical and user-friendly way for users to specify precisely who they want to have access to their files.

Unnecessarily having ACL that can allow files to be copied by all others would be nonprecise. If there's an explicit need to share files, use explicit ACL.

By the precise access policy, access by ACL should be maintained on an as-needed basis. When files are created, ACL should be initialized on a very restricted default basis. That means that access should be owner only.

The default directories' ACL controls the ACL of files created in them. The UNIX umask also works on all files that the user creates. Directory defaults and the umask are combined to produce the most restrictive result. In logic terminology, they're ANDed.

Once the default is to a restrictive ACL, changes to the ACL can be covered by an organizational policy. Permission to make ACL changes can be allocated by the organization to users that need to have it, such as file owners that

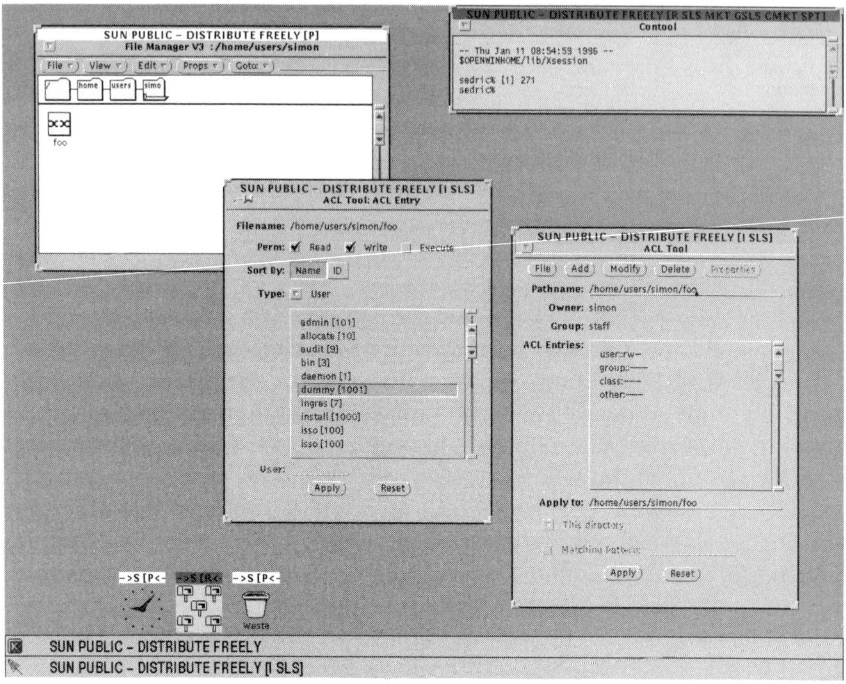

Figure 3.2 The user sets the file ACL.

manage their applications, such as databases. It can be done by allocating privileges to execute `chmod` (see chapter 5). In that context, you can focus your audit efforts on ACL changes, which can be indicative of an attempt to disclose or corrupt files. This is part of precise access policy.

Access Control Lists are the aspect of access control that a file's owner can perform, allowing or disallowing groups or individuals. It often is described as "discretionary" access control for that reason. However, organizations can set policy to limit changing ACL.

There are some basic guidelines for ACL that must always be followed within the default ACL setting for file and directory creation. Subsequent modifications to these ACL are subject to the organizational policy on ACL changing and can be monitored by audit.

The guidelines refer to user or system ACL. For the user, the focus is on files and directories in their /home directory, which they own. They shouldn't give write or execute permission for groups or others on directories, which prevents their files from being removed or even accessed.

This restriction can be set by the default ACL setting on the directories, which determines the default ACL of the files that are created. The default is inherited by the directories that are created. For default file ACL, users shouldn't give write or read for group or other on the default directory ACL.

ACL for system directories and files are maintained and monitored by system administrators and are owned by nonroot privileged administrative accounts, such as root, bin, or adm. Everything except the user home directories, /home, is the system. Other user file systems can exist for applications, such as databases.

The POSIX interface specification includes the ACL interface in its full functionality. This standard names the ACL management routines and describes their functionality, which allows adding identifiers to ACL, listing ACLs, etc.

There are three parts to an ACL entry: type, identifier, and permissions. As in pre-Secure UNIX, the types are the owner, group owner, and other. The new functionality of ACLs is that they also have entry types for users and groups of those other than the owners. Each has mode bits that indicate whether read, write, or execute permission is allowed or disallowed. The users and groups have identifiers, which are null for owner, group owner, and other (see Figure 3.3).

The listed users might or might not belong to the listed groups. If a listed user belongs to some of the listed groups, the ACL mode of their individual user entry is used to determine access. It might disallow access for them, even though they are members of groups that are allowed access (see Figure 3.4). This is the new ACL mechanism for disallowing access to individual members of groups that are allowed access.

If users belong to multiple groups on an ACL, they receive the sum of access granted for all of the groups. If one group that a user belongs to is denied access and another isn't, the user has access (see Figure 3.5).

Type	Owner	Group	Other	User	Group	User	Group
Id	NULL	NULL	NULL	User A	Group 1	User B	Group 2
Mode	*rwx*	*rwx*	*rw*	*rwx*	*r*	*rx*	*rx*

Figure 3.3 ACLs list more than one user and group.

ACL:	Group A	User 1
	r w x	*r - -*

(*Note:* User 1 belongs to Group A)

Figure 3.4 The user's ACL supersedes the group's. Users can be specifically denied access even if their groups have it.

ACL:	Group A	Group B
	r w x	- - -

(*Note:* The user is a member of both groups.)

Figure 3.5 Users can have access even though one of their groups doesn't.

Default ACLs can be placed on directories, and any files created in those directories will get them. Directories created within those directories will not only get those ACLs but will also have them as defaults (see Figure 3.6).

There is no change in the standard UNIX umask mechanism for the default permissions of files created in a directory (see Figure 3.7). Umask also masks the default directory ACL.

In addition, ACLs have maximum permission entries. They restrict the permissions of the users, groups, and owning group for the ACL (on ACL other than the owner or the other). (See Figure 3.8.) The value of the maximum is the widest allowed permission for the affected entries. On some systems, it initially is the mode of the owners group, but it can be changed.

`chmod` changes the owner, owning group, and other entry. Using `chmod` on the group owner permissions changes the maximum entry, which determines the maximum group owner permissions.

`chown` changes the owner. The owner can be a duplicate user on the ACL. `chown` use is restricted by the precise usage policy because its use could allow a user to pose a threat to file space usage limits.

You should not allow users to change the default access control lists of their files. Certain users, such as application administrators, might perhaps be excepted; otherwise, ACL changes must be coordinated with administrators. Given that policy, ACL changes will be conspicuous on the audit logger and can be reconciled with normal use, assuming its not an act of skullduggery.

Policy not withstanding, users still might change their file access, which gives impostors a way to steal or vandalize information. That's a reason why labels also are necessary. (See chapter 4.)

Database management systems will make extensive use of ACL and include a high-level interface to them, such as Secure UNIX versions of products such as SYBASE, Oracle, etc.

Major applications, such as databases, will be assigned application administrators who are responsible for determining who is granted access. By default, files are created with access restricted to the owner only. (See Figure 3.9.)

Basic UNIX Access Control

Let's review some basic UNIX access features that also are found in Secure UNIX.

The meanings of the permission modes are special when they refer to a directory. They also affect access control of the files in the directories. I'll look at the effects of each mode on files and directories.

Read permission on files allows users to open, read, and copy files. When a file is copied, the copy is owned by the copier, who then can change the ACL however he or she wants.

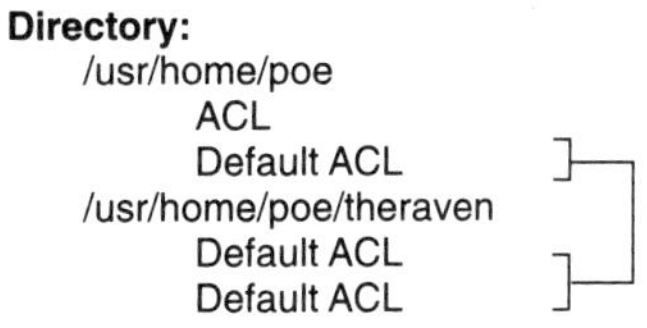

Figure 3.6 Directories inherit the default directory ACL.

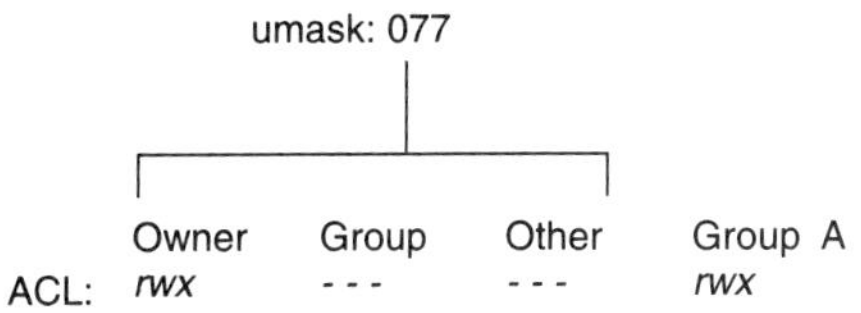

Figure 3.7 Umask still determines the default ACL, but only for Owner, Group, and Other.

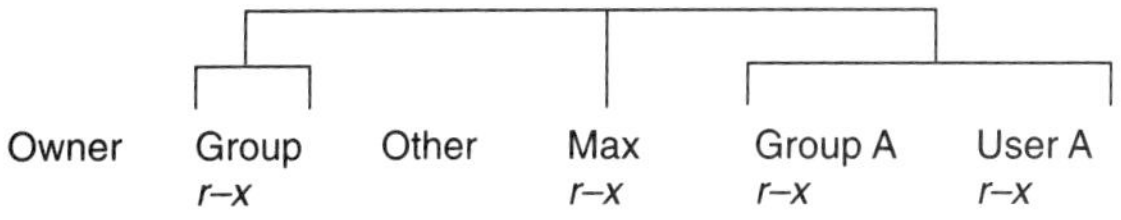

Figure 3.8 The Maximum entry gives the maximum allowed access for owning Group and additional entries.

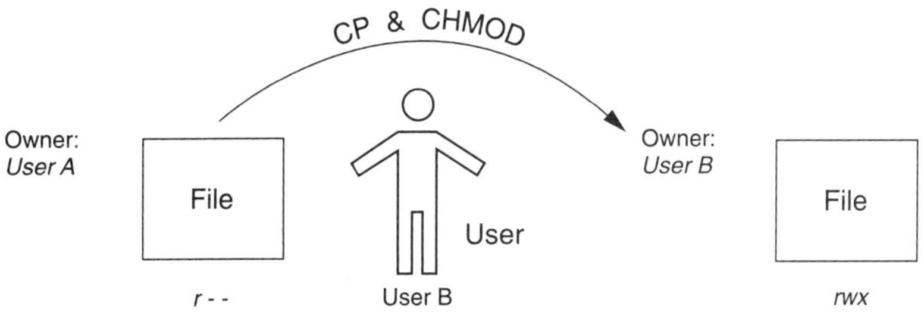

Figure 3.9 Copying a file can result in changed owner.

Read permission on directories allows users to list the contents of the directory but not to read files in it (unless they have read access on the file). However, read permission without execute permission on a directory allows only restricted information on the listing because the list can't include `stat` command information, such as the file length, owner, etc. `stat` requires directory execute permission.

Write permission on files allow users to write to, truncate, or modify files. Write permission on directories allows users to create, rename, and remove files, directories, and links in the directories, even if the permissions or ownership of the files deny it to them.

Execute permission on directories without write permission allows some search operations (see the following paragraphs) but not the ability to add and delete files as execute permission with write permission do.

These directory write behaviors make it essential to control the access mode on all of the directories of a file's path as well as on the file itself.

Execute permission on a file allows users the right to execute, or `exec`, executable files. Shell scripts also require read permission to execute.

Execute permission on a directory (called *search*) gives users the ability to change directories (`cd` or `chdir`) to it or its subdirectories, which is why it is known as *search permission.*

Search permission also "controls" access to the files in the directories by possibly allowing the files to be opened for read or write, if combined with other directory and/or file permissions.

Search with write permission confers the ability to remove, create, rename files and directories in the directory, regardless of the file's permissions or ownership.

Search also gives other search permission: With read permission, it allows listing with `stat`, long format list with file size, etc. Files can be executed and opened without read permission but not listed in the long format.

Setuid and setgid are meaningful on executable files. They are displayed as the high order bits of owner (setuid), group (setgid), and other (sticky bit). They determine whether a process will execute with the user or group identifier of the file owner and group, rather than or in addition to those from the user that executed it.

Setuid is de-emphasized on Secure UNIX and has largely been superseded by the privilege mechanism (see chapter 5). Pre-Secure UNIX files that were setuid root are notorious for being duped by hackers into giving them root privileges.

On a Secure system, root has been replaced by administrative privileges; however, to a much lesser extent, files that are setuid to a privileged user can be misused in the same way. However, as I will cover in later chapters, the privilege mechanism offers strong protection against that. Setuid root is moot because the root user no longer has special privileges. It's included for backwards compatibility.

You should never allow shell scripts to run setuid.

As implemented on some pre-Secure systems on directories, the sticky and setgid bit are useful for directories that are world writable, such as /tmp, and that will have files owned by various users, and so are "shared." Setting the directory sticky bit means that users cannot rename or delete other users' files in this directory. The directory setgid bit set means that files created there receive the group of the directory, not of the user that creates it.

Secure systems use multilevel directories for a similar purpose. These have subdirectories that have different labels.

System files are owned by system accounts and system groups. It is of the highest significance for maintaining security that no write permission for others be allowed on most system directories or files.

If the system files can be tampered with, they are as good as surrendered to the bad guys. Any unexpected change in the ACL of a system file or directory is monitored by the security audit alarm systems.

There is an exception to the no-write-permissions-for-others rule on system directories, and that's the shared spooler and temporary directories—such as /tmp, /usr/tmp/, and /usr/spool/uucppublic—that all users access.

Secure UNIX also manages labeling for labeled files in shared system directories by automatically creating labeled subdirectories, which are known as *multilevel directories*. Though files actually are kept in subdirectories that reflect the labels, users are presented with what appears to be the ordinary single label directory, such as /tmp (see chapter 4).

In addition to no write permission for others, many system files should have no read permission for others. These might be text files, shell scripts, or even executables that contain confidential information. Some of these are directories that hold the security attribute databases (such as /etc/security), the cron data file, and /usr/spool/crontab.

In addition to no write or read permissions for others, some system files also should not have read permission for group: the uucp data file /spool/uucp/L.sys, startup scripts, cron daemon scripts, any administrative scripts, or rc. Some pre-Secure UNIX scripts, such as /usr/adm/sulog (logs of super user password users), may not exist on Secure UNIX because there's no super user.

Some system files, such as /etc/password, need read permission for other. Secure systems keep the encrypted passwords in a private password file, /etc/shadow.

Publicly executable scripts (in /usr/bin) are readable, but executables aren't. Executables can be executed without read permission.

The /usr partition should be mounted read-only. Some /usr files are links to /var in the root partition, though mounting won't make the /var files read-only. Permissions on links affect the link access, not the file that they link.

Almost no /var files need to be writable by others. Unless they need it, remove write for others permission.

There are startup scripts on systems that can create files. They need to have umask 22 inserted in them to keep write permission off any of the files that they create. System V has /etc/initialize.d system startup scripts that create files every time the system boots. Putting umask 22 in the initialize script, which runs the init.d scripts, will ensure that the init.d script have it.

The same is true for most system scripts, or their creators, such as /etc/rmtab, /etc/rc, and /etc/rc.local or BSD startup scripts, which may use umask 22.

Device files have ACL. Terminal device file owners get changed to the user that logs in on them; on logout, the owner changes back to root. Secure computers change the terminal to root owned before it allows anyone to login. While the user is logged in, the terminal is *rwx* by owner only.

The system memory devices—/dev/kmem, /dev/drum, or /dev/mem—mustn't be readable or writable by others. They're owned by an administrative account, either root or kmem.

Disks are *rw* by owner only.

Chapter

4

Mandatory Access Control

Secure UNIX has two major methods of access control: DAC and MAC. DAC, Discretionary Access Control, is at the discretion of the file owner to control. It is the familiar UNIX file *rwx* mode bits and additionally, in Secure UNIX, ACLs (see chapter 3).

DAC allowed file owners to disclose their files as they wanted to. For organizations, that meant a lack of confidentiality.

When computer scientists pondered how to make systems more secure, they realized that DAC wasn't sufficient for organizational needs. What they envisioned was an access control "reference monitor" that was built into systems that would not be at the discretion of file owners but would be mandatorily imposed by the system.

The reference monitor would be an additional access check beyond DAC that even file owners couldn't circumvent. It would monitor information access and attempted user activity and ensure that it conformed to built-in access policy rules. It would allow organizations to control *what users did* with the information that they had access to.

The vision of a reference monitor was implemented in Secure UNIX as MAC, Mandatory Access Control. It was intended to enhance system confidentiality but, as implemented on Secure UNIX systems, confers much more, such as secure networking and practical auditing advantages.

I'll emphasize the more reader-friendly terminology of *MAC label*, or just *label*, when discussing MAC.

The Advantages of Mandatory Access Control

Secure UNIX provides many access firewalls. A *firewall* is literally defined as a building wall that prevents a fire in that room from spreading to the rest of the building. For example, a fryer might explode in a kitchen with a firewall ceiling and incinerate the entire first-floor restaurant but spare the upper floors. Firewalls are built in anticipation of problems in order to contain them if they occur.

If impostors have stolen passwords and broken in, Secure UNIX has system-guaranteed firewall limits on what information the impostors have access to and what they can do with it or to it.

A major access firewall is Secure UNIX labeling. You can organize your systems and information with labels such that you build in walls against information disclosure, vandalism, or system tampering. You determine what protections you require when you design your Trusted Information Base.

To explain briefly, Secure systems label not only files but directories, networks, databases, graphics, system software, application programs, printers, terminals, disks—all system resources that make up an information processing environment. User processes, such as their shells, also have labels. These labels all are compared in order to make access decisions.

Labeling provides wide-ranging system-access management because, whenever and wherever users, information, and systems interact, Secure systems compare their labels to make access decisions. Networks, file systems, and archives on removable media (such as tapes, terminals, and printers) as well as users and their files are all labeled.

These controls go far beyond determining which files a user can open. Communication connections are labeled, so data labels must entitle it to be transmitted. Tape archives are labeled, so they must be restored into a directory with a label that can accept them. That prevents the data from being restored by a user that isn't entitled to accept it.

The label of devices such as terminals will correspond to the physical security of their location. User shells receive a label at login that determines which terminals the users can login at and what data and devices they can access.

Users have a list of labels at which they can login. The login label will determine the users' session label, which is the label of their shell.

Whenever the user executes a program or command, it inherits the user's label. The system will base all access decisions on requests made by that process for all system resources on its label.

Labeling controls wide-ranging TIB access relationships. By it, an organization classifies its information by the information's importance to the organization, by which users it will allow access to the information, and what it will allow the users to do with the information.

Organizations have classified their information by using a labeling scheme that reflects the information's importance to the organization. "Importance" is a matter for the individual organization to decide, be it in terms of the data's need for confidentiality, protection from corruption or theft, monetary or strategic value, exclusiveness, etc.

Once classified, the information is labeled by the organization, and the label then is permanent, unerasable, and modifiable, even by file owners (modifications are possible but are heavily constrained by administrative privilege use).

When users login, they take their place in this label scheme. Whenever they attempt to access information, the system will compare their session label to the information's label and either grant or deny access. The system does this automatically for every type of attempted access, and the user cannot ever preempt, override, or circumvent this system power.

So it is then that labeling defines the relationship between users and information. Organizations assign label lists (called *clearances*) to users according to the importance of the information that the organizations allow the users access to.

Users benefit from this system in terms of confidentiality. For example, a directory that contains information with differing labels (called a *multilevel directory*) can be shared. The labels of the users can allow them access to some of the files or subdirectories, but not to others.

Users can take advantage of this confidentiality-boosting feature to as far an extent as the organization will authorize them, including providing the users with sole and exclusive access or providing access to a few highly select users. For example, a manager's secretary is sharing some files in a directory with other secretaries but wants to keep some of those files confidential.

This illustrates that, because labeling provides a practical way to keep information confidential, it also opens a new era in the openness and sharing of information. It is like the house with many rooms with secrets in them. Labeling makes each room in the house locked, so users will know the secrets of only the rooms that they have the keys to, and the house can be more open. That way, labeled information can be shared in unlocked rooms but still protected in locked rooms.

Access control is more than confidentiality; it meets other security goals, too. It protects information from vandalism and theft. It also protects the system from attacks that would bring it down.

Labeling is essential for all organizations, not just military organizations, national security, etc. Although it is best known for its confidentiality-boosting effects, labeling also is essential for system integrity and availability. The following paragraphs briefly state the reasons, which will be elaborated on throughout the book.

If, for whatever reason, you are not now inclined to utilize labeling, you can gradually "acquire a taste" for it with minimal impact on operating environment, user training, administrative overhead, etc., by using minimal labeling.

The most essential benefits of labeling can still be had with minimal labeling, wherein you label all users and their data at the same label. In this manner, users won't be required to design a hierarchical labeling scheme for their data and wouldn't feel very much of the effects of the label laws when they handle their data. Thus, the environment wouldn't appear very much different than if it weren't labeled.

Similarly, benefiting from labeling doesn't imply background checks on users or the need for monitoring of all system activity for confidentiality breaches.

Labeling provides an essential access firewall that maintains system (and user) integrity. This prevents users (or their impostors) from attacking the system files by corrupting them. It also prevents confidentiality losses by Trojan horses in the same manner.

As I will show you, the effect of the firewall is that users can read some system files, can't read others, and can't write almost all of them. These protections are in place even if an unauthorized user has stolen entry to the system or even privilege rights; thus it's an access firewall.

The firewall works both ways, too. By the label laws, administrative users can't access user files, except by use of privilege.

Another major reason that all organizations must use labeling on their information systems is that labeling provides a powerful, failsafe mechanism in the control and analysis of system auditing. Indeed, some of the most highly essential auditing capabilities wouldn't be feasible without it, including the auditing of access to the system files. Without control of audit by label, the data that was generated and needed to be analyzed would be overwhelming.

For that reason, labeling not only makes it feasible but also provides a failsafe mechanism, an ease-of-use feature. In a single stroke, it allows the auditors to ensure that they have included all of the system files in their audit configuration.

Another advantage of labels, beyond confidentiality, is auditing. Labels are integrated into the audit system and allow for precise selection.

Labeling also is needed to perform practical auditing of critical system activity, such as unauthorized system file access. Secure UNIX labeling also prevents disclosure because administrative users and nonadministrative users have separate labels and access capabilities. Thus, administrators ordinarily do not have access to user files. They do only if they invoke their privileges, which is restricted to specific administrators and tasks and is heavily controlled and monitored.

Secure UNIX labeling also has many purposes regarding protection of user data confidentiality. If desired, through the use of labels, it is possible to specify exactly which users can see a file, including limiting access to a single user.

Furthermore, with labels, it is possible to share file systems and still maintain confidentiality, no matter whether the sharing is with another coworker or with remote users. Previously, users doing remote logins or mounts lacked the practical ability to specify which individual users on the remote hosts they would allow access to. This sometimes resulted in remote users actually having wider access to files than if they were logged in locally.

Secure UNIX uses labeling and other security attributes as part of its networking protocols, and this affords a higher degree of user identification and authentication, resulting in better access control.

For example, there might be a particular file that you mustn't have "walk out the door" and the confidentiality of which you must protect. You can put a label on the file that would prevent it from being transmitted on network or telecommunications interfaces or being copied to tape.

The firewall aspect of this is that, even if the impostor had access to the file and even if they owned it, he or she still couldn't steal it by transmitting it over the network or making a tape copy. This "wall" is kept up by the Secure system itself and isn't something that the faker can get over.

Introduction to Labels

Secure UNIX implements MAC through a system of labels to organize files and other system resources. Labeling and built-in system label access control laws are at the center of what makes Secure UNIX more secure.

The labels are assigned to system objects by the security administrators and can't be modified by unprivileged users, including file owners. All access to objects and system activity then are regulated by a quasi-hierarchical label scheme, wherein labels are compared. That is the Secure UNIX reference monitor.

All objects, including files and devices, are assigned labels. Depending on your organization's requirements, labels of files might correspond to the fact that the information is exclusive to a few users, is a highly valuable asset, is very confidential, or any combination of those or many other factors. Each organization decides that when it designs its Trusted Information Base (TIB).

Labels also might reflect the level of trust an object has. For example, a communication line that is encrypted and offers strongly authenticated connections can be distinguished from one that is nonencrypted.

From the TIB perspective, label comparisons are meaningful, in that objects with some labels require more effort to protect or might be more exclusive or trustworthy. The labels can relate information by the amount of effort that an organization makes to protect it: it can be closely guarded, with auditing and security alarms.

Labels are compared as to whether they are "higher" or "equal" to each other. When it is said, from the TIB perspective, that a label is "higher" than another, there can be inferred some greater amount of the previous factors.

However, comparisons of labels are done by the operating system to determine user rights to access to a resource rather than to reflect any more qualitative TIB concept of how exclusive, valuable, or monitored that information is. Labels are compared and either are related in a certain required way to gain access or aren't. From the operating system perspective, a label that is "higher" might simply mean that it can allow its bearer access to resources, as I will explain.

The Label Laws

Secure UNIX allows organizations, embodied by the security system administrator, to label the objects such as files and devices. All system activity then is examined by the system reference monitor according to label laws, which are the built-in rules of the reference monitor.

(Conventionally, what I am calling label laws are called "Bell-Lapadula access policies," which is the policy that most UNIX systems use. I will refer to these access policies as the label laws to better distinguish them from organizational security policies and reflect how they are implemented on Secure UNIX.)

Labels are composed of a label level, which is an ordinal number, and a list of category names (see Figure 4.1). The level numbers are typically few, say levels zero through five, with five being the highest.

Label name	Level	Categories
Clerk	1	Expenses, salaries
Bookkeeper	2	Expenses, salaries
Accountant	2	Profits, expenses, salaries
Auditor	3	Profits, expenses, salaries, receivables

Figure 4.1 Auditor > Accountant > Bookkeeper > Clerk. Bookkeeper has a higher level than Clerk. Accountant has more categories than Bookkeeper. Auditor has a higher level and more categories than Accountant.

Category names can be any appropriate names. Conceptually, they divide the levels into compartments.

Labels are compared by operating systems on the following basis. Labels can be higher than, equal to, or unrelated to another.

Unrelated labels have different categories. Equal labels have the exact same level number and category names. (See Figures 4.2 and 4.3.)

A label is higher than another in these two cases:

Label Name	Level	Categories
Clerk	1	Expenses, salaries
Vice President	3	Strategic, operations

Figure 4.2 Vice President isn't higher than Clerk; it lacks some of Clerk's categories.

Level	Categories	
2	Expenses, salaries, receivables	*Not equal*
1	Expenses, salaries	
1	Expenses, salaries, receivables	*Equal*
1	Expenses, salaries, receivables	

Figure 4.3 Only labels with the exact same level and categories are equal.

- It has the same level number, all of the categories of, and one or more categories more than the other label.
- It has a higher level number and the same or more categories than the other label.

(A conventional, though I think less descriptive, term for "higher than" is *dominate*.)

The system never explicitly determines whether labels are unrelated or lower than another. It makes only two type checks to enforce the label laws. One is if one label is higher than or equal to another, and the other is if a label is exactly equal to another. It's a yes-or-no decision for both types.

It does either of the two type checks depending on what system activity is attempted. The activity can include reads, writes, or variations of them, such as copies and deletes. When it's a write, the system checks that the labels are exactly equal; when it's a read, the system checks that the labels are higher than or equal to. Systems do one of the two types of checks: greater than or equal to for a read or exactly equal to for a write.

Before I proceed, I now will summarize MAC labels as I explained so far and will tell what lies ahead about it. A system-imposed form of access control is implemented in Secure UNIX: System administrators assign labels to all system objects, which the system then uses for comparisons to make access decisions. Now, I'll relate labels to user processes to show how system-access decisions control user activity.

Users have a list of labels assigned to them, which I'll call their *user label list*. (Label lists are conventionally known as *user clearances*. That term evokes a world of military secrets, national security, and personnel background checks, which is in fact where secure computing was born. Organizations might choose to assign label lists on the basis of personnel background, but I'll call clearances *label lists* to avoid the emphasis on personnel background checks, which aren't necessarily required.)

For our purposes, a label list is defined as a list of labels that is assigned to users as part of their login accounts. When users login, their shell is given a label from their list and is said to be at that label. Any process that shell spawns will inherit that label. (See Figure 4.4.)

User Identifier	Label Range
User A	Bookkeeper, accountant

Figure 4.4 Label ranges are users' lists of labels at which they can log in.

The users' label lists are part of their accounts and are assigned to them by the administrator who creates them. The label list is very significant because it determines what information that user will be able to access. Users can login at any label within their range (which is to say any label on their label list), and having done so, their shell has that label. It will be used to compare the resource labels to check for access permission. (See Figures 4.5 and 4.6.)

The operating system does a comparison of labels to determine whether a user is entitled to access a resource according to the label laws. These

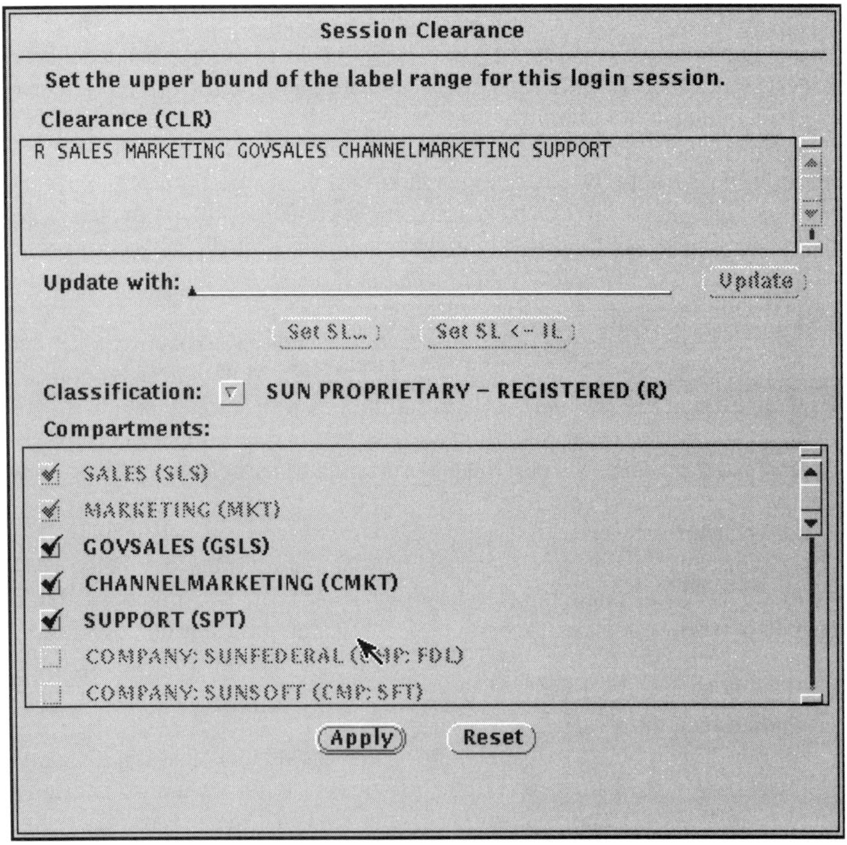

Figure 4.5 The system administrator sets a user's login label range.

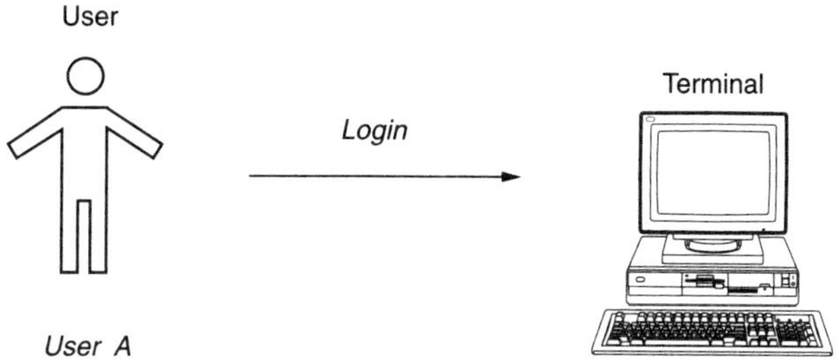

Figure 4.6 Users' login sessions are at a label in their label range. (User A has Bookkeeper in his label range.)

comparisons are made by the system among all labeled system resources—such as files, processes, and devices—and determine which operations users can perform.

Users then proceed to access system resources, such as files. Label comparisons carry out a built-in property of secure computers: They ensure that every operation conforms to label laws. In other words, whenever users read or write a file, the label of the user process and the file are compared and must conform to the laws.

Here are the label laws that the system will automatically enforce:

- To read a file, a user process label must be higher than or equal to a file label.
- To write files, a user process must have a label that is exactly equal to the file.

So, when file and user labels are equal, users can both read and write the file. When the user label is higher, users can only read the file (see Figure 4.7).

A major effect of this on the TIB is that label laws are enforced to disallow information disclosure to nonentitled users. Information shouldn't flow from higher- to lower-labeled users, because then it's being disclosed. So, higher-labeled users can only read lower-labeled information, but not write to it. Users can read information at lower or equal labels, but they can write information only if their labels are equal to it.

This not only effects disclosure, but integrity and reliability. All of the resources of the system are labeled, including system files. Users are barred from corrupting them by the label laws because their label list doesn't include the system label needed to write to system files.

You keep your information ordered by its labels. If information is able to change its label, or "float," either up or down, that could erode the organization that you impose to control your information. Information flowing down

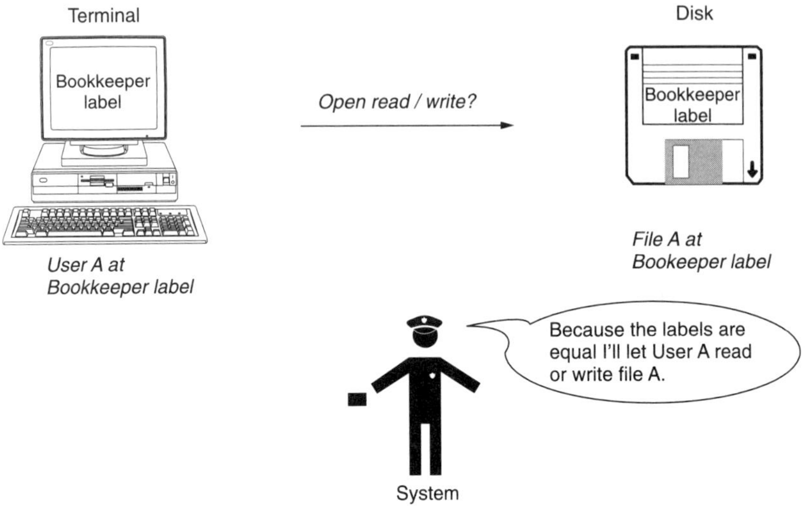

Figure 4.7 The user and file labels are equal, so the system will allow the file to be opened for read and write.

can constitute a disclosure of it; flowing up can cause an inaccurate TIB label height, which reflects how hard you work to protect it, etc.

Secure computing comes from the world of high-security where cold-war confidentiality was supreme. As it evolved, it became clear that solving the confidentiality problem led to computing environments that solved the general problem of secure computing.

MAC and Security Architecture

MAC (labels and label laws) is too often seen as solely a measure taken by cold-war agencies to protect national security secrets. However, MAC has a purpose in addition to that that makes it essential for general purpose environments as well. *You need not classify the secretness of your data at all to gain essential protections from MAC.*

Rather, labels will be an essential part of advanced security architectures because they offer support for secure networking, offer integrity protection of system files, make system auditing practical, etc.

Up until now, I've pointed out that the label laws (i.e., can't read up or write down) protect confidential information. Users with access to secret information can't disclose it or write it down to users without access.

Labels do much more. In a Secure UNIX environment, networking protocols include MAC labels. The networking interfaces throughout are sensitive to and handle the labels of the protocols. Networking services processes (e.g., telnet) are sensitive to the labels of the connections.

The effect is that the label embedded in the IP protocol by the network interface relates the connection to all objects in the environment. The label will reflect the trustworthiness of the originator of it.

All servers are label sensitive. For example, database-management system servers are label sensitive. That means that they accept connections only from labels that are higher than (or exactly equal for writing). Say, for this example, that connections to the DBMS server can be made only from the local area network or from a strongly authenticated private network. Given that, a dial-up connection cannot access that database because the interface to the dial-up lines would assign too low a label assigned to it.

What I described in the previous paragraph is the essence of 21st century security architecture. In the general sense, it is a built-in, highly distributed access firewall. It would work as a practical Internet firewall, too, but would do much more. It is a protection that extends to all system objects files, devices and processes, etc.

It distributes the firewall concept. Not only is login or network login the only point of authentication, but the concept of a user security credential is given to the users, and they must present it wherever they attempt system activity. The label becomes a part of their credential, which also might include privileges, system-entry information, and public-key certificates, and is carried via their network protocols and connections.

The label is embedded in the low-level networking protocol. When a connection is made over an interface, the listener (network or database server) process can accept only calls with a correct label. The connections that it makes have that label. Other server processes throughout the system will either accept or reject connections based on the label and the label laws.

Once connections are accepted, the server can only access objects that the label laws allow, such as labeled files or devices that it's higher than or equal to. The system compares the label of the file and the communications or tape devices and might determine that the file label didn't entitle it to be carried by the devices. Though the user had access to the file and the devices, you had precluded the devices' use for this file. You did this when you designed your TIB with labels that prohibited it.

Thus the labels form an enterprise-wide access firewall. You use them to discriminate among the trustworthiness of users. Users that come in over a LAN interface might be less trusted than the local workstation users, and their labels will reflect that. The LAN interface will label their connections accordingly. Users that dial in and that are strongly authenticated have appropriate labels, or the interface will give them low labels that restrict their access rights. Batch data that arrived over an unencrypted line might have a low label.

This way, no matter how users enter the system, their trustworthiness is recorded in their credentials, which can't be forged.

These kinds of systems will have a central role in the emerging global security architectures. They make practical today's Internet firewall-type approaches and eventually will supersede them.

Present firewall concepts are based on limitations of services to authorized host addresses and services by use of static configurations on dedicated communications hosts and routers. Processes called *proxies*, which emulate hosts and clients to local users, provide added protections, such as packet filtering and authentication, to services.

These approaches rely on the integrity of the dedicated boxes, limit connectivity, and have throughput limitations and area fault tolerance risk because they are bottlenecks almost by design.

Labels themselves constitute a firewall and do so without the problems and risks of current Internet firewall approaches.

A labeled environment would deal with networking and firewalls as in the following manner. Networking interfaces will "filter" network connections based on labels, not just IP addresses. The interface will insert labels into the IP protocols based on whether the connection can be trusted. It will determine that by how well it was authenticated when it was created, based on the integrity and encryption on the line, etc.

So the label of every connection will vary depending on how trustworthy it is. This is a crucial factor. Distributed environments might be modeled by entities that must determine the trustworthiness of other entities and that must persuade others of their trustworthiness. So when a server receives requests, it has to determine whether the request is a Trojan horse, a trusted local user, or a less trusted remote user.

In this model, authentication is distributed beyond system login. Processes, via networking protocols and public-key certificates, present their security credentials wherever they seek access. Credentials will determine how much trust (and access rights) can be given to the user.

Labels move into lower-level protocols—variants of IP, such as CIPSO—that carry a lot of other information to enable a credential's presentation.

I'll look at other relationships defined by labeling. All system resources are labeled, including devices: tape drives, terminals, printers, communications interfaces, etc. Whenever users attempt an operation on these devices, their session label is compared to the device's label. This fact can be used to specify exactly how activity is performed within a TIB.

A group of workstations on a local area network in a department might have file systems with important (high-labeled) information. You can allow users to print, make tape backups, and mail the high-labeled information, but only on the departmental network.

All users that you allow this access then would have the high label in their label lists. The tape and printer devices also have the high label, because the operations otherwise would fail. These users can login on the department workstations at the high label, because the terminals have the labels.

The workstations are part of your TIB. You are using all of the Secure UNIX facilities and principles in this book to keep it safe and monitored.

Additionally, in the controlled environment of the office, there is a high level of built-in trust. You can know that those people that are logged in aren't impostors because you can see them. You might have building entrance identification checks, bag checks, video monitors, physical locks on keyboards and other equipment, and room door locks.

This is how you would protect this important information. However, there is more than only this important information on the workstations. Secure UNIX handles information at many labels at once. Much information on these systems is not of the most relatively high significance to the organization, and some of it is even the ordinary electronic garbage that humans leave on computers. After all, security doesn't mean you have to try to make people perfect.

Not only is there low-labeled information on the system, there also are users whose label lists are low so that they can login on some of the workstations and access the lower information, but not the higher. The users with the high label list can access both high and low information.

Labeling and TIB

There's an important effect of this TIB approach. TIBs aren't isolated and walled off. They have all of the marvelous connectivity and communications services of UNIX. Yet often, there isn't any degree of trust about who or what comes in over an ordinary networking or dial-up connection. As I'll discuss in later chapters, trusted network connections soon might be widely available. For now, however, you need strategies to "contain" activity performed over most distributed networks.

For that, you rely on labeling. Keep networking services, such as FTP and e-mail, organized such that you distinguish connections made locally or over external networks.

You can do this because the connections themselves are labeled. You give a low label to ones that are made over the untrusted networks. You don't have trust that the user initializing it has been properly authenticated or that the line isn't being tapped.

The effect is that your high-labeled files can't be transmitted over these low-labeled connections. You can use them for general purposes that don't involve high-labeled information transactions. For example, the low-labeled users could e-mail or FTP over the network's low-labeled mail or files.

Similarly, labels are used to contain the importation of untrusted data. It can be done only on a low-labeled device (by an administrator) and will remain at a low label unless it has passed security scrutiny.

When you design your TIB, take into account the access requirements of your users, information, and system resources. The labeling that you plan will determine how information does, or does not, flow in your organization. When you label your TIB, you stamp the organization's access designs on its information, and users can't contradict it.

More exclusive or confidential information is given greater accountability as well, as you shall see.

You use labels to keep to the precise access principle that access is given out only to those who need it. They can be used to make access firewall protection in many other contexts, which I will describe in later chapters. They also serve the goals of data security, system availability, and confidentiality by their protections.

Any of the previous reasons, all addressed by minimal labeling with users and data at the same label, make it a necessity to have labeling in use on your information systems. I will be discussing the confidentiality-oriented advantages of more complex uses of labeling.

Label Interface

The label laws hold not only for users and files but also for users and any other resources. Other resources include devices, links, pipes, directories, interprocess communications, and processes. Within these, there are some special cases and interpretations.

A directory list operation is treated similar to a read: The user's label must be higher than or equal to the directory label.

A signal (kill) requires that the labels of the processes must be equal—similar to a write.

To read via a fifo, a process must run at equal label to the other process of the fifo. This is more restricted than the label laws, because, by them, a process can be higher or equal to a file to read it, yet here it must be equal to the process that it's reading. Because a fifo is an interprocess communications (IPC) object, the label laws are relative to the labels of the two processes, rather than between a process label and a file label.

Fifos are created within processes by a system call. Typically, it is followed by a `fork` and `exec` to create an interprocess system. To read the fifo, the `exec`ed process would have to be `exec`ed at the same label as the parent.

Other IPCs—including semaphores, messages, shared memory, and pipes—can be implemented as special files, which are labeled. When they are opened, label access control is applied. Depending on the implementation, however, they might have the same restrictions as for fifos.

The reason for the extra restriction is that, to read a fifo, one must write to it in the sense of a communication to the process being read or to the IPC object itself. Therefore, reads to IPC objects are treated as writes, which require equal labels.

This extra restriction precludes the abuse of IPC objects as covert channels. If the processes were at different labels, the higher-labeled process could attempt to pass information to the lower process by reading it, because reading sends a cue of some kind to the other processes that could be used to pass information to it—a covert channel.

Functions that read or write are subject to label access control; for example: `access`, `chdir`, `chmod`, `creat`, `exec` (and its variants: `execl`, `execv`, etc.), `fctrl`, `getcmd`, `link`, `mkdir`, `mkfifo`, `open`, `opendir`, `pipe`, `rename`, `rmdir`, `stat`, `unlink`, and `utime`.

Also included are user commands or system calls that access or modify the default directory ACL, audit buffers, information labels, and commands that manage processes, such as `exec`, `fork`, and `kill`.

Accessing file attributes requires read access; modifying them requires write access. Files are created with the same label as the creating processes.

`link` and `mkdir` require write label access to the directory that they are created in (the process and directory label must be equal). `link` also writes to the file's link count, so the user must have write label access to it, too. Both functions also search the directory, which requires read access (the process label must be higher than or equal to the directory label). `mkfifo`, `creat`, and `open` with create require write label access, too.

The label of a link refers to the link itself, not to the file.

Search access (directory list) requires read access to each directory in the path—from the root directory to the current directory—or the directory that contains the file. Due to this and because of the label laws, directories should always be nondecreasing labeled. To read, a process must be higher than or equal to.

Nondecreasing directories can be accessed until they get higher than the process. At that point, all subdirectories can be accessed. If a directory decreased then, a process with the lower label would be "cut off" from accessing it because the process couldn't search past the higher-labeled predecessor.

A nondecreasing directory has a label higher than or equal to the label of its parent.

The label of an open file can't be changed.

Information Ordering and Flow

I previously discussed the advantages of simple label schemes that have few user data classes and labels. The following discusses more complicated classifications of user data.

Labels are composed of a level number and a category list. This has many ramifications in your TIB design. Labels determine access. The level almost seems to divide labels into stepwise access levels; however, in practice, this is complicated by the effect of categories and user label list ranges.

This can be illustrated by considering different label numbers. A user label with the higher number might not be higher than the label on information with a lower number, because it might lack some of the categories that the lower-labeled information has.

Therefore, it cannot be said that label numbers divide information and access to it by an ordered scale. When designing a TIB, you decide such issues as what information or users should have multiple label numbers in their label list and whether categories should be associated with one label number or many.

Effective labeling of a TIB requires you to organize your information, and that is your guide to these issues. The goal is to identify the information that is most valuable, exclusive, and confidential so that you can control access and monitor it effectively.

A category can be used to describe a certain type of information. The same categories can be used on multiple label levels. By this, information of a category can be organized by label number according to the TIB protection required.

If required, a category can be associated with only one label level, which would allow confinement of users that require access to the category to that level. Confining users to a narrow label list is beneficial, because that inhibits information flow among label levels.

Files can be read by users at higher labels. By the label laws, it can be copied to a higher label. However, you should make it a policy that copying up is disallowed and require the use of privilege to change file labels to a higher label (known as *upgrading* them).

In a sense, however, if users have multiple labels in their label list, they could copy information to a higher, or even lower, label by memory. They also might have privileges to upgrade information, all of which might be undesirable information flow or even disclosure.

If information flows between labels unnecessarily, it might aggregate, degrading the TIB. It might needlessly flow up into higher labels where it overwhelms an organization's ability to focus on the most important information. Overused labels would grant users access to too much information.

Overused categories might cause information to aggregate. A problem of pre-trusted UNIX was lumping users into unwieldy groups where accountability was lost. So you now can avoid that by adhering to precise access and can keep labels allocated on as-needed basis.

When you label data, you must know who has those labels in their label list and is getting access. Labels should entitle access to only those who need it.

Label Categories

Categories should reflect general types of information. They are used to keep user access precise and should select the general types of users and information in your organization. They straddle label levels so that a single category of information can be organized by increasing degrees of TIB protection accorded it at each level height.

The use of categories also can confer confidentiality by providing a means to exclude access of high-labeled users. Categories found at the lower level, but not the higher, would keep the files private from the higher-level users.

I'll look at an example of what I mean by general types of information. If your organization is a hospital, it might have categories such as medical records, medical research, and claims proceeding, as well as categories that any business would have: inventories, personnel, accounting, etc.

Devising categories requires also considering which users need to have access to information. For each information category, permitted users will have the category in their label list, possibly at a few levels. In this way, access is precisely enforced by the system.

Upgrading the labels of information should take place only as needed or as part of a overall design. That way, only the information that is important to the organization as a whole, as opposed to individual users, will rise above the lower exclusivity levels. Of course, each user wants privilege of their data. However, if they want to give it the TIB protection provided especially for the higher-level information, they have to lobby the organization to raise its label level.

From the organization's point of view, upgrading is done only when the information has significance enough for the organization to expend the overhead of carrying highly monitored information. With this, information has to fight its way up.

There is an overhead for higher-level information. It is carefully audited and involves time-zero alarms and double-checked authorizations, which incur work on the part of staff. It might require physical access control to terminals, disks, and printers. Security alarms might require communication systems (such as dialers and beepers), phoning, meeting, or the use of video cameras by a building security staff.

Beyond that, there is the complexity of the TIB. Because it is a dynamic system, its ease of growth must be maintained. Adding information at higher levels might introduce unnecessary relationships among users and information. Keep higher level information at a minimum.

The automatic label-checking function of Secure systems is one of the main reasons that Secure systems are more secure than pre-Secure systems. However, just buying a Secure computer won't make a difference. It also requires organizing your information to make use of the automatic checking, keeping your eyes on what's happening, and being ready to act if something goes wrong.

Secure computers help you protect your information through built-in checks against disclosing or corrupting information. To do this, the system uses the label laws (can't read up and can't write down) with the basic effect

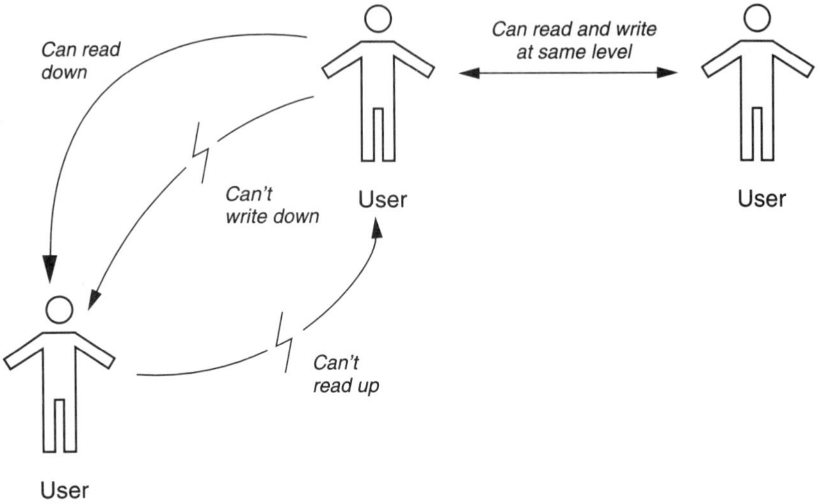

Figure 4.8 The label laws enhance confidentiality protection.

that users at a higher label can't disclose data to those at a lower label, and lower users can't help themselves to higher users data. (See Figure 4.8.)

Labeling and Information Access

There are many other effects of labeling on access and information flow, which the following will explore. Assume that there is an organization with users and information at many labels.

First, I'll look at how users and the operating system (commands, systems calls, etc.) relate. Access to system files and directories is kept restricted from users and processes according to precise access. Sometimes, the only users and processes that can access the system files and directories are administrators, system processes, and administrative scripts and programs.

One of the major ways that this restriction is carried out is by labeling. The others include access control lists and privileges.

The Secure system label database is the repository of all labels that are in use on the system. Labels are placed on all system resources, such as files, networks, and output devices. Users have a label list, which contains the labels at which they can login. Once users have logged in, their login shell and the commands or programs that they run inherit that label, and I'll say that the users or their processes are at the label.

Access to all system resources by the user is regulated by the system on the basis of comparisons between the user's label and the label of the resource.

Figure 4.9 is a facsimile of a Secure system label database file. From the left, the columns are the label names (which, in this example, reflect the label levels), the label level number (which is a hierarchical label ordering), and the categories.

The labels in Figure 4.9 are on all system and user resources, files, devices, and processes. They also are on the administrator's or user's label lists (I'll refer to nonadministrative users as *users* and to administrative users as *administrators*).

Labels are either system or user labels. The *system labels* are on the system files and processes. They also are on the administrator's label lists. Users are prohibited from using system labels for their files or processes. *User labels* are on users' files and processes. Users have them on their label lists and can login at them.

Multilevel Labeling

In the following discussion, I'll refer to labels in the context of a user that is logged in at a label and accessing a labeled file. I'll be discussing the case where users login at a user label, thereby getting shells at a label. The label must be one of the user labels on the user's label list. First, I'll be discussing what happens when these users attempt to access files labeled with the system label.

System labels are on all system resources, such as files, programs, and devices. Trusted system processes (daemons and servers) execute at system labels. Only administrative users, such as the security administrator or auditor, can have shells or execute programs that run at the system label. Only they have system labels, and only system labels, on their label list. Administrators assume their label and privileges through an administrative interface, rather than by login.

User labels are on all user files. Users have user labels, and no system labels, on their label lists, which allows them to login and run processes at the

Name	Level 1	Categories	
4 a	4	ABCD EFGH Z	
3 b	3	DEFGH Z	
3 a	3	C Z	
2 b	2	ABCD Z	
2 a	2	E GH Z	
1 c	1	D EFGH Z	
1 b	1	E GH Z	
1 a	1	B D Z	
0 b	0	Z	*Can read*
0 a	0	YZ	*Can't read*

Figure 4.9 Users can read those system files with the Z category only, but not those with the YZ categories.

user labels. Thus, mutual exclusion of system and user labels is maintained. The label level number of the labels (which I'll refer to as their *levels*) is zero for system labels and greater than zero for user labels. This is how the user and system labels are kept totally separated.

In Figure 4.9, labels 0a and 0b are system labels. Their level is zero. One has the category Z, and the other has the categories Y and Z.

The labels with levels greater than zero are the user labels. Note that all users labels have the category Z. Therefore, all users will be able to read the system files that are labeled 0b, as their levels are higher and they have the same or more categories. Because many users' labels are higher than some system labels, they can read some system files.

Some system files shouldn't be read by users (for example, the Secure system label database file, /etc/security/label). To ensure this, users can't have a higher label or equal label to the system files so that the users can't read them.

Reading is prevented because those files have a category in their label that no user label has. Therefore, because users all lack a category found in some system files, they can't read the files.

For example, in Figure 4.9, system label 0a has the categories Y and Z. Although users labels have higher level numbers than the systems, they lack 0a's category Y. Therefore, the user labels aren't higher and cannot read system files labeled 0a.

One thing that you don't want happening in any case is users writing to system files. That would be a security threat, as the users might damage the files by accident or might even deliberately attempt to plant an attack there. As mentioned, users can read many system files because their labels are higher; however, to write (by the label laws), you must have equal labels. (See Figure 4.10.)

To prevent users from writing to system files, user label levels never go as low as the system's levels. That is, labels with a zero number never are in a user's label list, so they can't login at that label, get a shell, or run programs or

Name	Level 1	Categories	
4 a	4	ABCDEFGH	Z
3 b	3	DEFGH	Z
3 a	3	C	Z
2 b	2	ABCD	Z
2 a	2	E GH	Z
1 c	1	DEFGH	Z
1 b	1	E GH	Z
1 a	1	B D	Z
0 b	0		Z
0 a	0		YZ

Can read down

Can't write down

Figure 4.10 Higher-labeled users can't write data to lower-labeled users, but they can read lower-labeled users' data.

commands at that label. The result is that users can never have an equal label to system files; therefore, they can't write to the system files by the label laws.

In Figure 4.10, the system labels are 0a and 0b; the others with the higher level numbers are the user labels. User label lists would have user labels only, precluding the users' ability to login at a system label and to write to system files.

The lowest user level is one. Because user processes and the files would have to have equal labels for users to write to files, users will never be able to write to system files. This is handy in order to stop Trojan horses from being planted in the system files.

The only way to have write access to system files is by becoming a privileged administrative system user via an administrative interface. To do that, you must invoke the trusted path, which insures that the administrative interface is authentic.

The interface program is setuid to an appropriate administrative or privileged user that would have the system label in his or her label list. Other system programs also can be setuid to users who have system labels. These can be users such as bin and adm that also own these system files or can be administrative users such as security administrator. However, it is not possible to login as an administrative user.

Once users assume their administrative users' identity, their commands also can invoke privileges appropriate to the administrative role. It is through these privileges that the administrative user processes can also gain access to nonadministrative users files, overriding the label laws, which would disallow access.

System File Labels

I'll look at how system labels would prevent administrative access to nonadministrative user's files. The system/user label access firewall works both ways. Not only are users restricted from access to the system files, but administrators also are restricted from access to users files, unless they invoke privilege.

Administrators at system labels, such as 0a or 0b, are barred from access to files labeled with user labels at level 1 or higher by the label laws: can't read up and can't write down. Because they can't read up and they're not higher than any user files, they're barred from reading them.

Because administrators don't have user labels in their label lists, they can't login at or have processes that run at users labels. Without equal labels, they are barred from writing to user files.

However, administrative users also can assume privileges that allow them to override the label access protections of the label laws. These allow them to read and write user files, despite the label laws. This separation of administrative and user label lists, and of the labels of system files and user files, is a major access firewall of Secure UNIX.

The system has lower label levels than users. You might find that odd because you'd think that the system ought to have the highest levels. The "low and high" relationships on it are more than just an increasing scale in that the zero-level labels are reserved for the system. As I will show, higher-labeled users don't always have greater access powers. However, labeled user information is on an increasing scale in the sense of the TIB protection afforded it, such as security alarms, according to its value to the organization.

The relationship between users and system files is a model for how to relate an organization's data and users. You design the labeling to meet disclosure, integrity, and information-flow requirements.

I'll assume that you have many users labeled at various information labels from low to high. Each might own or have access to data at those levels. What are the typical relationships that you find among these, and how do you avail yourself of Secure system benefits in the design of our Trusted Information Base?

You design the TIB labeling so that you differentiate the data that is more exclusive and give it the highest label, with only the most exclusive users given those labels on their label list. Otherwise, you might lose much of the benefit of the protection provided by Secure systems and labeling. If you lump all of the information at one label or let data be upgraded in level too easily so that it piles up in one level, you might tend to allow too many users access and lose the ability to focus monitoring on the important data.

High-Labeled Information

I'll start the discussion with the highest labeled data. Highly valuable, confidential, or exclusive data, which you monitor most carefully with audit, has the highest label.

Data is available to users on the basis of their label list (the labels that they can login at). Depending on what labels users have in their label lists, I'll refer to them as high- or low-labeled users.

High-labeled users will not be able to disclose high-labeled information to lower-labeled users, because by the label laws information cannot be written down-level. They are the most exclusive users because fewer users labels go that high.

In general, it is possible that the highest labeled users also might be those who have the widest access to information because their labels are the highest and have the potential to be higher than most of the other information labels on the system. They would be able to read lower-labeled data, provided that their label had all of the categories of most of the lower data.

These effects of labeling can be employed to provide confidentiality when you design your TIB. As I explained earlier, user programs and commands that run at a high label can have read access to a wide range of information.

I'll discuss a TIB design strategy utilizing labeling. An organization might find it desirable to keep information accessible to an exclusive group of directors. Naturally, this group and the information would be high labeled.

In most cases, this wouldn't be sufficient to maintain the information, as there are other users needed, such as data-entry or other assistant staff. To keep access precise, you should avoid giving the high label to those users.

The label laws allow you to do that. You can provide the assistant users with a lower-labeled data-entry program that allows them to enter "raw" data, perhaps with code numbers rather than names. The programs, files, and directories for this are all at a lower label than the directors.

The directors at the higher label have read access to the assistant's data. They could run programs at the higher label, which would read in, analyze, and display the data. This keeps the information restricted to users at the higher label.

Database management vendors will provide Secure products that allow databases to contain records at multiple labels. For such a system, users at multiple labels might get different access rights to the same databases.

High-labeled users not only could have more read access, but as I'll discuss next, they also could have more write access, in that they can have a wider label list.

A label list is the difference between the highest and lowest label on the users label list. Those labels determine what labels a user can login at. Users must have equal labels to the files to write to them. If your users had a wide label list, they could login at various labels and write to data at those labels.

The label list directly determines which users can write information to which files. If users can login at a file's label, they have an equal label to it—a prerequisite for writing to it. To minimize the write access to files, keep users' label lists as precise as possible by not including labels of files that they don't need write permission to.

Even if a file's label isn't on users' label lists and so isn't writable by users, it still might be readable by them. That is because the labels on the list still might be higher than the file. So, if the users login at higher levels, they will be at a higher label and can read the file.

If users were abusing their wide label list, they could copy, by memory or by using a print out, information to lower labels in order to disclose it. This form of threat is known as a *covert channel*, which is defined as the deliberate use of a legitimate system resource or property to disclose information.

TIB security alarm detectors monitor resources to detect these threats. For example, users that change labels unnecessarily might be a cause for an alarm. Another defense against this threat is to slow changing labels down. On an X Window interface, pasting among different label windows is deliberately slowed by an interactive prompt.

In terms of label laws, creating a file or directory within a directory is similar to a write operation; users must be at the same label as the directory. So, users could copy files only to directories with the same label that they are logged in at. Copying a file won't change its label.

If users were at a lower label, they couldn't access a higher-label file to copy it. The only way to copy a file to a lower-label directory is to have the administrative privileges needed to do it.

Users can create files and directories that are higher or equal labeled than the directories that they are created in. However, it should be a policy that all directory hierarchies on the system ascend or stay equal in label; don't create directories whose labels are not higher than or equal to their parents. Security alarm detection will check that that's carried out.

The reason that a policy that states that directory labels must ascend is necessary is so that directory access can be kept organized by increasing labels. The label of a directory should reflect the label of the files in it.

If a lower-labeled file is copied to a higher-labeled directory, it will retain its low label. To keep the directories organized, the file should be upgraded or have its label changed to the higher label. Upgrading should be restricted by policy and also can require privilege. It would degrade the TIB if files were upgraded unnecessarily.

If a higher-labeled user wanted to change directories to a lower-labeled directory, the operation would fail because that is treated as a write. Therefore, a lower-labeled directory would be inaccessible. To `cd` to a directory, a user's label also must be higher than the whole path.

High-labeled information and users most likely will be monitored by audit to a greater extent.

Higher-labeled users can read down, so far as their labels are higher than or equal to. Here is an odd-seeming idea: you might want to exclude the highest-labeled users from reading data available to lower-labeled users. A high label might not give you access to everything on the system (i.e., an executive might not need to have access to another executive secretary's files).

All that is needed for that protection is to not give the higher-labeled user some of the categories used by lower-labeled users and their data. A missing category on some of the lower-level files would be selective, denying access to the executive that lacks only those categories on those low-level files.

Not only can't high-labeled users read files with such labels, they also can't write them either. Those users won't know that the files are there; the users can't even list them. This not only prevents bumblers from accessing data that they might not know how to handle, but also lessens the impact if an intruder has gotten in and is masquerading as the high-label user. This is one of the major advantages of Secure UNIX—one that is effective only if you design your users and data with care.

The same means are used to relate users at less exclusive labels to other users and their data.

Middle-Labeled Information

Users at a middle-level clearance can read information at a lower label as long as their labels are higher, they have all of the categories or more, and they are at the same or higher level. If you want to exclude them from reading lower-level data, include a category on it that they don't share. If you want to let them read it but not write it, don't let their label list go down to the level of the file. That way, their label can be higher but never can be the same, which is a prerequisite for writing.

Middle-level users, therefore, can read down if permitted by having higher labels than the downward information.

Always begin the design of the TIB with information flow inhibited by allocating overlapping labels among users and information on an as-needed basis. Seek to minimize the flow to known, "appointed" users so that any other instance of that flow can be recognized as a suspicious event when audited by the systems auditor.

The label lists given to users will have an enormous impact on what information that they can access, what they can do with the information that they have access to, and ultimately on how secure the entire TIB is.

There is another place that information can flow, besides among users at different labels. The most heinous break-ins that have occurred so far have involved hackers or their attacking programs coming in over a communications network. Information also can flow over networks to output devices, such as printers or terminals, or to removable media, such as tape or disk.

You manage this flow much the same way that you manage information flow among users: all output devices (such as disk drives, tape drives, and terminals) and system services (such as a networking or printer spooling) are labeled so that users and these resources are related as the users are to their files.

If you can have confidence that highly confidential, valuable, and exclusive information is kept safely at high-label level without being leaked down and spread out to "junk" bin directories at lower levels, you can keep an eye on it, on who accesses it, and where it is copied or transmitted to. Because your communication channels, file systems, removable archive, and printers are all tuned to the label level of the information that they handle, high-labeled data will be transferable only on these exclusive means. With exclusion comes the ability to focus your efforts and effectively maintain control and keep useful logging records.

Low-Labeled Information

Finally, there are those users at the lower-label levels. They might have access to only a few files if their clearances are confined to low levels. They can have read and write access to the files at their level if they own the files or are put in files access lists by their owners. Otherwise, below them are system-level files, which are not writable, and only in some cases readable, by them.

As a rule, unless you want to have an upward information flow, you don't want lower-level users to get higher-level files disclosed to them or to have the opportunity to vandalize or misuse them.

It might be that many higher-level users can read their files or write to them if their label list is low enough. The number of users that are labeled low enough to write to lower-level files should be kept to a minimum. Lower-level files might need to be accessed only by lower-level users. Other users that don't need to write lower-level files should be kept in a nonoverlapping label list, either by having a higher level range or by having a different category set. It's better to keep users separated by nonoverlapping level ranges, because this is a clearer distinction. Over-reliance on categories will have a tendency to overpopulate them with users who don't need access, which has been the major problem with pre-trusted UNIX.

If information needs to flow up, user label lists should overlap (categories, levels, or both). If higher-level users need only read access to lower-level data, they should not be labeled as low as the data. Only files that need to be passed to higher-level users should be upgradable. The owner of lower-level files shouldn't unnecessarily have a range that allows overlap to higher users.

As users are labeled to lower levels, they potentially are entitled to write more files. For each file, determine which users will require either read or write access. Keep users who don't write files out of range. Lower-level files are those that, in general, will be writable by many users and categories, so those users who aren't writing files need not be labeled to that level.

Categories are apt to be used on multiple files. Many users might need write access to at least some files on the lower levels, so the lower levels shouldn't be too exclusive.

Generally, higher-labeled users have wider access to information, and lower-labeled users have less. Keep users confined at one level, except for where information flow is necessary. Start with the high levels, then move to the medium and low levels. Assign users to the levels by the exclusivity of the information that they need. Lower-level users are bounded below by the system.

Keeping categories associated with a level can maintain order.

Label Lists and Information Flow

As I've discussed, the width of the label list effects TIB organization, from the aspect of possible upgrading, and presents a possible covert channel threat. The width of the label list has another effect on the organization of information and labeling. A wide label list might enable a user to increase the label value of information, upgrading it, thereby causing information to flow between labels. When it does, the information also might be flowing between users, because information labels determine who can access it, and a user's label list might have prohibited him or her from accessing the information at a lower level.

If not restricted by policy and privilege, users, as their file owners, might be able to upgrade the level of their own files within their label lists, perhaps to a label that overlaps a higher-level user's label list. If the user also lists that higher-level user on the file's access control list, the user has passed information uplevel. In some kind of a cover-your-tracks scheme, this action might constitute a part of a covert channel, although a covert channel usually is associated with a disclosure of a higher-labeled file to a lower-labeled user.

If there is no need for information to flow between users at different levels, it can be prevented by not allowing their label lists to overlap. Overlap can be stopped by either keeping user labels at different label levels or by not sharing categories among them. If users create (own) a file, it is given the label of the users' login label. It can't be upgraded to another user at a higher level that doesn't have a category that label has.

By precise access, try to achieve the following in the TIB design:

- Higher-label users should not be higher than files unless the users need to read the files.
- Users should have overlapping label lists only if files need to be passed among users.

Also, the upward information flow path doesn't hold true for passing information downlevel. Even files' owners can't downgrade them because this would permit divulging of information to lower-labeled users, which is a potentially major security problem. Some systems give users the privilege to downgrade; however, in general, it's not how TIB operates.

Information flow has many side effects besides possible user access flow. It also tends to aggregate information upward, which can cause a loss of data organization and distinctiveness of labeling.

For these reasons, upgrading of information is a serious step with potential global effects on the TIB, and it should be covered by the precise access. Only users who need to be at a wide label list should have it. Only users who need to upgrade information should be allowed to do it. Organizational policy should prohibit it otherwise. Upgrading is detected by security alarms, and on some systems, privileges can be used to restrict and detect it. These might be needed to protect the integrity of your TIB.

Covert Channels

Covert channels are the bypassing of system access controls in order to disclose information by using some feature or component of the system. They can be used to subvert ACLs, labels, or privileges in that they can be used to pass information among unauthorized users and override those access controls.

Covert channels use shared resources or observable system characteristics to act as a signal among users to transfer data. Most methods involve abnormal repetitions of some activity that can be detected and inhibited before large amounts of data are compromised.

An example is using the state of system resources as a signaling mechanism. If users could tie up all of the /tmp file space so that they could cause other users' attempts to use it to fail, that could be used as a signal. All that is needed is some sort of protocol between them and a code. Each time that the receivers try to use /tmp, they either can or can't use it, which is a bit of information passed between users that tie up /tmp and those that try to use it.

Covert channels are either timing or storage channels. *Storage channels* use the state of some system resource or object. *Timing channels* use a time-related signal, such as response time or some conspicuous event frequency.

Most covert channels will show up on an audit trail. If /tmp access keeps failing, that would raise audit alarms. Failed access on system objects is audited.

Strategies to avoid them include randomizing all system-allocated resource identifiers—such as file system data, such as inode numbers, etc.—or introducing delays on some system calls or operations in come contexts to inhibit their use as channels.

Information Labels

Secure systems have a method of associating descriptive text with files that is called *information labels*. Information labels are printed on page headers or displayed on X Window frames and included when files are exported or archived. They are not a part of and don't affect label access control.

Information labels describe the current information content of files. They can change automatically to follow changes of the content, which is called *information label floating*.

The labels are kept in a database called *label encodings*. Encodings determine how to concatenate labels when differently labeled information is combined, requiring its label to float.

The labels can serve as information handlers, a log of how the information was derived, warnings, software release data, user access lists, or whatever might be useful. Each organization determines what labels are appropriate for its information.

Although information labels have no effect on label access control, the descriptions might reflect it, perhaps by stating its significance, a text name for it, or handling instructions that are related to it. For example, the high-labeled files might be labeled "Confidential % Proprietary % No Unauthorized Use, Under Penalty of Law," whereas the low-labeled file might say "For Public Distribution."

These labels cannot only play a role in proper handling, they also can be crucial in establishing your claim to your information. By U.S. law, it can be essential to have a proprietary claim of some kind attached to your information to keep your rights to it.

Because the information label reflects the current content of a file, it can offer a contrast to the access control label of a file. For example, a newly created file at a high access control label can be initialized with the mildest advisement as an information label, because it's empty. If data from a low access labeled file is copied into it, the information label then can float up to a somewhat more urgent label. Still, the information label can be less severe than what you'd expect from the fact that the file has a high access control label.

This serves as a commentary on the accuracy of the access control labels of your information and, as such, can restrain unnecessary information upgrading.

Chapter 5

Privileges

One of the biggest security problems of pre-Secure UNIX was superuser. Superuser had unlimited access to system and user files and could execute any command. Frequently, many users would require superuser powers to do their jobs, with the result that the superuser password was spread around. The superuser account, root, was an anonymous user ID and lacked accountability.

Superuser is a vestige of the origins of UNIX, where a laboratory minicomputer was shared by a cozy group of programmers. In those days, the priority of security was secondary to that of optimizing the development environment.

Superuser had many other problems besides bad password use and the lack of accountability. It was the worst case regarding precise access. Superuser privilege was the only form of privilege, even if limited privilege was needed, such as read access for a backup.

Pre-Secure administrators sometimes would login to administrative accounts, such as line printer or bin, and either get superuser privileges by that, or they could `su` to root, which meant more of these same problems. Secure UNIX privileges have eliminated this type of administrative login, too.

The menace of superuser not only referred to users that abused the account but also to rogue processes that ran with root privilege. Many UNIX break-ins involved duping a root process into giving hackers or their worm programs root privileges. I am going to discuss exactly how privileges put an end to that threat.

Rather than superuser, Secure systems use privileges to control access to system resources and the use of system services.

Secure UNIX restrained superusers by eliminating them and dividing their powers into what it calls *administrative privileges*. Each power requires that the user be explicitly authorized to use it by a privilege authorization. All users must login as ordinary unprivileged users. They then can assume administrative privileges if they are authorized.

The hundred or so privileges cover file, network, process, window, database, as well as system access control. Privileged users administer and control applications, such as databases or networks.

Privileges can control access to specific system modules, system calls, system files (such as the password files), and administrative commands. The separation of privilege powers not only conforms to the precise access principle but also to the principle of accountability.

Privileges are the linchpin of confirmed authorization policy, which states that all use of administrative privilege must be confirmed to be authorized. That means that, whenever administrators act in a way that can have security implications, another administrator (the auditor) or an administrative security program confirms that it was authorized.

Because processes have privileges, their use of privilege is confirmed to be authorized, too. This is done by auditing and by administrative security programs that create profiles of activity, including privilege use by programs. As programs execute, their privilege use is confirmed against their profile.

Accountability is maintained, and the activity is audited. Therefore, auditors will be notified. By confirmed authorization, there will be a system in place whereby the auditors will be able to confirm that a resource's use is authorized and that the administrators or their processes are not impostors and are doing their legitimate jobs.

Administrative users are associated with a list of special powers, which are known as *privilege authorizations*, that determine what privileges they can impart to their commands.

Some systems also list commands in the authorizations, which might list what commands users can execute with what privileges. Some commands are organized into task-oriented sets called *roles*.

Privileges are assigned to users by privilege authorizations. They allow users to make privileged system calls. A *privileged system call* is a system call that requires privilege to make.

Privilege authorizations can include a number of privileges that confer the right to make privileged system subroutine calls. Therefore, authorized users will be able to make those calls from the programs that they create or the system commands that they issue.

Privilege authorizations are assigned to user login accounts by the security administrator. The authorizations are assigned either individually or by a set identifier (if they are handled that way by the vendor). They also can be assigned precisely to specify each command that the user can be authorized to use.

Authorized users pass their privilege authorizations to the processes that they execute. Thereafter, the processes are able to invoke the authorized privileges, subject to other considerations that I will describe later. (See Figure 5.1.)

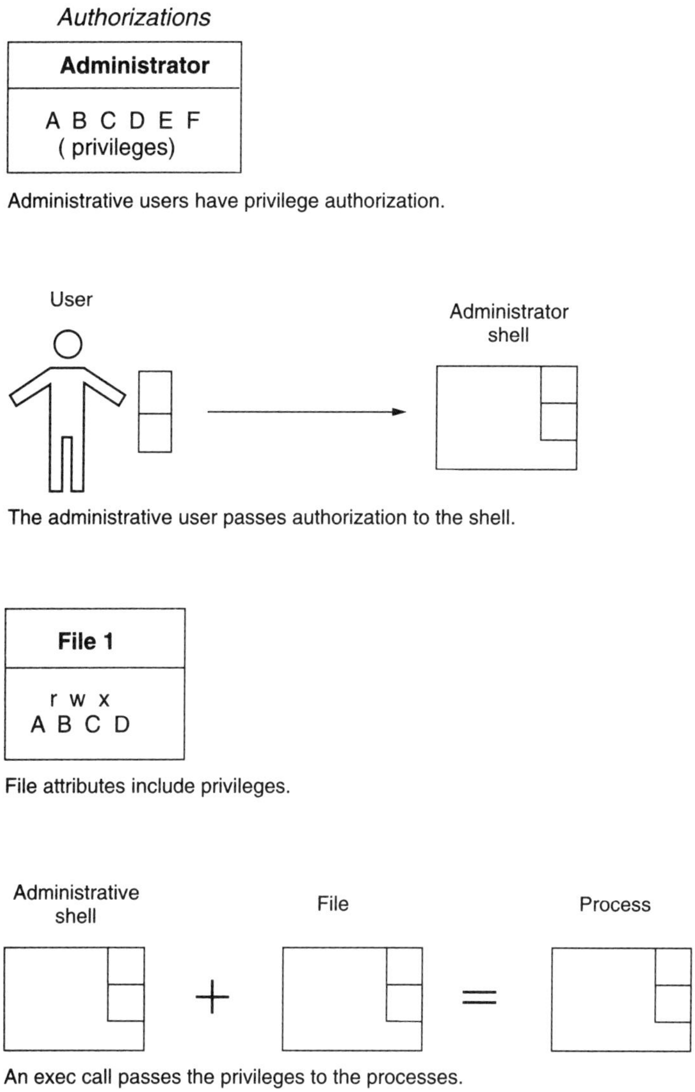

Figure 5.1 The privilege mechanism.

Privilege authorizations sometimes determine which commands the user can execute and with what privileges. Some systems refer to these authorizations as *command authorizations*. They can organize the commands by administrative roles, where each type of administrator has a list of which commands they can use, or they might be smaller lists that administrative "assistants" can have. For example, the authorizations can have the following commands:

- Security administrator: `label`, `privilege`, `chmod`, and `chown`
- System administrator: `install`, `fsck`, and `mknod`
- Auditor or audit operator: `boot`, `line printer`, and `mount`
- Line printer: `lp`

These commands can make privileged system calls, so using commands might require both the command authorization and the privilege authorization for the privileged system calls that the commands make. (See Figure 5.2.)

Security administrators assign users to command authorizations, but these assignments might not rely on the same mechanism as privilege authorizations. Authorizations have identifiers, which name a set of command authorizations. Users are assigned to the identifiers.

Each command authorization also can include the specific privileges that the user can invoke with it, or users can pass the same privilege authorizations to all of their commands. As I'll describe later, the command might not accept all privileges from the user.

Users would have privilege authorizations and authorizations for the commands so that they could issue the commands with privileges. Some systems might associate specific privileges with each command in the authorization.

Secure UNIX systems check users' authorizations if they attempt to make authorized commands. *Authorized commands* are those that require user authorization for their use.

Figure 5.2 System verifies authorization for all process activity.

Privilege use typically is made by authorized users who access their privileges by assuming authorizations in the form of administrative role, subsystem, application, or command authorizations. Administrative roles include security administrators, system administrators, auditors, operators, and application administrators; other authorizations include subsystems (such as printers and networking), applications (such as X Window), or individual commands (such as such as `mount` or `shutdown`).

No users can login as privileged users. If users are authorized, they can assume their privileges by invoking an administrative interface for the trusted path. That way, they aren't giving their privileges to a Trojan horse, and their login identifier can be maintained for accountability. Because they login as themselves, then assume an authorized administrative role, their individual identifier is associated with all of their administrative actions on the system audit records.

Processes also have privileges. (A *process* is an executable program file that is executing.) Users pass their privileges to the processes that they execute, subject to limitations on what privileges the file will accept when it is executed. System processes can have privileges *inherently*, without having been passed them by an authorized user. System processes aren't owned by a login user account identifier.

Executable files have privileges in their security attributes that specify what privileges they will have unconditionally when they execute and also what privileges they can assert while they execute.

The processes' privileges then are derived from the authorizations of their executers that match the assertable privileges of the file and the unconditional privileges of the file.

Processes carry those privileges when they run. The system verifies that processes have the required privileges whenever the processes attempt to perform a privileged operation.

Thus, users, files, and processes are related by privileges, and administrators and their processes are authorized to use privilege to do their jobs. Privilege authorizations get put to work to precisely manage special administrative powers by relating users, files, processes, and system resources.

Files also can have privileges called *file privileges*. When users execute them, the process derives its privileges from its own file privileges and its executer's privilege authorizations, which are passed to it. Some of the procedure's privileges might come from the procedure's file privileges, so they don't require user authorizations.

Any privilege can be part of the user authorizations, processes, or file privileges.

The security administrators are the sole managers of privilege assignments. They assign privileges to files and add users to privilege authorizations.

Roles

Some systems group the command authorizations (possibly specifying privileges with them) into special authorizations called *roles*. Users that assume roles are the major administrative users of privilege.

Roles are the authorization for the use of commands and privileges by administrative users, such as the security administers, the system administrators, auditors, and operators. Some system environments can make roles for applications administrators, such as networking, X Window, and database.

The security administrator will manage the authorization files with commands to create authorizations or add users to them. Users are assigned to roles or authorizations, which entitle them to use privileges.

Authorizations and roles are similar to groups in that they contain an identifier and a list of user identifiers. By being on the list, the users are "authorized" to assume the role. By assuming the role, they can execute commands and perform tasks that require privileges.

The security administrators manage which users are assigned authorizations by using the administrative interface commands that access the system authorizations database file. They also create authorizations by specifying the commands and privileges associated with the authorizations by using the administrative commands.

Privilege Classes

Privileges are required in order to perform administrative tasks. They can be grouped into basic classes: administrative, security, user, and application.

The distinction that I'll make between administrative and security privileges is that *administrative privileges* are the privileges that are the Secure UNIX replacement for the pre-Secure UNIX superuser's privileges, whereas *security privileges* are privileges that Secure UNIX added to support the new security mechanisms. *User privileges* are policy-optional restrictions on the pre-Secure user capabilities.

Each class can have subclasses: system call privileges and override privileges. *System call privileges* allow the execution of privileged system calls. *Override privileges* override access control mechanisms or other system-enforced policies or mechanisms.

Administrative privileges

Administrative privileges are those that delegate the tasks performed by system administrators or operators and system processes that are the controlling operations and maintenance processes. These privileges are those that unwove the pre-Secure UNIX superusers net of privileges into its individual strands. Included among these tasks are adding users to the system or performing backups. They are assigned to system administrators, with operators having a subset of them. Security administrators also have many administrative privileges.

There are two subclasses of administrative privileges: those that allow for override of system access control or other system mechanisms and those that allow the execution of privileged system calls.

Administrative override privileges are used to override system access control by labels, ACLs, or addresses or devices reserved for the kernel. These can empower commands to access resources that the user otherwise wouldn't have access to because they aren't permitted by the ACL or are prevented by the label laws.

I refer to privileges as an access mechanism because holders of privilege are allowed to bypass access control, such as ACLs and labels. A user doesn't need to be on the file's ACL or have a label that's higher than or equal to the file label to have access. Administrators need those privileges because, for example, they need to access the files of all users, not just their own, to make backups.

Override privileges can be invoked by a wide variety of commands, from everyday ones such as `cp` to special purpose administrative commands such as `fsck`, and are assigned to most administrative users.

Security privileges

Security privileges are the keys to the management of the security configuration, attributes, operation, and maintenance of the security protections and environment of the system. They allow the completion of security administration commands and access to the resources, such as the password or label security data files, that are the blueprint of each organization's TIB. Other security privileges allow control of the audit system: programming it to collect data about system activity and users, its management utilities, and the data that it creates. These security privileges are largely assigned to security administrators and auditors.

Security privileges also have system call and override subclasses.

User privileges

User privileges implement restrictions on nonadministrative user capabilities that used to be unrestricted on pre-Secure UNIX, such as the capacity to give ones files away or to execute setuid programs.

Application privileges

Application privileges are those that pertain to various applications, such as networking, X Window, and database-management systems. They can be assigned to application administrators or to the other administrators.

Permission to use privileges is assigned to users by the use of privilege authorizations. Sets of commands, possibly with specified privileges that can be used with the commands, are associated with command authorization identifiers. Authorized users then can assume the identifier and its privileges.

Override privileges

Override privileges allow processes to bypass system access controls on system resources or user files. These are the privileges that allow administrators to access users' files and system resources that they otherwise aren't given access to. Without privileges, administrators would be bound by the same access controls as any other user. These privileges can be included in a wide range of authorizations.

There are privileges for many types of overrides. Some bypass label access or ACL permission checks to read or write. These would allow an administrative command (which runs at the system label) to access user files that are labeled with user labels. Similarly, the administrator doesn't need ACL access to access the files.

Other privileges override the requirement that a user own a file to change its ACL or its owner or to kill a process with a different user identifier. As I'll cover later, there are separate privileges to execute the `chown` and `chmod` commands. Users that only have the `chown` privilege, and not the owner override privilege, only could change the owner of files that they owned. If they had both privileges, they could change the owner of other users' files, too.

Other privileges

Other privileges allow execution of task-related administrative commands, either by allowing the commands themselves or the system calls that they make. These privileges are for administrative commands that require particular privileges. Commands can be individual commands or related groups of commands.

Not all commands that administrators run require privileges that are special to the commands. Commands can be executed with no privilege or with privileges that are not particular to them, ones that are, or both.

The areas of commands that require specific privileges include security, audit, printer, network, or database administration.

Security privileges empower users to issue the commands that alter the security state of the system, which can have critical security effects. These users can modify the system security databases and the labels, ACLs, or privileges of system resources or user files.

Security commands display and change file labels (higher [upgrading] or lower [downgrading]); ACL attributes for permissions, owner, group, setuid, or setgid; and file privileges.

These commands require specific privileges. For example, even if a user had the privilege to override ACL access control, he or she still would need the task privilege to execute the `chmod` command to change ACLs.

Most critically, some security commands change the system security databases: the label, group, password, and privilege authorizations. Others affect information labels and audit identifiers.

Security privileges include the audit privileges that confer to users the power to control the audit system. Audit commands control turning auditing on and off, selecting which events are audited for each user, and allowing access to audit record buffers and files.

There are many miscellaneous system-administration commands that require particular privileges to perform, including `link`, `mkdir`, `mknod`, and `shutdown`.

Privilege Classes

I'll examine privilege types in greater detail. Throughout this book, I'll make a generic description of privileges. I'll use the draft POSIX conventions as a starting point and, beyond that, the shared base among the major Secure UNIX systems manufacturers, as well as other notable features.

Override privileges

Override privileges give any process the power to override system access controls. They often are used by system startup scripts, system recovery, and system control.

ACL override privilege allows a process to access a file, device, pipe, or other ACL-mediated object even though the user or group identifier of the process isn't granted permission on the ACL. It's part of administrators authorizations and is an allowed privilege of the backup command, for example. When authorized users run a backup, they pass the override to it and can back up all users' files without requiring ACL permission.

Each part of the ACL modes can be a separate privilege: execute, search (the execute mode on a directory), read, and write. Without the privilege, an attempt to `open` a file or `cd` to the directory without ACL permission would fail.

Interprocess communication objects (IPCs) can have separate override privileges.

Label override gives a process the power to violate label access control. If it tries to open a file for read a file at a higher label or to write data at a lower label file, it won't be stopped by the system.

Overrides of label control of read, write, and search are separate privileges. Process objects might require a separate label override privilege from file objects. Label override is used by startup scripts, system and file system initialization, and system recovery.

For systems with information labels, a privilege allows processes to write to a file without floating its label.

Kill privilege overrides are able to send interprocess signals only among processes with the same user identifier. Administrative scripts, such as `shutdown`, use them.

Owner override privilege allows users to change the ACLs on files that are not owned by them, provided that the users also have the security privileges that allow use of the respective commands to do that: `chmod` or `change_ACL`. Without privilege, only owners are entitled to change the ACLs of files. IPC and processes objects can have separate owner override privileges.

Owner override privilege used to be part of superusers bloated powers. It now is found only as a forced privilege on system programs such as `login`, `initialize`, and `su`. No users have them as authorizations. The programs require owner override privilege to rewrite system data files and logs. It is one more privilege that cannot be used by a user that has broken in to an administrative account, because administrators don't have it.

Other owner override privileges separately control owner access operations besides changing the ACLs.

Modification of a process owner or effective or group identifier is allowed with an override privilege, which is useful during system initialization. Processes also can have a privilege that allows them to override their own label list, information label, or label.

A privilege can allow a process to override its maximum process limit. This is a resource limit that prevents excessive processes from affecting system availability.

A privilege also can allow a process to override delays introduced to combat the threat from covert channels. (See chapter 4 for more information on covert channels.)

Security privileges are privileges that allow the configuration and modification of the security attributes of the system, including ACLs, labels, and privileges. They are used exclusively by the security administrator and some system processes. They include the privileges to use the commands to change file ACLs, labels, and privileges.

Privileges to change labels have separate privileges for upgrade and downgrade. This is because downgrading can have a more severe impact on confidentiality than upgrading. Downgrading, or changing the file label to a lower label, is allowing actions that normally are prevented by the label laws to prevent information disclosure. Upgrading is less of a disclosure threat; however, if it is performed unnecessarily, it can degrade the effectiveness of your TIB by creating useless monitoring overhead.

Typically, only the security administrator will have change_label privileges. System and application processes might have them to provide a multilabel interface. For example, a mail server might manage mail with different labels, or a database server might accept input from processes at different labels. A separate upgrading privilege might upgrade up to the top of the owning user's label list or to the highest label in the TIB. (IPC objects can have separate change_label privileges.)

Audit privileges

Audit privileges endow the auditor with the rights to control the audit system. Privileges include the power to program audit events for users or the system and to manipulate the audit buffers and output records.

Other audit privileges are for trusted processes, which are privileged system daemons or servers. These privileges allow the daemons or servers to execute without generating any audit records or to generate audit records themselves. For some procedures, such as an audit system daemon, it would be an initialize loop if the procedures generated audit records, so the daemon runs with auditing shut off.

Other processes, such as administrative interfaces run from the trusted path or audit analyzers, can audit themselves. They first would shut the system auditing off for themselves, then do the job themselves. In which case, they'd require both privilege to shut off system audit on them, as well as privilege to generate their own audit.

Administrator privileges

Administrator privileges are associated with administrative commands that aren't exclusive to managing the security state of the system and the security administrator. They can be shared in part by the security administrator and the other administrators and operators. Not only can administrator privileges be assigned to the exact administrator that needs them, they also are used by the exact programs that need them.

The following commands are affected by these privileges: `shutdown`, `startup`, system accounting, system attributes (such as `date`, `time`, or `node` name), `chown`, `chroot`, `chmod` (suid and sgid), `debug`, permission to execute suid programs, `limit`, `mknod`, file system (`format`), `link`, `lock`, `mount`, multilevel directory, `mkfs`, `nfs` (`rmount` or `export`), `nice`, resource limits, `remote` (`nets` and `X`), privilege to redirect the console, device control (change attribute and access system device), driver sensitive, override file system range, `backup`, consistency checkers, printer (`label`, `jobs`, and `queue`), memory (`ps` and `who`), `password` (other users'), `df`, and tape (`tar`, `cpio`, and multilevel tape).

The system accounting, chroot, debug, kill, limit, lock, mknod, mount, owner, remote, processes identifier, shutdown, and system attribute privileges are examples of the division of superuser powers and concisely illustrate how privileges dispersed the excessive and dangerous powers.

I'll begin with a select group of these that primarily is relegated to trusted processes in the form of forced privileges, as opposed to passed to them by users or administrators privilege authorizations: chroot, kill, owner, process identifier, audit suppress, and audit write.

Pre-Secure UNIX system daemons, such as initialize, and administrative commands, such as shutdown, ran with root privileges. Secure UNIX uses new, more precise privileges to allow these processes to do their work, yet it obviates the need that the processes be owned or executed by an all-powerful user.

On Secure systems, the chroot system call is mostly used by the login program. chroot defines the file system root directory for a process. Pre-Secure environments used chroot to implement restricted shell and guest logins. Secure systems rarely use the chroot system call or the chroot command except during login because the need to control or restrict file system access is better met by features such as ACLs, privilege, and labeling.

The only Secure UNIX programs that need to make the chroot system call are login and the chroot command, and they are the only programs that have that privilege. login has it as a forced privilege; it's run by a getty system process (the terminal- monitoring process), so it doesn't require that its executers pass it privilege by their authorizations. As a consequence, login doesn't have to have superuser privilege to make the call, only precisely what privilege it needs. By barring user use of the chroot command, no users or administrators need have the privilege authorization to make the call.

I'll observe what a revolutionary, powerful, grandly comprehensive security mechanism that use of privilege is. login has the forced privilege for the chroot system call. No users can have the privilege authorization for it, not even the system's administrators.

Thus, it now is that no users can write and execute a C program with the chroot system call in it. Because they lack authorization, they cannot pass the chroot privilege to their programs. Also, the program wouldn't have chroot as an allowed privilege, because all of the allowed privileges must be assigned to programs by the security administrator. For those reasons, the call attempt would fail.

For the same reasons, no Trojan horse binary can sneak on and execute chroot. No users that have stolen an administrator's password can sneak on and plant a Trojan horse that uses chroot, because no administrators are authorized for chroot privilege and it won't execute without the privilege.

The only entity that can execute `chroot` is the system `login` program, because it is the only one that has the `chroot` privilege. It has `chroot` as a forced privilege and doesn't require its executer to pass the privilege to it. It can be executed only by system initializer or getty processes.

What works for `chroot` works for any of the other potent system calls that sometimes were used on pre-Secure systems by malicious programs to deceive. Thus Secure UNIX privileges are a highly effective new security mechanism that, in a thorough and noncircumventable manner, redress the heinous security problem that was the pre-Secure UNIX superuser. I'll be fully describing the other means whereby privileges provide the cure.

`kill`, or sending interprocess signals without having privilege, is allowed only among processes with the same user identifier. Kill privilege overrides that and allows the termination of processes with different identifiers. No users or administrators are authorized for kill privilege. It is assigned solely to administrative scripts, such as `shutdown`, to kill all user processes and system daemons, such as the audit daemon.

This again demonstrates how an excessive power that used to be granted to superuser accounts is removed from use by all users and is confined to where it really is needed—an administrative script that runs with only the privileges it needs and no more.

Pre-Secure UNIX would run `shutdown` as root user with all privileges. Also, any user that become superuser (and there often were too many of those) would have the 007 license to kill processes (even users that might have borrowed the root password to unclog a print queue).

Shutdown and startup privileges either are assigned to the administrative scripts or commands for those purposes and allow them to make privileges system calls or are assigned to users as privileges that allow them to execute the commands or scripts. Those privileges usually are a part of most administrator and operator roles.

A setuid privilege allows a process to change its process identifiers, owner, or group. It is a forced privilege on `login` to create new login session processes and on `su` to change process owner. No users are authorized to use this privilege.

System accounting privilege

System accounting privilege allows the use of the system accounting command, which gathers system statistics, such as process scheduling and disk use. It is an essential part of the system administrator's task of performing system- consistency checking by use of consistency alarm detectors.

System attribute privileges

System attribute privileges are privileges that allow commands to change the system date and time, node name, etc. The commands with these privileges usually are run from system startup scripts. The system administrator also can have this privilege, if necessary. It's better to avoid possible misuse by leaving it to the script because these scripts rarely change.

The system attribute privilege illustrates how superusers powers were confined. Using privilege, it isn't necessary to give the power to change the system date to any users, because it can be granted solely as a file privilege to the system startup script, which has precisely the privilege that it needs.

Previously, the script would have had to be owned by superuser and have had absolute privileges, which was in itself a risk. Also, there would be the superusers who could execute the command as well.

Debug privilege

Debug privilege allows use of system debugging, which can be used to alter memory, such as buffered system data structures and data files. It should be restricted to a dedicated debugging account that has few other privileges.

Limit privilege

Limit privilege allows users to exceed limits (file size, message queue, etc.). It is used for recovery.

`mknod` privilege

`mknod` is an administrative command that creates device special files. `mknod` is exclusively executed by the system administrators at systems installation or systems reconfiguration to add devices or device drivers to the kernel. Device files belong in /dev, and it would be a menace if they were anywhere else. Conceivably, a crook could use an unauthorized device as an eavesdropping tool or for other foul deeds.

To ensure that only system administrators execute `mknod`, only systems administrators have the mknod privilege authorization, which allows execution of the `mknod` command. The system administrators can impart the privilege to an administrative interface program that has it as an allowed privilege. However, no program has it as a forced privilege. The only way to execute `mknod` is by having the mknod authorization.

The same administrative interface program can be used by all of the administrators. For example, it might consist of a menu whereby users select either security administrator or systems administrator command submenus. Only systems administrators have the mknod privilege authorization, even though the interface has the mknod privilege as an allowed privilege. Therefore, the system administrator can run `mknod` from the interface, but the security administrator can't. The interface can inherit the privilege from the systems administrators because they have the authorization. The only program that the systems administrator can pass the mknod privilege to is the administrative interface, because it is the only program that has mknod as an allowed privilege. The security administrators can't execute `mknod` from the interface even though it has the mknod allowed privilege, because they don't have the mknod authorization.

This is an example of how the privilege mechanism wiped out the egregious excess of power of superuser. It provides not only protections, but also a dependable and flexible means to promote shared resources, such as an administrative interface, that guarantees that users can't gain a drop more power than they need to do their jobs.

Backup and `mount` privileges

There are two types of backups: user and system. It's one thing for operators to be able to backup and restore all user files, or even for users to do their own files; doing system files is another matter.

As perilous as it was, on pre-Secure UNIX, users that needed to do backups had to have superuser access, laying open the crux of the system's ability to defend itself. As an absurdly obvious yet deadly example, the kernel executable /unix could be switched with one that is full of trapdoors, Trojan horses, etc. by users who ostensibly wanted to make a backup floppy of their Moria game files.

Privilege to the rescue. The overall procedure of backup is regulated by scaled privileges that allow varying degrees of system access. Various backup privileges can allow read-only access to user file systems or read/write access to system file systems. The Moria users would get the former and be unable to wreak havoc on the kernel.

Closely related to backup privilege is mount privilege. Mount privilege allows the `mount` command. `mount` is necessary for the system to interface its system files, as well as its user file systems. Mounting these is done upon system startup by the system startup processes. They subsequently can be unmounted or mounted by operators to do system backups.

The power to mount file systems is dependent on whether the users have privileges to perform backup. If they have read-only backup privileges, they can only mount file systems read-only; if they have system backup privileges, they can mount read/write. In either case, they also must have mount command privileges.

Needless to say, only the system administrators have system backup privilege authorizations. Operators have the read-only backup privilege authorization. The effect is that users that lack backup privileges cannot execute the `mount` command.

Privilege Mechanism

Administrators get their authorizations by logging in at the system label and by invoking an administrative interface via the trusted path. The interface will `exec` shells with the privilege authorizations that the users have.

So now you have privileged shell processes, which will `exec` the users' commands with privileges. This has to be done so that privileged commands can't use more privileges than are appropriate for the job or so that the commands can't `exec` any other processes that will gain their privilege needlessly. This limiting of the use of privilege is the Secure UNIX access firewall that fixed the superuser problem.

Process privileges

When a process is execed (with the UNIX `exec` system call that starts a process from an executable file), its privileges are derived from the authorizations of the execer process (the old process that makes the exec call) and the privileges of the file that is execed (the new process that results). The following paragraphs will focus on how this is achieved.

Processes have three sets of privileges: inheritable, permitted, and effective. A process receives its inheritable privileges directly from its execer. It then can change those before it execs another process. It gets its permitted privileges partially from its execer but also from the file it was execed from, which I will soon describe.

Inheritable privileges Inheritable privileges are the users' privilege authorizations that are given to all of the users' shells, commands, and subprocesses, which are transmitted by `exec`. These privileges can be asserted or retracted by a process to control what privileges the process will pass to a process that it execs.

Execing processes is the fundamental method of process creation in the UNIX environment. In it, a running process overlays itself with another executable program, resulting in an entirely new process. Secure UNIX has enhanced `exec` to manage privilege transfer between the execer and the execed process.

Permitted privileges The permitted privileges are the maximum privileges that a process is allowed to assert. To keep privilege use precise while it runs, a process will adjust its privileges to meet its requirements but can only assert those privileges that it is permitted.

Effective privileges Effective privileges are the privileges that the process currently is asserting. The system will use them to judge whether the process has the privileges to perform a privileged operation.

File privileges

So far, I've been describing the privileges that a process has. Processes are execed from files, which have different privileges than processes. The file privileges are: allowed, forced, and set effective. (See Figure 5.3.)

Allowed privileges Allowed privileges are used when the file is execed to calculate the processes' permitted privileges. They are an essential side of the firewall because they limit the powers of the processes, no matter what the powers of the execers. That way, if the execers are rogue administrators, their powers are restricted, no matter how great their authorizations are.

For the execed processes to receive a permitted privilege, it must be listed by both the inheritable privileges of the execer processes and the allowed privileges of the file.

Forced privileges The forced privileges of files are passed to the execed processes' permitted privileges without any comparison to the execer processes' privileges. They are the "inherent" privileges of the file that become effective when it's invoked, no matter what the authorizations of the invoking user.

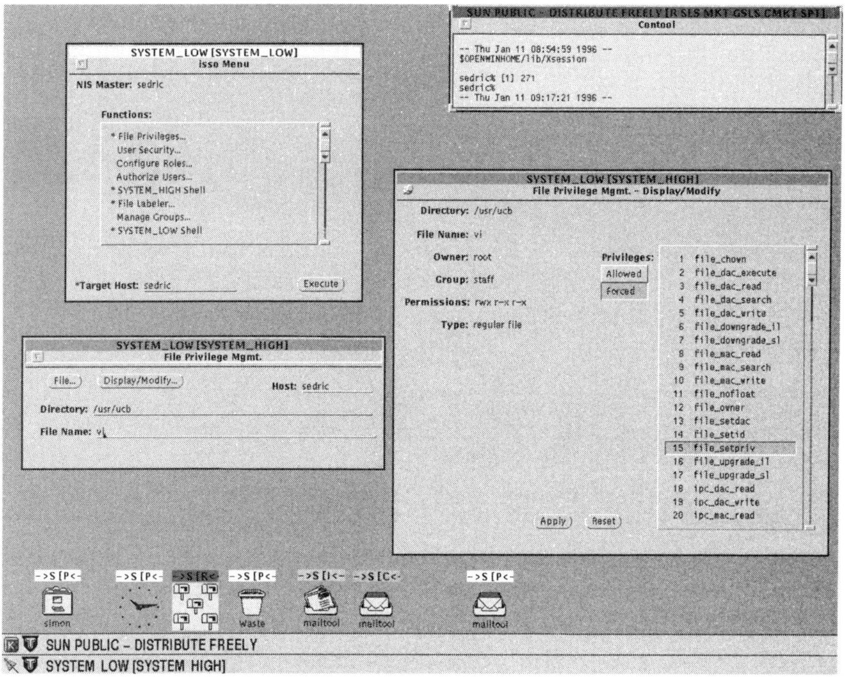

Figure 5.3 The system administrator sets privileges.

Forced privileges of Secure UNIX have replaced pre-Secure UNIX setuid. Setuid still exists, but its former job as the primary means to provide user access to system resources by setuid root is gone. However, the general concept remains. In effect, forced privileges (and previously setuid) are used to provide privileges to unprivileged users.

Privileges are needed to allow users to access system resources, such as print queues. You don't want to give those privileges out to all users because they might not be qualified to directly perform detailed system operations, among other security reasons.

The solution is provide interface programs, such as `lp`, that can expertly manage system resources. This management requires a method to temporarily give the required access privileges to otherwise unprivileged users. Secure UNIX uses forced privileges to provide these. When users execute a system interface command, the command's forced privileges allow the user system access, as setuid used to do.

Forced privileges are far more precise than setuid in that they bestow very select privileges to the invoked command, rather than allowing it to get root privileges.

I'll bring together the processes and file privileges in order to describe how privileges are passed via `exec`. The permitted privileges of an execed file are derived by selecting the inheritable privileges of the execer processes that also are allowed privileges in the execed file and adding those with the forced privileges of the execed file. They become the execed file's permitted privileges. (See Figure 5.4.)

The execed processes' inheritable privileges are copied straight from the execer processes' inheritable privileges. These become the new processes' means to pass privileges with any execs that it does.

Set-effective privileges The final privilege of files is the set-effective privileges. If they are matched to the permitted privileges of the execed processes, they set the execed processes' effective privileges. (See Figure 5.5.)

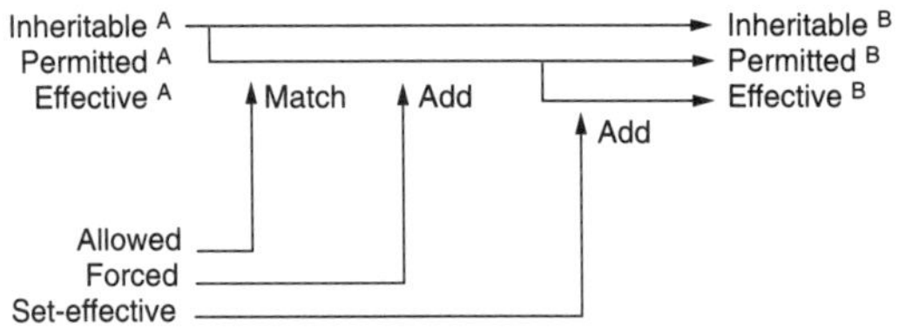

Inheritable^{A} = Inheritable^{B}
Permitted^{A} = Permitted^{B} that match A, plus any Forced
Effective^{A} = Permitted^{A} that match Set-effective

(Match = bitwise AND, Add = bitwise OR)

Figure 5.4 How privileges are derived.

Before process			File 1				After process	
Inheritable	ABCDEFG		Allowed	ABC	HIJ		Inheritable	ABCDEFG
Permitted	A CD G	+	Forced		FG XYZ	=	Permitted	ABC FG XYZ
Effective	A D		Set - effective ABC				Effective	A C

Figure 5.5 An example privilege derivation.

That is the final step in the method to pass privileges via `exec`, and thus keep privilege use precise, and is an effective access firewall.

Some observations

There are some observations that you can make about this privilege system. Inheritable privileges are the users' privilege authorizations that are used on all of the users' shells, commands, and subprocesses. Allowed privileges are configured on a file's security attributes by administrators in order to limit the privileges that the file can acquire as a process.

When a file is execed, the execed processes receive the execer's inheritable privileges if these privileges also are the file's allowed privileges, plus the file's forced privileges. The result is that the execed processes might have more permitted privileges than the user is authorized for, because of the file's forced privileges.

Any privilege can be a file privilege or authorized to a user as forced, allowed, or permitted. There are no privileges that are restricted by the system as to how they can be used. The security administrator can assign any privilege to any users or files.

Summary

In general, if users attempt operations for which they lack privileges, the operations will fail. Also, all privilege use is audited.

Backup privileges are examples of privilege authorizations of commands. Some privileges authorize processes to make system calls and, therefore, only indirectly authorize the use of commands. For example, mount can have a privilege for the mount system call and the `mount` command. Backup is a command privilege authorization. Backup can call the `mount` system call, but one need not have the mount command authorization to make the `mount` system call.

Other system calls that require authorizations can be made by one or more system commands. The `mount` and `backup` commands both make the `mount` system call. The privilege to make the `mount` system call is implied by having the authorization to issue either the `mount` or `backup` command.

Some system call privileges indirectly control the use of commands, rather than having an explicit privilege for the use of the command. The `chown` command, which doesn't have a command privilege authorization, makes the `chown` system call, which has a privilege authorization for it. In that way, the command is indirectly controlled by the system call authorization because, without it, any attempt to issue the command would fail.

Chown privilege allows users to run the `chown` command (or system call) to change the owner of files that they own. This is required by some system programs, such as mail.

A privilege can allow a process to set the setuid and setgid bits on a file. On Secure systems, setuid is no longer used extensively; it has been replaced by the privilege mechanism itself and, to some extent, the use of setgid.

Chapter

6

Audit

On pre-Secure UNIX, there was very little way to know who did something after it was done. This was a lack of accountability—the ability to know "who did what to what." There were even many instances whereby users could be anonymous.

Secure UNIX systems have an entirely new facility that changes all that. It's called *Secure UNIX audit*. There's nothing like it in pre-Secure UNIX. It's a way to provide accountability for all system activity—from file access to networks and databases.

On pre-Secure UNIX, file access—whether authorized, desirable, or otherwise—happened in effect anonymously and secretively. After a file was accessed, there was no way to know which user had accessed it. There was no way to be informed each time the file was accessed.

Worst of all, there was no way to record system activity to anything near the necessary level of detail for management of it or no way to discover and provide evidence of misuse.

This can't be overstated as a historical problem of UNIX. It is a major reason why mainframe environments have persisted to the extent that they have since they offer this capacity. Major organizations must have it to meet regulatory and internal audit mandates.

Systems services, such as communications and database servers, also didn't keep a log of user actions. This was due to some serious accountability and auditing shortcomings. Anonymous logins were allowed.

Lack of accountability was true for most other types of system activity, such as use of printer or tape output.

Activity on the system is audit logged by compiling records, called *audit event records*, that describe all aspects of system activity. They are classified into classes, such as administrative, authentication, privilege, etc. Audit information describes most system and user activities.

Each audit event record (called an *event*), such as a user login, is formatted into fields, such as the relevant event type, user ID, file names, and time.

Administrators preconfigure (or "preprogram") the audit system to collect selected audit events, usually restricting it to events that will yield the most significant information lest too much information make auditing overwhelming.

Audit is a continuous activity-logging facility. It can be used to maintain a system activity log that is a complete record of every user's (and administrator's) actions, such as what commands they issued (including the command line), what resources they accessed from their programs, or their login sessions. However, it usually is important to select critical activity rather than collect it all.

Secure audit also records all system-related events beyond those attributable to users, such as system failures, the workings of the system processes (such as login), and the state of system resources.

Audit preprogramming to select which records are collected can take place from selectable perspectives such as for a specific user, for file objects, for all users or files at a specific label, or by event type.

Audit information is gathered continually whenever a system is running. You can direct it to printers, disks, or any other output or communications channel.

To maintain accountability using audit, you must go beyond deciding what audit event records to preprogram to collect and setting up the system to collect it. Once you have collected it, you must analyze it, monitor it, respond to problems, and finally store the records in archive.

Once the important information is preprogrammed and auditing records are generated, they are examined by a program, expert system, or audit administrator. A program can simply format audit records, perform statistical analysis, or attempt to identify suspicious activity. Expert systems are best at the latter, partly because they allow input of complex conditions to monitor.

I will be describing which events are most important to preprogram to audit for and when these events constitute situations that should raise your concerns. Audit records that seem to indicate problems are called *audit alarms*, and the programs that analyze the records for alarms are called *audit alarm detectors*.

The auditors, who are privileged system administrators, are the only users that can control the auditing system. They preprogram it and analyze the records.

In any case, whether or not programs just format and display audit data or "reduce" it to statistics, alarms, or mail notices about suspicious activity,

Secure-system auditors must have the job of evaluating it. They, their alternates, or programs must be "on call" at all times to detect or receive alarms about possible suspicious activity.

Alarms might require action on the part of the auditors. The auditors might have to respond to a violation that is occurring or make follow-up inquires. Auditors should understand the "normal" system activity that they perceive in the audit trail. Any signs of abnormal behavior should be followed up with an inquiry to the user, with fast, blocking action or maybe only focusing more detailed auditing on the activity.

Auditors are special administrators that have exclusive control of the audit system. It's a separation of powers; the other administrators can't shut down the audit system to do something sleazy. On the other hand, auditors can't perform the privileged actions of the other administrators and conceivably attack the system.

On a Secure system, administrative tasks are divided among a team of administrators. They must coordinate their activities with the auditors so that, as events show up on the log, auditors have a reasonable assurance that the events are legitimate.

It is not only administrators that must reconcile their actions with the audit log. Users, when acting upon data that has been identified and labeled as important, also must reconcile similarly.

Reconciliation can be a formal procedure. Administrators can keep written logs of operations, which can be manually or automatically compared to the audit log. Programs can process the audit trail listing multistep operation sequences and comparing that to online administrative transaction logs.

Online reconciliations can be a part of an automated system-monitoring procedures based on an expert system.

Manufacturers provide tools to format audit records, which initially are produced as binary data, into data that can be fed into an audit analysis program or displayed as text. Statistical analysis can be displayed along with highlighting for problem indications. Other tools include a database manager for event records with a query language.

Alarm-detector programs can be made from the tools offered by manufacturers or supplied by third parties. Alarm programs can analyze audit data as it occurs for alarms.

Auditors analyze audit records to catch problems that might have occurred. They try to detect problems as soon as they occur or even while they're occurring.

Alarms are named by the problems that they refer to. Alarms might be due to breaking organizational policies (such as inappropriately changing a file ACL) or blatant evidences of system tampering (such as corrupting a system file).

In some cases, the alarm-detector program can take an action in response to an alarm, such as terminating a user session. Urgent alarms are literally alarms. The program might attempt to notify an administrator by beeping a system monitor terminal, e-mail, or telephone beeper. It also could set off a burglar alarm.

The audit alarm detector is an important part of the confirmed authorization principle. Using it requires that administrators, application administrators, and users work closely and coordinate their activities with the auditors.

For the alarm detector to be able to distinguish unauthorized activity from legitimate system use, activity that potentially could effect the security of the system or its highest-labeled information must be coordinated with the auditors. The auditors must be notified in advance of it, either by a written schedule or other means.

The auditor then can program the information into the alarm detection system so that the activity will be accepted as normal when it is detected on the audit records.

Each user has an activity description database in the audit alarm detector that keeps configurable user activity data, such as when users can login or invoke privileges, as well as dynamic statistical values that are kept as indicators of normal user behavior. (See Figure 6.1.)

Other user activity will be reconciled after it is performed, perhaps by using written notes or keyboard captures of user activity to justify with the audit records.

The audit records are accessible only to privileged auditors. The records can be analyzed by their record fields, such as activity type or user identifier.

With the audit means in place, you need policies that can guide the use of the Secure UNIX features to meet your security goals.

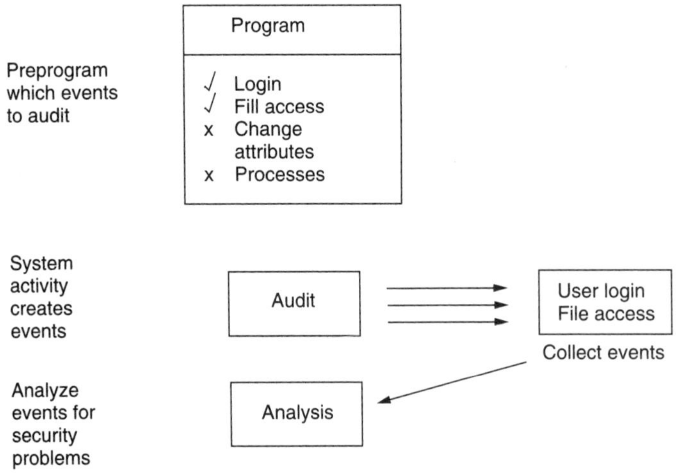

Figure 6.1 Audit overview.

Suspicious events on audit reconciliations can be responded to on an appropriate timescale. An unexplainable system shutdown or open of critical files requires immediate investigation. Other events are less an emergency.

Responses can be remote shutdowns, phoning the building security staff to check a video monitor, or, if all else fails, unleashing the Dobermans.

The events that must be audited are access of the system files and the files that control the system security, repeated logins, etc.

There is a wide range of responses to audited events. If you've wisely done your trusted information base (TIB) design, audit information is manageable. You can perceive what is due to regular use and what is of concern and requires action.

Audit events can be organized into classes in order to prioritize and handle them by their potential security implications—the degree of security concern that they raise. This is essential because, if you don't audit efficiently, auditing quickly becomes unmanageable. With prioritizing, the features and strategies of the audit system allow you to have a powerful, efficient, and essential capacity for confirmed authorization.

Total accountability is available for all system activity. Application server processes—such as communications, databases, and graphics—are all integrated with system audit facilities to describe user activity in detail by user.

What makes the audit effective is organization. It takes organization because there is an overwhelming amount of information that can potentially be generated from auditing. You have to be able to keep the important information in sight. By judging what information is the most important, you can make an additional effort to audit it. Keeping organized keeps the most important information distinct.

You also need to persist and be ready to respond if something is suspicious. Auditing must never cease for the time that your systems operate, nor should your ability to respond.

When some types of activity occur, you must ensure that they are legitimate system use. For example, there are times when the system is highly vulnerable, such as during system shutdown. This type of event must always be audited.

However, it's not enough to just audit it, to see that it happened. You need to ensure that it was legitimate. It must be a policy that system critical operations have to be reconciled with the audit log as part of confirmed authorization.

That policy implies procedures that take place after the fact. To as great an extent as possible, reconciliation must take place as events occur.

Another major benefit of labeling your information is that you can organize it by its importance to your organization. More important information—in terms of its confidentiality requirement, economic significance, etc.—is labeled accordingly.

You concentrate your auditing work on actions affecting this information. This requires keeping information organized by its importance.

Audit records consist of specific events types such as "file open" or "chmod command." Classifying events aids you in selecting which events to audit. Audit event classes are a way to name sets of events to simplify inputting them to the audit system. The events are related by function and the importance of auditing them, so they usually would be input to together. Some systems implement audit-event classes; otherwise, the events that compose the classes can be input individually.

The activity of the users can be audited by using the users' identifier and their other security attributes as part of the audit information. System auditors will "preprogram" the audit system, requesting it to audit the security relevant activity for each user. When activity is audited, a record describing it is created and can be output for analysis.

Although the option to audit all user activity is available, it usually won't be used. Only the security-significant activity of users, such as their assuming privileges, is always audited. The commands that they issue within their privileged roles are tied to their individual user identifiers, not to their anonymous administrative role identifiers.

Auditing of security-relevant actions is done for all users at all times and is not selected to be audited on an individual basis. Security relevant actions are selected on a global, systemwide basis, covering all users and their processes, as well as system processes.

The security-relevant activity might include: login, file open and removal, and administrative activity. The information in the audit record includes the commands that the users give, the arguments of the commands, the time, the location, the files or devices affected, and the return state of the command.

A central advantage of the new Secure UNIX audit technology is auditing administrative activity. The administrative audit event class consists of audit records that describe the activity of the system administrators: security administrator, system administrator, operator, application administers (database, network, X Window, etc.), and users that have some administrative powers. Events in this class can include evocation of an administrative interface and issuance of administrative commands.

Typical administrative events include creation of a user account, assigning a login label list to a user, and assigning a label list to a device, tape backup, etc.

Another event class is the file access audit event class. The data included on events include date, time, user and statistical information of the command return, labels and attributes on file open or remove events, and terminal identifiers for authentication events.

All file access now can be examined immediately after the fact with audit records, including the user identifier, the file name, the time and date, the privileges used, etc.

All other activity is similarly described. The information provided is tailored to the activity. Login audit records also would include the terminal or communications service (such as `rlogin`) used.

Audit events, especially if collected on a write-once device such as a WORM disk drive, make excellent courtroom evidence.

Audit data is kept in a binary format in a *kernel buffer*. The buffer uses some sort of flow-control scheme whereby data must be output to disk before it fills up. If audit buffers get full, the system should shutdown.

Managing the buffers can be the job of audit daemons. They keep the buffers free by outputting audit data to disk. Usually what they dump from the buffers still is in binary or compressed format, and the auditors or analysis programs must run formatted programs on them.

The policy of confirmed authorization is that you must be aware of all activity on the system, confirm that it's authorized, and be ready to act if its not. The pre-Secure UNIX days, in which you didn't have a firm grasp on what was going on, are over.

Audit Objectives

Secure UNIX audit is an essential new facility. One of the major reasons why UNIX has not replaced mainframes is that it has lacked the type of activity auditing found on the mainframes. Auditors at large organizations, along with federal regulators, demand this type of activity auditing.

Secure UNIX changes that. It now is possible to satisfy the same auditing requirements as is on mainframes.

For audit to be effective, you must be selective about what activity you preprogram to audit for. You do this by keeping in mind objectives that are feasible to reach on Secure UNIX.

The objectives are audit of:

- Access to system files and high-labeled data
- Use of administrative commands and privilege
- Access to critical data
- Login and other system entry
- Resource control
- Changes of access control

To meet these objectives, use a combination of preprogramming strategies. In some cases, there are specific audit classes that you can preprogram that meet whole objectives. You also might have to limit some audit classes to administrative users or use MAC labels to precisely specify which objects you audit for each audit class.

In the following paragraphs, I'll briefly describe the objectives and how to preprogram Secure UNIX audit to cover each of them.

Access to system files refers to unauthorized modifications of those files, which could be due to accident or foul play. The only time that access to system files is acceptable is during system installation, upgrade, or maintenance by authorized administrators.

However, this is a difficult objective to meet. File access is too common an activity to audit it all and look through the events for system file access. There'd be too many records. This objective can be met only by auditing file access by the MAC label of the system files, which limits the amount of file access activity that is audited.

Critical data refers to files, such as database files, that contain an organization's most confidential, valuable, or guarded information. This data also has to be audited by its label, so an organization must assign such labels sparingly, or audit of access will overwhelm the effectiveness of the whole system.

Other objects besides files might be critical, such as network connections or devices. Audit by label also is the practical means to preprogram them.

The use of administrative privileges and commands must be confirmed to be authorized, including all users, programs, processes, scripts, and administrative commands.

Unlike access to system files, all activity involving administrative privileges and commands must be audited and checked for authorization. There is no way to limit it to that done by or to a particular MAC label, because it could be any or all MAC labels. It's the unexpected occurrence that you might be most interested in.

So, for this objective, it's best to preprogram for all administrative and privilege activity, then analyze it to check its authorization. This requires not only checking who gave what commands, with what privileges, why, and when, but it also is a matter of what privileges were invoked by what programs and whether they were expected.

Checking all of that requires sophisticated analysis programs that use behavior profiles and rules. It also might be beyond the capacities of some environments. In which case, not all of the events of the class can be turned on to audit. Some privileges have less power than others. At the least, however, all actions by the major administrators must be audited.

Audit Programming

There are flexible methods to preprogram the audit system to establish what system activity, users, and resources will be audited by it. You "program" the audit system in the sense of providing it a list of events or event classes for which it will output an audit event record whenever the respective system activity occurs. (See Figure 6.2.)

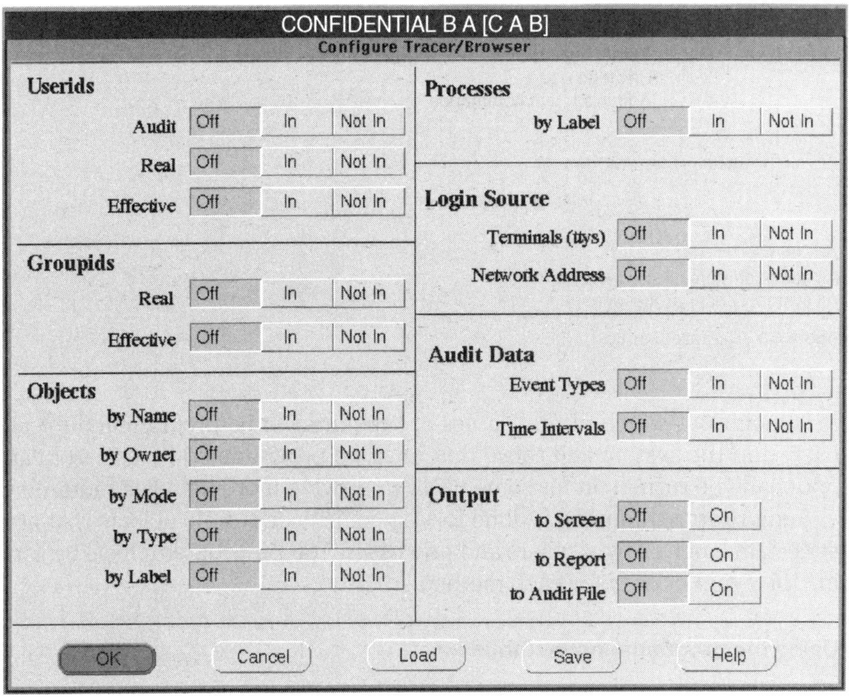

Figure 6.2 Configuring the audit analyzer. *(Courtesy Haystack Laboratories, Inc.)*

Audit events might occur due to user activity, such as the issuing of administrative commands, or to system activity, such as a failed login.

Audit classes can be preprogrammed to be "required" so that the audit system will audit for all users and system activity. All users' events (though not individually programmed for it) and system-derived events will be audited if programmed to be required. (See Figure 6.3.)

Audit classes also can be preprogrammed for individual users, whereby the audit system programs audit for their activity only. For users, including administrators, the programmed-by-user and the required lists are combined, and those audit records are generated by the users activity.

The same classes can be programmed either as required or by user. The distinction is made as to whether the whole system or an individual is being programmed.

Auditors program the audit system. Required auditing is programmed by setting an audit system-wide audit configuration parameter, whereas individuals have an audit security attribute set on their accounts that determines their individual user audit programming. Required auditing can't be overridden by individual auditing.

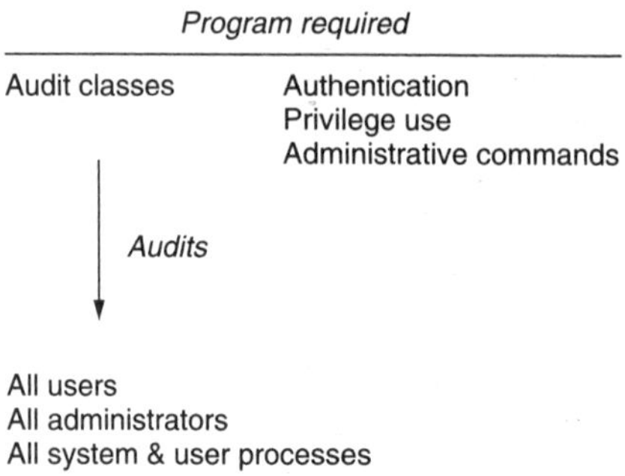

Figure 6.3 Required audit.

I'll point out which of the classes are required to be programmed for all users and the system and those that must be programmed by users or can optionally be turned on for some users to provide more detail as required.

Audit preprogramming is done for a specific user, for file objects that are at certain label, or by all users and processes. You preprogram these by listing the event classes for each method.

Using the programming methods

The following paragraphs will describe how these programming methods are used to efficiently and securely audit.

The required class is for events, such as administrative activity, that must be audited under all circumstances. By using the required class, you avoid having to list the classes for each user. You also protect against the threat that a user account somehow is created or modified so that it doesn't audit the required events. That could be caused by crooked administrators, their impostors, the impostors' programs, etc. With required audit, you know that, whatever happens, you've got an underlying protection in place.

Administrative privilege use, login/logout, and access of system file space are examples of activity that must be programmed as required audit.

You should make the administrative privilege class required auditing (done for all administrators, users, and system processes, rather than by individual users) because you want to catch its unauthorized use by either administrators, malicious programs, or ordinary users.

That demonstrates the use of required audit programming: to program administrative privilege use on a required basis so that use of it by any user, administrative user, or system process is audited.

When programming by user is advantageous

All administrators also must have a higher level of auditing programmed by user than ordinary users. They are the ones that can wreak the most havoc if they are bent. Although you don't normally program detailed event classes (such as file access) for ordinary users, you need to for administrative users.

So, here is a case where you program individual users (in this case, the administrator) for more detailed auditing, such as for file access, than you'd perform on nonadministrative users. (See Figure 6.4.)

The reason that you should audit administrators more than other users is that an administrator could have devised a Trojan horse using his or her privileges. Therefore, heavily audit the administrative users to be sure that all of their privilege powers are exercised using legitimate administrative interfaces for authorized purposes. Do this even though administrative interfaces (by which administrators exercise their privileges) might control their own auditing and even though you trust them to give you credible audit data to audit the administrative activity.

For example, I'll say administrators have created a process that they switch for a backup utility. Rather than do backups, it attempts to send the files out by the public e-mail to your competitor. This is an outrageous abuse of their privileges to override ACL and label access control. You require audit for all privilege use, but you expected this "backup" to use privileges.

To ensure that administrative programs are authentic, you need to have much more detailed auditing for administrative users. In this case, you would detect the queer activity of the backup because you are auditing administrative users for file access at the lower labels (the public e-mail), where you wouldn't be auditing the nonadministrative users.

That explains why you'd audit by individual user, rather than use required for all.

The need for auditing file objects by label

Up until now, I've been discussing auditing events in response to the activities of users or system processes. In these cases, you audit for a limited set of classes to keep the amount of data manageable. For example, you should

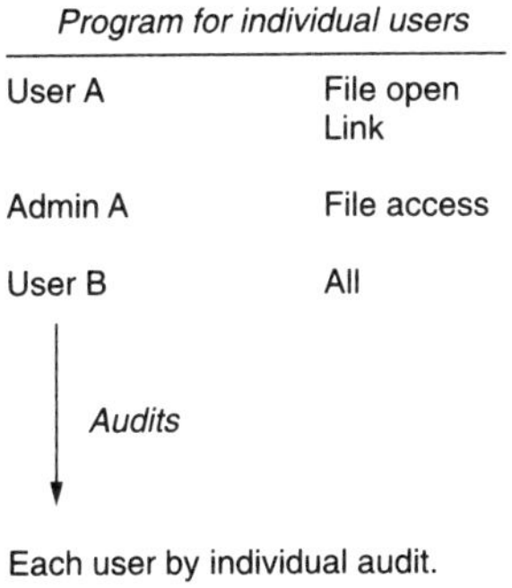

Figure 6.4 User audit.

require the audit class for all users for unauthorized use of privilege, but you usually wouldn't audit them for the file I/O class because that would amass enormous, but not very useful, amounts of data. (See Figure 6.5.)

However, this presents a dilemma. You need to audit some files, such as the system files, for file I/O to make sure that there hasn't been any unauthorized user access of them. Yet, you can't audit the users for the file I/O audit class, because they heavily access their own files (or their group's), and it would ruin your capacity to audit if you had to analyze all of that data for a rogue system file access.

To solve this dilemma, you use another important audit feature. This feature audits events caused by user or system processes. The solution is programming the audit by file objects and labels, which audit relative to file objects rather than processes.

Label programming is done by associating a list of event classes with a label so that those events will be audited for all file objects at that label. It is necessary to restrict the audit to a label to provide necessary precision. It would be a mess if all objects were audited because the record volume would be overwhelming, and the data would be of little security value.

Therefore, to audit file access to system files, do label-class programming on the system label with the file access event class. That way, opens for read or write access of any files, directories, or devices at that label will be audited. You also can use this method on your highest-labeled files.

Using label-class programming on your highest-labeled files can be used to provide a highly precise audit of some essential system resources. This is the pay off to your efforts to keep your TIB organized so that the information that you want to protect the most is kept separated at high labels. It also is reason enough to have a system that supports labeling, just to audit the system file access.

With a flexible audit control feature that includes required (i.e., system-wide), user, and object/label audit control, you have a highly efficient foundation for critical auditing: privilege use, administrative activity, access to system, and high- labeled files.

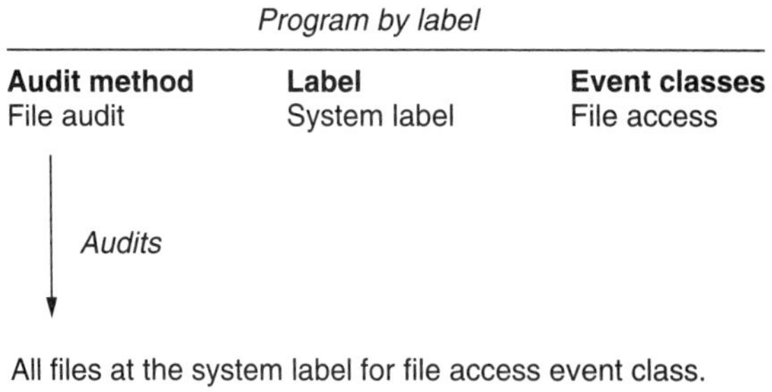

Figure 6.5 File audit by label.

Use required audit for all administrative and privileged command use, use object audit for system files and high-labeled data, and leave the rest of your requirements on a per-user basis. By that, you audit the required activity and no more or less. With audit, efficiency is the name of the game. The audit system has the capacity to overwhelm your system with data if the audit system is not controlled efficiently.

By required audit, you ensure that the minimum auditing of all users includes administrative and privilege classes. This avoids any oversight on individual users' classes that would permit unobserved use of privilege. By object/level audit, you ensure that all access to system and high-labeled data is audited. This is immensely more efficient than auditing the access of all users, then sorting out the system access.

That leaves the auditing that you select for each user. This can include much less clearly security-alarm-raising events, such as linking.

The previous uses of required, user, and object programming of classes, such as administrative privilege and file access, are highly efficient and powerful new security methods. They precisely log the use of administrative privileges and system file access for all users and their processes without incurring a bit of unnecessary or too burdensome overhead in audit proceeding. (See Figure 6.6)

In other words, all of the audit records that it generates are needed to do the job; you don't have to sort out the less relevant ones. Every event is necessary for your complete picture of all administrative and privilege activity by users and processes, which is a task of the highest importance. If done properly, this most crucial task could be accomplished with a manageable amount of record-proceeding overhead.

There are a relatively small amount of records generated by administrative command execution as compared to, say, disk I/O. The same is true for access to system files, which should be a highly distinct event. How often does an administrator need to open the etc/profile? Yet, there would be a much larger amount of files access events if they were collected for the whole system, and you then would have to pick out the system accesses.

After events are collected, they can be analyzed by any of the data that is logged in the record: user, object (such as a file or directory), time, or device (such as communications port or terminal).

Some of the collected events are essential to analyze, such as access to system files. Others might be of lessor interest, such as a user's access to his or her own files, and can be archived or compiled into statistics and discarded.

To meet your objectives, your strategies depend on what facilities are provided by the audit systems. In the most efficient way possible, you must audit all access to system and high-labeled files, use of privilege, logins, etc.

Effective auditing requires efficiency judgments. How can you get the most security given your limited capacity to process audit data? Which au-

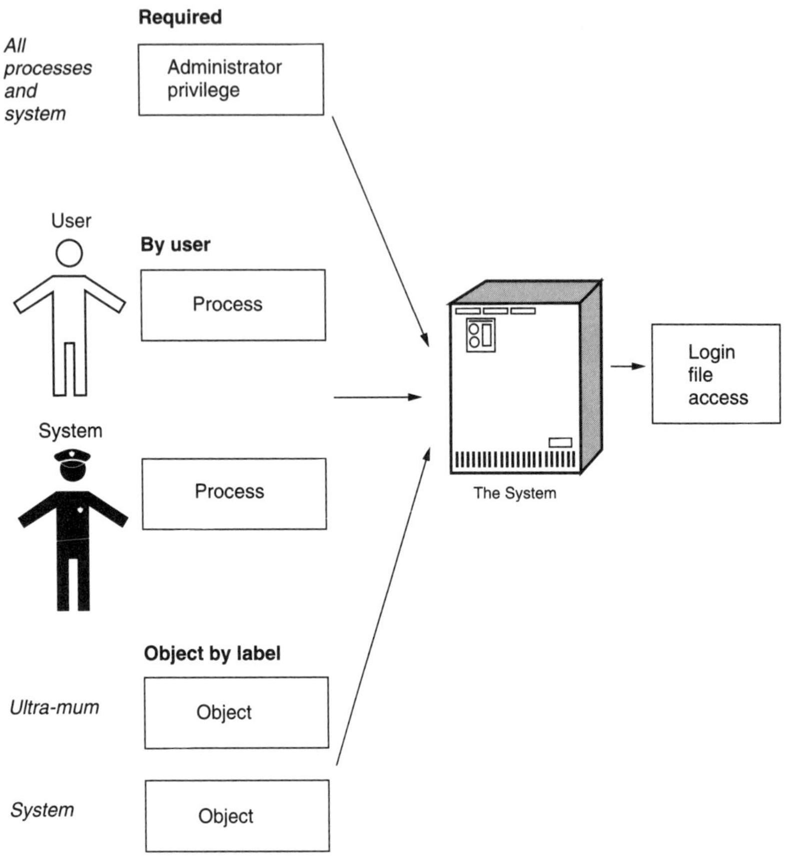

Figure 6.6 Programming methods.

dit records do you program and collect that are likely to have security value without generating too many records that won't?

There is some audit that is of the highest priority in maintaining security: administrative use of privilege, access of system files and high-labeled user data, and the use of the authentication system.

Making the judgment calls

I have described three types of audit programming: required, by user, and by label of object. Through these methods, you efficiently audit the most critical activity. All administrative actions and authentication must be audited; programming those event classes to be required will audit them no matter how the activity originates. You audit system and high-labeled file access by programming by label of object for efficiency, without generating excessive audit data from other user activity.

That much auditing is mandatory. Beyond that lie the judgment calls: How much record proceeding overhead can you afford? Is the additional level of security worth the resources? There is overhead in terms of machine processing, auditor labor, and archiving facilities.

Each Secure UNIX system will implement auditing differently so that audit efficiency will vary among systems even if they're programmed similarly. The way to tell how much auditing your system and staff can afford is simply by trying it out. Establish your limits: Start with the critical auditing and turn on more until auditing becomes too much.

You'll need to prioritize what programming is most necessary, weighted by what is most efficient (in the sense of generating a high percentage of security relevant events). You'll quantify this somewhat by rating importance/efficiency of the audit classes. The point is that you can't audit everything. I'll offer guidelines so that you can make judgments about what to program to audit based on your environments and security requirements.

There is a great deal of work done on how to quantify "risk" and therefore, in this case, the amount of auditing required. Rather than expend our energies on those deliberations here, I have laid out reasonable methods that any organization can use to be very secure—as secure as a general purpose data processing environment ever needs to be, even in this world of sophisticated threats. I'll leave the quest for the ultimate in security protection to those with unlimited resources to pursue it.

Efficiency is a factor because, given your limited resources, you might have to choose not to audit an event class if it is too inefficient to audit it, even if the event is somewhat security valuable. To hyperbolically illustrate, if auditing it generated a terrabyte of audit data per a second (of which a byte a year was interesting), constantly ground down your procedure while clearing audit buffers, and drove the auditor to become a hacker, you might have to choose the next event class of similar importance that was more efficient.

However, I will describe how it is practical for all organizations to do their important auditing in an efficient and acceptable manor.

Audit Events

I now will analyze the audit events in detail. I'll mention their security significance and how to program them for both audit importance and efficiency. I'll examine the event classes in detail beginning with the classes that are programmed as required events. (See Figure 6.7.)

Event classes that are required for all users are the Administrative and Audit classes, which have the events for the use of administrative commands (mostly with privileges) of the security administrator, system administrator, operator, and auditor. It is required that you audit all users for these classes, not just the administrative users, because that is one way that

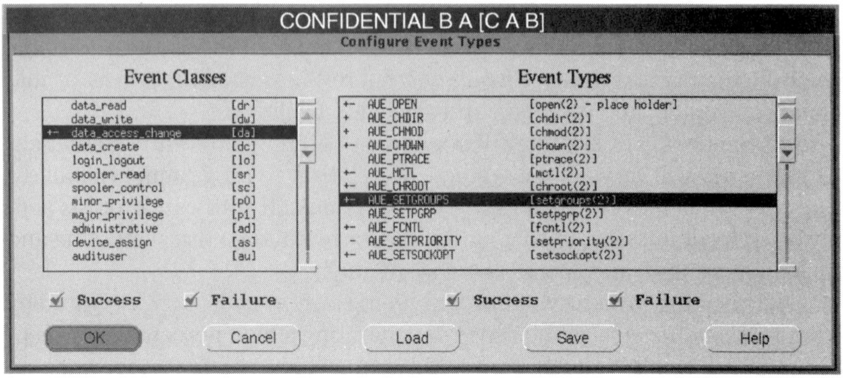

Figure 6.7 The administrator preprograms the audit system.

you would catch unauthorized use of privilege by a nonadministrative user. (See Figure 6.8.)

An even more compelling reason is that it allows you to confirm the authorizations of all administrative actions. Thereby, an administrative impostor or their Trojan horse processes would be detected.

The corollary to required audit for the Administrative class is required audit for the Privilege class that audits privilege use. Here's where you catch the "Hunt the Wumpus" game that actually is a Trojan horse that is copying the password file.

Administrative event class

All Administrative event class events are of security concern and are important events. Administrators are authorized to use privilege, so they can override or otherwise circumvent system defenses, have control of the most valuable data, or make the system unavailable.

Administrative activities that produce these events are all administrative tasks allocated to the various administrative roles: security administrator, system administrator, operator, application administrator (networks, databases, X Window, etc.), and (in an interdependent relationship with the other administrators) the auditor.

Administrators do their work by using an administrative interface program, so the events that you will get from administrative activities can come exclusively from the interface and describe the specific tasks performed.

For example, if the system administrator adds a user to a class, the administrative interface program might produce an audit record of that. However, because it controls its own auditing, it might not produce other records that are part of that transaction, such as the execution of the add_user command, the use of privileges, or the access of the class file.

As described in chapter 5, roles are flexible depending on your organizations resources. The most essential requirement when planning roles is to separate the roles of administrators and auditors to provide the capacity for confirmed authorization— the principle that use of administrative power must be confirmed to be authorized.

Security administrator events The Administrator event class contains the events that log the activity of the security administrators, who control the security configuration of the system. These events log the use the interface commands that manage the security attributes of user accounts (such as events logging the login label list, privilege authorizations, and role assigning), the system security databases (such as the label, information label, level, and class data files), and assigning label lists or markings to system devices (such as disks, printers, and tape). Any changing labels of objects or information on the system, such as information downgrading, also would be under this rubric.

All security administrative events can spell abject disaster if they're unauthorized. They all must have confirmed authorization by coordination between the auditor and administrator. The following paragraphs describe the audit events of the work that the security administrator does and the events' security implications.

The user login label is the label or label list at which users can login and is part of their system accounts. Thereafter, the session label of the shell that they get (and resource ACLs) directly determines what information they can access, as well as what they can do with it. See chapter 4 for more on how the label list determines access powers.

As most of the security state of the system, it is rarely changed once it is made. Users are assigned labels according to such factors as their work assignments or job roles—things not likely to change so frequently that they couldn't be planned and coordinated among security administrators and auditors.

Privilege authorizations are how users are designated administrators— the granting of a limited amount of superuser's powers to them. Users are associated with the privileges by listing them as assigned to administrative roles (sets of commands with specified privileges) or by directly assigning privileges to them. Sun uses the former method, which is a highly precise access mechanism.

Event classes	Events
Authentication	**login, cron, nfs,** x client, e-mail
Administrative	**add user, change label, mkfs, backup**
File access	**open,** file I/O, **create, delete, mkdir**

Figure 6.8 Audit classes.

The giving or taking of authorizations is given to a small class of administrators. A large organization might have any number of administrators. Administrative authorizations could be assigned to more than one user (e.g., two users could be security administrators). The typical number will be small. Those that fill the administrative roles should be highly qualified, expert technical and security staff. This event should be relatively rare and is always planned and coordinated.

Not all authorizations are for administrative roles. Some are for lesser privileges, such as the privilege to make backup tapes or to use the line printer. All use of the administrative interface for authorization control generates audit events.

Security administrators also create events when they manage the label-access security database files. These include the label, level, and class files. These are accessed via the administrative interface, which generates the event. Also included here is the information label database.

These files are the foundation label-access control system. The class and level databases list the class names and level numbers, which are information attributes that are a part of the labels. The label database has label names, number, level number, and classes list. The labels are on all system resources and determine access control by the label laws.

The information label files contain the information labels and information label encodings, which determine how information labels are floated.

Labeling files is the basis of system security. Tampering with them could result in the loss of all security protections. These files should rarely change. In general, they are laid out when the system is installed and can be built upon, but they don't have major changes unless the entire TIB is being revamped.

If this database were tampered with, it would allow the plundering of your information by lowering the identifier number of the level names. (See the section "System Label Database Change Unexpected" later in this chapter for more information.)

Device label lists determine the allowed label of users that access them or of the files that they can operate on. Unauthorized changes in device labels can leave your system wide open to loss of your most valuable data. Devices are assigned labels or label lists. By the label laws, the labels and label lists determine both which users can access the device and what files the devices can handle.

Some trusted processes change the labels of devices. When users login, their terminal device is assigned the temporary label that they login at by the login processes. The users retain this label until they logout. Some systems require that users temporarily assign devices, such as tape drives, to themselves at their session label, which their backup command processes for the duration of the backup. The labels assigned would have to be within the device label range. The data handled, such as that backed up to tape, would have to conform to the label laws (i.e., be equal to the tape device label). It can be data at more than one label.

As with other trusted processes, this label change might not be audited. The trusted processes can control its own auditing of its activities.

Other devices, such as disks or communications interfaces, have labels that are fixed and are accessed only by the system. Therefore, the label lists of devices are planned into the TIB basic design because they determine how the organization controls its information.

Any unauthorized event of change in device labels might be an attempt to subvert basic security protections.

Administrative events that the security administrator elicits also include assigning labels to all other system file and directory objects and, in some instances, to user files. Part of the installation processes, and a key step in implementing the TIB, is assigning labels by use of the administrative interface and the appropriate commands.

As is the case for much of the system, system file labels are a foundation that wouldn't change except for slow growth and development, barring some major overhaul.

User file labeling and label changes might be a more common event, depending on your organization's needs, but these changes are always highly controlled and subject to confirmed authorization.

Changes in file labels that lower, or degrade, they might constitute information disclosure; raising, or upgrading, they might have the effect of diluting the TIB's ability to order information by its value to the organization. If information is downgraded, it might be that high-labeled confidential data is changing to a less confidential label and will be disclosed. If it's upgraded, unimportant or public files might be being put into the high-labeled directories where they'll needlessly require heavier expenditure of organizational overhead to protect and monitor.

In light of these considerations, the ability of users to change file labels is severely restricted. It requires privilege authorization to change file labels. Downgrading is forbidden by the label laws to all users and is the exclusive domain of the security administrator. This keeps that activity at the highest level of confirmed authorization.

Upgrading is more variable by organizational policy. Privilege authorization to upgrade is held by the security administrator and possibly by some application administrators, such as database administrator, or some special users.

It should be organizational policy as much as possible to restrain upgrading by users to clear necessity. Preferably, that means that only the security administrator can do it. Any upgrading should be confirmed to be authorized.

Most upgrading, if necessary, will be done by trusted processes—applications running with privilege. A likely scenario would be a process running at a high label that has upgrading privileges. It can read or upgrade some data at a lower label and place it at the higher label.

There are database files that are the central repositories of the security state of the system. For example, /etc/password on pre-Secure systems contained users' passwords, home directories, shells, etc. These type of files give you an overview of how the system is laid out in many key aspects.

System administrator events The Administrative event class contains the events that are generated by the activities of the system administrators—those users who install, configure, and maintain the workings of the system environment. This class pertains to events caused by using the system commands that build the system; install, configure, and manage user accounts and classes; set the system date; make special devices with `mknod`; run the system consistency alarm detectors and file system check commands; and set system resource limits and defaults, such as default ACLs.

System administrators and security administrators have separate roles. They have different privileges to issue their respective tasks' commands. The separation keeps the actions of the security administrators distinct. This is desirable mostly for reasons of precise access. It allows for one or more system administrators without the need to give them security administrator privileges, and vice versa.

A user can be both security administrator and system administrator if necessary, but it is highly insecure to mix auditor and the other administrator roles in one person. Organizations should avoid it if there's any possible way to.

Another reason for separating security and system administrators is to make security actions distinct by user to aid audit analysis.

Systems administrators do system builds, installation, and configuration. System installation would take place from the single-user state, where no auditing would take place. Auditing requires an audit daemon that wouldn't be running yet.

Administrative events created by systems administrators include system installation and configuration. System build is a remake of the kernel from the system object files and configuration file source, which would require access to the system libraries, editing of system configuration files, use of the `make` command, and finally the placement of a new kernel in /unix. Again, use of the administrative interface via the trusted path is required. Unauthorized system builds can lead to the inclusion of a security threat into the kernel that is supposed to be providing the protection.

Other administrative events created by systems administrators include management of user accounts. The assignment of security attributes to user accounts is done by the security administrator after the accounts are created by the system administrator. These include user login labels and privilege authorizations.

There are other security-relevant aspects to accounts that are determined by the system administrator. Password management for the user is selected, including whether the password is machine-generated or user-supplied (if both options are available), the expiration period, etc. Within these, parameters might be configurable that would allow for guessable passwords.

The choice and reliability of user home directory, shell, and classes can be a security factor. For example, they might allow an impostor to substitute a Trojan horse for a user's shell. Home directories have default ACL and login profiles, so an improper choice could lead to a vulnerability. Just the fact that an account is being created could be an attempted break-in. Once in, the trespasser could use his or her account for other schemes. The assignment of users to classes has the effect of granting them access to whatever the class has access to.

All account events that are a result of system administrator activity must be subject to confirmed authorization.

The date command event is from system administrators setting the system date. The system date provides basic data for the reconstruction and comprehension of audit event sequences. (See the section "System Date Change Unexpected" later in this chapter for more information.)

The system uses the date to timestamp file access times. For example, this is part of how configuration programs and users identify files.

The `mknod` system call is used during system installation, when device files are created in /dev. That's the only place where they belong. Device files created anywhere else are a menace because they could be a part of an attempt to sneak onto system disks or eavesdrop on communications. `mknod` also would be called whenever devices, such as a disk, are added to the system.

The `mkfs` command event also is generated by the activities of a system administrator. `mkfs`, the creation of filesystems, also usually is a part of system installation and is performed to load raw disk space onto an inode free list. Performing `mkfs` on top of an existing filesystem would destroy any data stored in it. `mkfs` also would be called whenever a new file storage capacity is added to the system.

The event of system administrators running `fsck` as part of routine maintenance could be security relevant because it could effect filesystem integrity if improperly executed.

System administrators generate an event when they run the accounting programs, which display the state of system resources and activity such as disk space, processes scheduling, and CPU usage. Resource statistical information should be fed into a consistency alarm detection system. It allows for the detection of the abnormal use of resources that might constitute an attempt to disrupt the system by tying the resources up.

Commands regarding the setting of resource limits, such as per-user disk quotas, also can create events. Permitting excessive resources could allow an availability attack, and too little resources could be an attack in itself, as it might deny practical use of the system.

System administrators operate the system consistency alarm detection program. Although independent of the audit system, in that its statistical and alarm display is primarily to the system administrator and not the auditor, the system consistency alarm detection program also can generate audit event records to record anything that it might detect, such as access of a system file.

Operator events The Operator events also are part of the Administrative event class. Events stemming from operator activity include routine maintenance and operation of the system, such as system boot and shutdown, tape backup, mount, printer, and mail control. This class can include events from users that aren't operators but that have a limited amount of privileges (e.g., to mount floppies).

Administrative commands that affect the setting of limits of resources are audited. These include commands that control the user limits for the number of processes, disk use, memory (process size), or processes' priority.

Events from tape backup should be part of managing information confidentiality. Backups of files at higher labels are of particular concern.

Secure UNIX creates backups that must include the file security attributes. The backup should take place on devices labeled according to the information being carried on them.

Events from the printer also are part of managing information confidentiality, including printouts of files at higher labels. Printer events also include controlling the markings of the information labels on the pages, which shouldn't be suppressed or misleading. Information labels are used to provide print markings. Changing the marking on the printout is known as *printer marking override*. Other events include spooler control, which should be directed towards improved throughput.

Audit event class

The Audit event class includes the audit events that describe the operations of the audit system itself. Events include audit shutdown and start, audit bin switch, audit record formatting, and the configuration of which events, users, and objects to be audited.

The auditing system has configuration files, processes (daemons) that do its work, sets of control and configuration commands, and directories and files where audit records are kept. (See the section "System Audit State Change Unexpected" later in this chapter for more information.)

Another of the most critical time-zero alarms is illegitimate use of administrative privilege. To detect this any time that it is used, you have to be aware of the use and know that it's legitimate.

You can do this by many means. The use of administrative privilege is an auditable event, which you should always audit. When it is detected by the monitor program, the program checks the activity statistics and configuration records. Each organization must design a strategy around this mechanism for ensuring that the use is proper. I'll explore a few possible ones that a secure UNIX organization might have.

Special administrative privileges include control of system accounting, setting of privileges, printers, creation of devices, scheduler, or administrative interfaces.

Administrative privileges can be combined into special sets called *roles*, such as the auditor or security administrator role, but more than one user might be authorized to assume that role. (See chapter 5 for more information on roles.)

The next objective is to audit all access to the system files. This requires auditing the system files by file object at the system label for the event class. The event class is the file access audit event class that includes the audit events regarding user or administrative user file object creation, access, or deletion. File objects include files, directories, links, and symbolic links. I also will put interprocess communications objects, unnamed pipes, fifos, messages, and shared memory in this class, although they are implementation dependent and might not be implemented as files.

With audit programming by label of object, you can attain efficiency for this objective. The important events are those of access to the system files and high-labeled user data, which are the labels that you program.

User activities logged by these events are open for read, write, append, or create; delete; copy; move (rename); link; symbolic link; directory and fifo creation and removal; multilevel directory creation; directory access (`cd` or `opendir`); alias; touch stat; and access.

The Audit events include file open for read. Some system commands read system files (e.g., the `pw` command reads the pw file). Users therefore have read access to the password file via their setgid privileges, which allow execution of the `pw` command and which run setgid to the owning class of the password file. Note that the owning class, such as bin, doesn't confer any privileges to the user. No user could open a system file for write, append, or create.

Administrators are audited for all opens, which must be confirmed authorized and be executed via the interface.

Making a link (hard or symbolic) to a file consists of creating a link file in the current directory. It also updates the link count in the file that is linked, so users require write permission to perform the link. A link to system files by a user would be disallowed by label laws.

Directory creation is governed by the write access control of the parent directory. Multilevel directory creation might require privilege.

User activities logged by directory-creation events are open for read, write, append, or create; delete; copy; move (rename); link; symbolic link; directory and fifo creation and removal; multilevel directory creation; directory access (`cd` or `opendir`); alias; touch stat; and access.

Security Sensitivity of Events

I'll examine the security implications and how best to audit each of these events.

The File Open audit event could refer to opens with read or write access of any file objects, such as devices or fifos. Opens of system files, high-labeled user files, and any other files that are to be especially protected are monitored by auditing this class.

You need to audit file opens, rather than reads and writes, to monitor file access efficiently. Otherwise, you would gather an overwhelming amount of data of little security value. However, in some cases, you can turn on more detailed auditing with the File I/O class for read and write if a file is opened unexpectedly.

With audit, you could do an after-the-fact review of the access control checks of access control lists of system files. In other words, audit can be used to verify that users that have opened files are authorized to do so, which would doublecheck the accuracy of the ACLs and would be a break-in detector.

System files must always be audited for file open to detect unauthorized access. In many cases, the only users that should be able to open system files are administrators who can login at the system label or who are privileged to override label access control.

Trusted processes (system programs with privileges, such as daemons) also might have access. However, as trusted processes, they are in charge of their own auditing and might have auditing for access shut off.

Every system file open must be confirmed to be authorized. If an administrator needs to upgrade a system file, the upgrade should be coordinated with the auditor. Trusted processes and administrators should be opening the system files that they're supposed to.

I should note that all users access system files regularly. The type of access that you want to prevent is access that is beyond what users need or what is appropriate for each administrator.

For example, users might have execute and occasional read access to the files in /usr/bin, but users never require write access. Chapter 3 gives more detailed analysis of what the appropriate ACLs are for user access to the system files.

The file open audit must be set to audit all opens of system files and be used to ensure that the opens are appropriate. Any other files, such as high-labeled application or user files that must be protected, are likewise audited.

For example, a user should never be opening database files whose access is managed by a database management system. That would constitute a clear intrusion.

An unwarranted open of a file might mean that the file's ACL is incorrect or that users are granted access on it that they shouldn't have. It also might be that a user has somehow stolen the privilege to override the ACL.

Most system devices, such as hard disks, shouldn't be opened by users. Ordinarily, terminal devices can't be opened by users either. System programs, such as login, exclusively open them and then can assign them to users.

Administrators are entitled to open files that are appropriate to their role. Auditors can open the audit configuration files, security administrators can open the security database files, etc.

As previously discussed, to audit high-labeled and system files for access, you cannot resort to programming on a required basis—auditing all users for the file access event class—as that would deluge your capacity to interpret what would ensue.

The efficient way to obtain the desired protections is to program audit by label of file object, rather than by required or user audit for users. You program the file access event class for file objects at the system label and whatever other high labels that you want to audit for. The law is back in town, partner.

In that way, any unauthorized access to system files by users, administrators, or privileged processes will be detected without producing any "junk" file access audit records as would occur if you audited users for file access.

If you are pondering whether you need label access control protections: I think you do, no matter what your environment. You can use it to do some necessary jobs, like the one that I just mentioned, without having to introduce anymore complexity than that into your information systems. For that purpose alone, it's a necessity.

If you don't want to incur any overhead for label protections, label access can be used to protect your system software, and the rest of your user information and users can be at the same label. This is another reason that label access control is a necessity. So, labeling is worth it, no matter what the risk analysis/cost tradeoff deliberations. Labeling is found on many Secure UNIX systems; hopefully it is found on yours.

You must keep the integrity of the system software that you rely on to build your TIB. Auditing must be kept on it with a time-zero alarm. (See the section "System Access Unexpected" later in this chapter for more information.)

File Attribute Events

The next Audit event class is File Attribute Changes. Attributes include security attributes, file labels, ACLs, default directory ACLs, and privileges. Other attributes include filename, time of last access, and any other attributes that might be kept by the filesystem to manage files. The events log user activities that change ACL (`chmod`, `change_acl` calls, and changes of owner or class owner), time of last access (`utime` and `touch`), file attribute displays of any of the previous attributes (`ls`, `stat`, `access`, `ls_privilege`, `ls_label`, and `ls_ACL`).

The Change ACL audit event can include `chmod`, `chown`, or `change_acl`, all of which change a file's ACL. At most, users should be able to change the ACLs of files that they own and not of system files or those owned by others. The restrictions are much greater than those on opening a file, as users should not control who has access to others' files but might have been given access to by others.

Change ACL auditing should be in place for the entire system and at least all high-labeled files.

File owners can change their ACL, at least as far as UNIX is concerned. However, organizations might have a policy that even file owners cannot change file ACL beyond the defaults. Low-labeled files owned by users might not be so restricted, as they are less in need of TIB protection. ACL change requires privilege and can be restricted by giving it only to administrators.

Certainly, however, unauthorized users shouldn't be changing the ACLs of high-labeled data, system files, or devices. Administrative users' system ACL changes, possibly by use of privileges, must be coordinated with the auditors.

Process Events

The next class of audit events is Process events. These events can provide a log of process creation and execution by users and the system.

Many audit events are related to processes' activity, such as `exec` (and its cousins `execl`, `execv`, etc.), `exit`, `fork`, and `kill`. All of them should be recorded for all processes, as they concisely describe an aspect of system activity that has important security value: process creation and exit.

By recording process activity, you have a complete log of what commands users made or what processes their programs executed, all recorded with high efficiency. It also provides a means to measure the rate of process creation for the purpose of fending off system availability attacks.

The Exec audit event should always be recorded because it provides a log of privileged processes invocation. (Chapter 5 has more details on how `exec` manages privileges.) To summarize, the `exec` system call provides a precise mechanism for dynamically assigning privileges to processes. It maintains control of the privilege authorizations of the user throughout the successive entities, yet it also allows the execed file to veto some of the user's privileges and also to contribute some of its own when it derives the processes privileges.

`exec` therefore is the moment processes attain privileges. By recording every `exec`, you can assure that privilege use is appropriate. Users don't have administrative privilege authorizations, so processes that they `exec` shouldn't inherit any from them. Administrators can give their processes only the privileges that administrators are allowed in their authorizations.

Monitoring `exec` also verifies access control. A user shouldn't have execute permission for an administrative file, so the user shouldn't be able to `exec` it.

The Fork, Kill, and Exit audit events complete your record of process activity. `fork` more or less duplicates a process (makes a child process), including its privileges, so you won't be alert to process children that don't die when they should or that `exec` when they shouldn't.

This is used to spot processes that aren't what they're supposed to be or that aren't behaving as they should. A Trojan horse process would pretend to be doing a normal and expected act but actually would be stealing a user's privileges and access authorizations. You would detect this with process auditing.

The Kill audit event is an interprocess signal, which might result in the termination of a process. `kill` is subject to label write access rules. If attempts are made to kill inappropriate processes, it might be a sign of an attempt at system disruption.

The Exit audit event completes your ability to make a full accounting of process activity in the audit log. Upon logout, if all user processes don't exit, it might indicate that a process has disguised itself by means of privileges, etc.

Authentication Events

Authentication is the single most critical security action. It's when the system gives out access powers to users and when break-in attempts must be controlled. The following paragraphs will discuss the audit events monitored for this alarm. Related actions, such as setuid and `cron`, are included here.

Failed login, either by entering a bad user identifier or invalid password, is audited. If a user has entered a correct identifier with an incorrect password several times within a few minutes or on other repeated occasions, it's necessary to take an action, such as terminating their session if he or she gets on and changes his or her password. Your response to this situation mustn't be locking the terminal or the user account, as that might create a system-availability problem. Afterwards, the cause of the problem has to be investigated. However, as a time-zero alarm, you act first, then ask questions later.

The number of failed logins and the time intervals are configured in the system monitoring database.

Another login alarm situation is when a user successfully logs in but at a time not allowed. The alarm monitor will check the user activity database to determine whether a login is allowed at the time of day or day of the week. If users need to login at an unforeseen hour, they need to notify the system administrators in advance, or they will trigger this alarm.

In this case, the response can be to log the user off and lock their account. The risk of an availability attack is low as a mass theft of passwords on a secure system would be highly improbable for many reasons: Passwords files have labels that keep them away from the public, access to them is allowed only by highly monitored administrators with a high enough label, there's no superuser, etc.

Timed program executers, like `cron`, generate audit events. They should be treated as mini-login sessions in that they have the same time restrictions as login. Out-of-schedule jobs must be alarmed and removed.

The other alarm related to authorization is setuid. For users or programs to perform it, they must be listed in the user activity database.

System entry events, such as login attempts at an unauthorized time or location, are audited.

Many administrative commands, which are audited by required auditing, require specific privileges to execute. Administrators have privilege authorizations to run many other commands with privileges. The presumption (which must always be confirmed) is that their privilege use is authorized.

Yet, secure systems have other instances of processes that use privileges besides those that administrators run. System commands that ordinary users use, such as `ps`, have privileges, even though the user isn't authorized for them, whether or not the command is setuid, too. So auditing for privilege use is a low-efficiency protection.

Commands are compared against descriptions and profiles.

Audit Alarms

Secure UNIX systems presently come with basic auditing tools: a programming and control interface, an audit record database management system with query and report capabilities, and some monitor/statistical displays.

In the following paragraphs, I will identify what situations constitute security threats, which are called *security alarms*. Once you've programmed and collected the audit records, you analyze them for alarms. The determination of a threat might require contextual or statistical information beyond what is gathered from the audit records. For example, a login might be a threat only if you know that the context that the user isn't scheduled to login at 3:00 A.M. or the statistic that it's failed repeatedly.

I will describe the audit events, contextual information, and statistics that allow you to recognize alarms. Alarm detector programs that would automate this analysis come with some Secure UNIX systems or will be available commercially.

Events are programmed to show signs of trouble, must be corroborated by contacting the user, or must be monitored and investigated. You then select those events to be audited, taking care to get the most protection for the least amount of record generation.

Next, you analyze the audit record and maintain highlighted alarm displays by using programs, statistical methods, and expert systems. The typical activity of users is constantly kept updated in a activity description file. Abnormal behavior (that an impostor might exhibit) can be detected by comparing activity to the activity averages and histories in it.

Activity descriptions are kept for the system and each user. They are tabulations and analysis of activity, such as command usage and file access. Statistics, such as the number and percentage of failed access attempts, are kept updated on each login session. There also are activity configuration settings, such as the time of day when the user's logins are allowed.

These activity descriptions form a norm that monitors can use to detect an impostor. For example, a higher than normal percentage of access failures during a login session as compared to the history's percentage would trigger an alarm. I'll be exploring this feature throughout the remainder of this chapter.

Actions that circumvent the activity settings also might cause alarms.

Alarms

An *alarm* is one or more audit events that require you to respond to verify their legitimacy or take immediate defensive actions. Determining whether events are alarms often requires checking audit activity statistics and configuration databases that are maintained by the audit analysis programs for the system and for each user. For example, login audit events are a possible time-zero alarm, but only if they fail three times in a row or occur in the middle of the night by a user who is disallowed night-owl hours.

(*Note*: Manufacturers can assist security by providing a UPS (uninterruptable power system) that will enable machines to have the emergency power to enable the audit system alarm to function during a power failure.)

It is of the utmost importance that users performing an action receive their own alarm. That way, if an impostor is performing it, he or she will receive the alarm, say, at home and know that he or she has been detected. Ordinarily, users receive their alarm at their terminal.

Alarms are generated by audit-monitoring programs called *monitors*. These monitors examine the audit event records that are generated by secure UNIX systems. Alarms occur when audit events fit some predefined pattern of a problem. To monitor alarms, the audit events that might indicate the problem must be audited. Most times, the events will be checked and found not to be a problem but simply part of legitimate use.

Alarm monitors use user and system activity databases that include statistical data that is kept dynamically, as well as activity parameters that configured by administrators.

Critical Alarms

Alarms are rated by the urgency by which you must respond to them from most urgent (time zero) to least urgent (time three).

The alarms of the time-zero alarm class include Authentication, Administration, Integrity, Audit, Disclosure, and Critical Object. Many of these also are time-one alarms under some circumstances. Worsening conditions can raise the alarm urgency, as you recognize identifiers.

Time-zero alarms are events that are absolutely bad. If someone is trying to guess passwords, it's not subject to any decision making about whether it's bad. It is something that you immediately want to know about and stop. Therefore, you must always audit events that might be time-zero alarms and be ready to respond immediately with actions, such as interrupting sessions.

Your information systems embody your organization's assets, as truly as does the organization's bank. In every real sense, a computer break-in is as much a criminal act as a bank robbery.

Given this, not only should time-zero alarms be processed by the normal mechanisms, but they also should be alarmed to multiple physically secure output facilities and terminals and, if possible, sent over a communication channel to a designated remote system that isn't controlled by the alarm-originating machine, because it is possibly going under attack. These facilities should be monitored somehow by a human, hopefully in real time, if not daily. The remote alarm receiving system should be capable of dialing human administrators, building security staff, or the police with the news, 24 hours a day. No doubt services will appear for that purpose. Let's not forget triggering the good old burglar alarm.

Once informed, the administrator should have emergency powers to intervene by remotely powering down the system, controlling physical access, having the building security staff investigate, or riding in on the police squad car.

Time-one alarms are those that might have critical security effects, yet might correspond to legitimate use of the system. Any privileged administrative action is in this alarm class. These are the events that you must not only be aware of but also must also corroborate to the actions of authorized, legitimate users, ruling out impostors or inside abusers. Audit events that might be time-one alarms also must always be audited.

At the time-two alarm class, you begin to have to make the hard choices about your resource expenditure and the degree of safety that you require.

At the time-three alarm class, you are including events that don't need (or can't have for lack of resources) timely analysis. These events are those that you audit to uncover problems using long-term statistical analysis. It's a job that might involve heavy costs with only a modest expectation of there being a security benefit.

Types of alarms

Alarms are named by the problems that they indicate, such as "login during login-disallowed times." To describe the alarms in the following sections, I first will state what the alarm is, why its a problem, what events must be audited to recognize it, what the activity descriptions are that must be checked, the alarm classes with the reasons for them, how to response to them, and any additional comments.

Mandatory alarms I will begin with alarms that are mandatory that you be alert to. Among these are the irregular use of administrative privilege, unexpected access of data that is system level or high-labeled, certain system call failures, abnormal logins, and excessive use of system resources.

Administrative privilege must be used in a planned and scheduled manner among the auditor and the other administrators, such as the security administrator, the systems administrator, and the systems operator. The goal is the Accountability Principle: All activity on the system is accountable to a legitimate, specific user. I'll look at administrative actions in regard to alarms.

System State Change Unexpected

System state transitions refer to system stop and start, wherein there is a transition from system boot to single user to multiuser state (the sequence of system start). The only remnant of the pretrusted UNIX superuser privileges is within the single-user state. A secure administrator can shutdown or bring up a system into single-user mode. Users of a single-user-state system are very nearly the old UNIX superuser. They can act on the system without access restrictions and with no audit log. It's a necessary tool, but if hackers get there, they control your organization's fate.

System state transitions are events of the most crucial significance imaginable. Not only must they be audited events, but they also must never occur without the knowledge of the security administrators.

The events that you must audit to be aware of system state changes include the executing of administrator commands (such as `initialize` or `shutdown`), the occurrence of audit events (such as `powerdown`), or the use of privileges (such as `reboot`).

None of these events are bad in themselves; however, in every case, they must be verified to be legitimate use by using activity schedules and norms.

If it isn't scheduled or takes place during a restricted time, it's a time-zero alarm, and preemptive action must be taken. Likewise, booting the wrong kernel or using the wrong boot device are time-zero alarms.

If the event is scheduled, its use can be compared to user activity norms or activity codes (secret command use codes). If the events fail these tests, it's a time-one alarm. The user can be redundantly authenticated (such as by phone) or can be verified retroactively against their activity logs or by a subsequent inquiry.

System Date Change Unexpected

The system date is a pivotal component of a trusted system. It provides key audit data for the reconstruction and comprehension of event sequences. Tampering with it can provide a means to obfuscate such activities by shuffling event sequences. It also provides the scheduling clock for processes that might be audit analyzers and alarm ringers. Wedging the clock hands would prevent their detecting an intruder.

The event that needs to be audited is execution of the `date` command. Unscheduled system date changes are an example of an event that is a clear-cut indication of wrongdoing and are a time-zero alarm. Unless you're switching to the Aztec calendar, they take place on system installation only.

Preempt first, ask questions later. If scheduled, they are time-one alarms. Either redundantly authenticate, inquire later, or verify against the administrators log.

System Label Database Change Unexpected

Secure systems have an internal database where labeling data is maintained. The data is the security level names and their identifying numbers, which will be placed on your organization's TIB. If this database were tampered with, it would allow plundering of your information by lowering the identifier number of the level names. Such an attack would be a *de facto* lowering of the security level of your most important information, which would allow it to walk out the door.

Levels are the foundation of the TIB design. Once you build a building on a foundation, you almost never change the foundation.

The events to audit to stay informed about this possible alarm are events that indicate access to the label database file, execution of commands that do that, or the use of privileges required.

Unscheduled, this event is another clear-cut sign of trouble and a time-zero alarm. Although labeling-related operations, such as changing file security levels, might generate volumes of audit events, they are not necessarily of concern. However, corrupting this file, which is internal to the secure system, would affect all of the data contained and protected by the TIB.

System User Database Change Unexpected

Each user has security-related attributes, such as a clearance range. Attempts to alter user or class attributes might give unauthorized users access to an organization's most exclusive information.

The events to audit to stay informed about this possible alarm are events that indicate access to the password file, execution of commands that do that, or the use of privileges required.

System Audit State Change Unexpected

The auditing system has configuration files, processes (daemons) that do its work, sets of control and configuration commands, and directories and files where audit records are kept. That's a lot of territory, but let's not have any spiked chopmeat given to the watchdog. You rely on your auditing systems to protect you, so changes to the configuration files that determine its strength mustn't be touched. A really slick intruder probably would attempt to hit these files first to cover their tracks.

This brings up a problem. Other alarms are brought to the attention of the auditor, the basic idea being that, if the user and the administrator coordinate on activities, the auditor will have a sense that the activity that it observes on the audit system corresponds to legitimate use of the system. Legitimate means that the user isn't an impostor and that he or she isn't doing anything that he or she isn't supposed to do or is not acting maliciously.

In this case though, if the auditor is an impostor and shuts off the auditing, checks and balances breaks down. Ways to avoid this situation include having two auditors. The second auditor's function can be merely to receive events related to the functioning of the audit system itself and coordinating them with the other auditor. Other measures might include using extra authentication security for the auditor, such as allowing auditor login only on a physically restricted and video-monitored terminal.

The events that must be audited are events relating to the state of the audit processes, the commands that control the audit system, access to audit files, and the privileges needed for any of these events.

System Accounting State Change Unexpected

System accounting is used by the audit alarm program to make decisions about whether events constitute alarms. Accounting evaluates the state of system resources, such as disk usage and processes scheduling. If system accounting were off, the system might be vulnerable to availability attacks.

The events are the accounting control commands and privileges involved. If the event occurs without being scheduled, it's a time-one alarm.

Other time-zero alarms Another major type of time-zero alarm includes alarms that involve irregular access to either system files or high-labeled user data. These will be described in the following paragraphs. Even if secure computers did no more than keep access to the system monitored, they'd be worth getting. One of the most damaging attacks can be smuggling on a fake system file.

System Access Unexpected

You must be cognizant with unfaltering persistence of the integrity of the system software that you rely on to build our TIB. Auditing must be kept on it with a time-zero alarm. Any unauthorized attempt to modify it or to change its access control lists, labeling, or privileges might be an attempted attack. If you can't protect it, all of your efforts are worthless. A discussion of which files makeup the system software of a secure system is give later in this chapter.

There are many events that might indicate such a threat that you must audit and analyze. You must know when they happen on the system software. There are events that are caused by alterations of discretionary access control, labeling, and privileges; by the commands that do the alterations; and by the privileges needed to execute them.

You also must audit events that describe other events, such as creating and opening system software files. It isn't advisable to attempt to audit reads or writes to system files as that would produce heavy audit generation and wouldn't be giving very much more protection than just auditing the opens.

Another inefficient audit strategy would be to turn on auditing for access of all files, then select the events about system files. More efficient approaches would be auditing access events on the label of the system files or auditing the individual files and directories of the label of the system files.

The ability of secure systems to audit by the label of files or directories is one of their most powerful auditing tools. In this instance, to audit access to all system files, you setup audit to audit all access to files and directories with the unique system label. Alternately, you could audit each file in the system software individually.

If this event is unexpected, there's no more urgent an alarm. Detecting this alarm is why secure systems are secure. It is a time-zero alarm.

User High-Labeled Data Access Unexpected

With secure systems, you have the capacity to identify the data that you need to protect the most carefully. This might correspond to data that is most monetarily valuable or is of the most crucial importance to your organization's competitive stance. It is a judgment that each organization makes when it designs its TIB. It might emphasize the need for the data's theft-, vandalism-, or disclosure-protection requirement or the exclusivity of the users that you allow access to it.

Once you have made this judgment, you give this data a label that you will refer to as high—hence high-labeled data. The benefit of making this distinction is that you can identify data that you are going to be extra careful to protect.

Protection is provided by coordination and scheduling that is much the same as between the auditor and the system administrators. In this case, however, it is perhaps more appropriate to have an application manager and the users coordinating, with the auditor passing the alarms to the manager and the manager passing user scheduling and activity logs back to the auditor.

The event that must be audited to protect high-labeled data is the access of data with that label. In other words, configure audit to generate access events for that label.

Once there are events such as that, it is a time-zero alarm if the access is unexpected, either occurring during a restricted time or when not scheduled. If the access is scheduled but abnormal, its a time-one alarm.

Programming this event for users sometimes is done to provide a detailed audit record. This can be done for individual users when there might some problem to look into or when the users exact activity that needs to be recorded for some reason.

Session Unexpected

This type of time-zero alarm has to do with attempts to penetrate the system in an unauthorized manner, either at 4:00 A.M. or by guessing passwords.

For secure systems, it is no longer acceptable to allow logins unless the user is authorized to login at those particular hours. At other times, the administrator must ensure that the account is disabled for logins. However, it is prudent to verify this on the audit log. You don't want some hacker impersonating a user to log in at 4:00 A.M. There are other login circumstances that you want to consider before you accept the fact that a login session has taken place.

Each login event gives the terminal on which the login took place. The login might have taken place over a network or a dial-up line as well, or it might have been from a host or a user on another host. Any combination of these factors can be used to specify precisely who may login, using what means, and at what time. The Access Management Principle must be followed, and these logins must be allowed on an a precise as-needed basis.

If you don't restrict logins, you make your system far more open to impersonators and network-borne attacks.

This same alarm can be applied to jobs run by `cron` or `at`. Not allowing login sessions to continue after a scheduled time and limiting the number of login sessions allowed at the same time is similar to this.

The activity descriptions for this alarm include per-user login and job schedules and restrictions on the terminals, network services, network hosts, and dial-in lines that the user may use. The norms include typical login times, length of their sessions, command-use profiles, and the level at which they login at.

If the login is unscheduled, uses the wrong terminal or network, etc., it is a time-zero alarm; kill the login session and lock the account. If the norm isn't followed, its a time-one alarm.

System software defined What is the "system software" of a TIB? I'll now go into some detail on that. Firstly, the traditional UNIX system software is included: the kernel, system calls, and device drivers.

I also include user-level commands—many of which have been modified to support security—found in directories other than the conventional UNIX ones and symbolically linked from the conventional to the secure directories to preserve the familiar UNIX interface. For example, many /usr/bin commands will be links to /usr/sbin. In general, Secure UNIX preserves the pretrusted interface conventions.

Similarly included are system data files, directories, device special files, named pipes, symbolic links, and trusted processes.

Trusted processes are commands issued by a system administrator in single user mode. They also are system daemons, administrative commands, or applications that execute with administrative privileges. They can control their own audit generation.

In general, commands in pre-Secure UNIX that performed a user level setuid or setgid to root, adm, sys, or tty; that update security related system files; or that are used in administrative shell scripts are included in the TIB system software. Secure UNIX no longer performs setuid of this sort, except in a mock way to maintain compatibility with old software. Under Secure UNIX, such processes are assigned precise privileges to do their jobs rather than require setuids.

The utilities included are the directories and file management, systems administration, user environment, encryption, editing, interprocess communication, line printer, systems performance analysis, spell, system headers, C development, the security system, and auditing.

Other software considered part of the TIB system software include products that might not have achieved the rigorous security certification of secure kernels but that often are included out of necessity. They include networking, RFS, uucp, X Window, ufs, the Internet, NFS, and RPC.

Vendors of established UNIX applications are developing secure versions of products, such as database-management systems, which will be included.

Secure administrators also can allow software into the TIB system software if they have insured that it's trustworthy. This software typically will include shared programs or utilities.

I'll examine the TIB system software, aside from the convention kernel files, down to the detail of directory organization.

There's /etc, with the system startup file, initialize.d, cron, line printer, as well as etc/sbin.

Secure systems have many new database files that have complex interrelationships. For that reason, it is essential to use the administrative interface routines when performing security administration, such as assigning or changing the user login labels.

You shouldn't manually edit security database files. The complexity of the Secure databases goes beyond file relationships, such as that changes in one might necessitate updates to many others. This alone rules out "manual" editing of database files in that it would be too error prone, introducing internal inconsistencies in interrelated files.

Also, secure systems sometimes implement object reuse, which insures that deleted objects really are deleted without a trace before reallocation. For files, resources—such as the disk space—are scrubbed clean of data.

In the case of an administrative operation, such as deleting users, the administrative interface can not only remove users' entries from the /etc/password file but also perform a whole slew of scrubbing work too, such as deleting them from all file ACL on the system or deleting all of their files.

Another reason why manual editing is no longer to be done is that secure systems have consistency-alarm detectors, which are programs that are constantly scanning the file systems looking for inconsistencies with descriptions of them that the programs maintain. So, another job that the interface would do is update those descriptions. Manually that could be done only by the system administrator (not the security administrator).

The final consideration of manual editing is that you are auditing for manual access to the system files. The auditor would assume that access to the file without using the interface is an attempted break-in. So, the auditor and the system administrator would have to be involved.

Due to the previous considerations, it should be organizational policy that administrators must always use the administrative interface to modify the system security database files. Not only is manual editing too difficult and error prone, it would involve the work of a few administrators and is too disruptive of systematic routines.

To uphold the principle of confirmed authorization (that system activity is confirmed to be authorized), you must audit all use of administrative powers.

Secure systems provide an administrative interface with which to do all administrative activity, such as changing login labels. It is available only through the trusted path, ensuring that no Trojan horse programs can be involved.

To perform the administrative task, the interface will perform all access of system security database files, such as /etc/password and /etc/security/classes. It also will do all necessary auxiliary operations, such as an update of any related database files, object reuse of user data and system data structures, update to consistency alarm detector records, etc.

The audit trail first will show invocation of the security administrator's interface, then subsequent access of security database files. There should not be a case where the security database files are accessed without the interface event first.

In this way, confirmed authorization is kept. You will expect the administrative activity because the auditor and the administrators plan it and reconcile it afterwards. It occurs through the interface, so you know that it used the trusted path and isn't a Trojan horse. You know it has properly managed all aspects of the transaction.

If the audit event of a file access upon a security database occurs with no audit event of use of the administrative interface first, it's a time-zero alarm—a sure sign of trouble.

Any audit event of access to a security database might be a problem. The administrative interface is a *trusted program*—one that runs with administrative privilege. A major aspect of that is that they can do their own audit system control.

As such, the interface certainly will inform the audit system that it is being evoked, what task it has directed to do (probably including the command-line arguments), and what data objects it is accessing, such as the database files.

However, it might not explicitly elicit the File Access audit event when it accesses the database file, because, depending on the implementation, it might have shutdown the auditing of its own actions. In that case, it would be generating events describing its activities by itself, rather than relying on the system to do so.

So the moral is: When designing the your audit alarm detection system, know your system.

Administrative work could be scheduled in advance, on a weekly basis. Specific users could schedule specific tasks at specific times. This schedule should be made accurately each week and fed into the monitoring program activity database. When the administrative privileges are invoked, the monitor verifies them against the schedule. If its unexpected, a time-zero alarm is generated.

This approach would ensure that administrative activity happens as scheduled. The greater the detail, the more the assurance. If user X schedules a sequence of administrative commands, the sequence could be used as a sort of code. Randomizing the start times and sequences each week would provide assurance. For example, the system operator might schedule a backup of /usr at noon, mounting /mt1 first.

These types of strategies would provide a post-event qualification—a sort of secondary authorization of the administrative user. If nonscheduled actions need to be taken, notification to the auditor should be made first.

Another approach to ensuring legitimate administrative privilege use is the activity description. As any user might do, administrators often routinely perform role-related tasks. Therefore, they would establish a pattern of privilege use in their history, which can be compared to the use in each session.

This is an opportunity to build "secret codes" into activity. For example, administrators' roles can be divided among users by file system, time of day, files or devices, processes, commands, or other objects. These could be used to plant randomly disallowed combinations of these factors that an impersonator would have no way to avoid.

The monitor program, which has been fed these arbitrary policies, would alarm if an administrator stopped observing them.

The total effect of these strategies is a secondary form of authentication, which is validating the identity of a user. Other authentication means, such as biometrics or a surveillance camera on a terminal, might be more accurate but are not practical on inexpensive or networked systems. Double passwords aren't advisable in most cases.

However, by careful design work, you can add a second level of authentication beyond the login password using secure audit. That helps with the impostor problem.

It is harder to deal with an insider that abuses their access rights. Checking the activity database would stop sudden erratic behavior, such as perhaps would occur if an employee discovered that he or she was to be fired. So here they weren't "acting like themselves" or were trying to do things that they weren't allowed.

The restrictions on what the user could do helps for that reason. However, what about the worst case, where a user cunningly abuses their legitimate access rights in a way that gives the appearance of normal activity, such as an administrator that deliberately imports a malicious user program?

In that case, the audit record of the privileged actions would slip into the audit archive. Presumably, the program would be cornered by other defenses of the system, and the origin of it would be pulled from the archive.

Auditors work with the administrators. Auditors protect the system from unauthorized use of the administrators' powers. In that, they are all teammates. I say that because the auditor seeks to verify, with full cooperation, the activities of the administrators. Auditors, therefore, must never act in any way that might cloud the openness that best serves the organization. For example, this might be disclosing the activities in some circumstance that might compromise the administrator or entering into any sort of competitive relationship with them.

The point is that, in the real world, it might take a certain amount of confidentiality for administrators to share their activities with the auditor. Just as a hypothetical case, it might be embarrassing to someone that he or she had to redo something due to a foolish error, and he or she would rather it not get around. It is the responsibility of the auditors, and of the corporate policy about the auditor's records, that auditors maintain confidentiality of administrators doings.

Not only will this help keep the essential openness of their cooperation with the administrators, but it also is another dimension of security. The activities of the administer should be kept as confidential as possible, as the divulgence of these activities might assist impostors in their crime, especially in the case of an inside job.

In this way, the audit system performs a unique security function. All of the access controls of a secure system—such as labeling, ACLs, or privileges—are controls that prequalify user access to a resource. When you examine audit records, you view what already has occurred and what access has been granted, and you have the opportunity to correct inconsistencies with information that hasn't been checked by the access controls.

Therefore, audit serves as an additional level of access control. In the monitor program, statistical data files and activity databases are information needed to perform unique checks of some operations, such as checking the time of a login against the user's permitted login times.

These checks are especially useful in spotting impostors who have stolen a password and are assuming the identity of another user and also in spotting inside abusers who are abusing their legitimate access rights.

Doing the monitoring requires overhead: There would have to be coordination between the auditors and the file owners or application administrators about which users are on ACLs. For lower-labeled files, the overhead wouldn't be worth it.

Here's where you benefit from the work that you do to maintain your TIB. You keep your information organized by how valuable it is in the sense of how much work that you do to protect it. If you wanted to super-protect files of higher labels, you could afford to enact this double-check for them, but not for lower label files.

Chapter

7

Secure Applications

Secure UNIX has security-enhanced versions of databases, networking products, and X Window. I'll explore some of the new features of these in this chapter.

Secure Networking

Security doesn't mean isolation. Remote users come in over the networks that UNIX is famous for. Now though, you can either network with secure systems or, if the remote system isn't secure, deal with the connection and what comes over it appropriately.

Secure UNIX networking is most conspicuously different from pre-Secure networking in that it offers a much higher level of identification, authentication, and accountability. Many of the users or hosts that network to a secure system are authenticated much like local users. Of equal importance, those that cannot be authenticated are kept restricted on the basis of the label laws and other access restrictions.

To provide higher levels of authentication, Secure UNIX introduces new networking protocols at all levels and secure versions of networking system applications and processes. A major innovation in the protocols is to include the users' security attributes at the transport level with protocols such as CIPSO. Using that, secure versions of applications such as NFS and NIS are subject to the label laws. These provide security for local area use.

Pre-Secure RPC-based systems such as NIS were a major weakness in the protection of the password file. The SATAN or ISS security testing programs check for the presence of RPC-based programs.

Beyond the local area, Secure UNIX will be securely distributed with the application of digital authentication using public key technology or other means. The new protocols will carry encrypted user authentication credentials over the Internet and public data networks.

These two features—digital authentication and protocols that carry security attributes—will be used together to form the linchpin of Secure UNIX networking. This will be done by using network interfaces (gateways, firewalls, or intelligent network adaptors) that will assign MAC labels to connections according to security factors, such as authentication strength, encryption, etc. Network connections that lack security attributes or credentials also will be labeled accordingly by the network interface.

The label will be carried by the networking protocols throughout the local environment to determine the trustworthiness and the access rights of connections. The benefit is that impostors and spoofers are kept out. Also, the effectiveness of firewall gateways is greatly improved, because they are a part of the access firewall provided by mandatory access control.

The bottom line is that network users now are held up to the same high standards of identification and authentication as are local users. The pre-Secure days of accepting connections and providing services to poorly authenticated hosts and users are history.

Secure wide-area networking, such as that provided by public packet-switched data carriers and the Internet, is going to appear in the near future. What some might have considered a pipe dream suddenly is here, and you should take it seriously in your planning now.

The technology and the infrastructure already are here. However, due to some failed attempts to deploy it and some standardization considerations, secure wide-area networking has been delayed, and a perception is out there that it involves hard-to- implement technologically. It doesn't. Within the next year, secure networks will be the norm. This chapter strives to anticipate them, in that it deals with some issues that will accompany secure networks and how you can plan your TIBs now to take advantage of secure networking when it comes online.

Networked digital authentication

I'll begin with the two flavors of digital authentication: symmetric (secret) key and asymmetric (public) key. Although it has had shortcomings, Kerberos is an available method of networking authentication based on secret keys. It has a future on the Internet. PKC (public key cryptography) is a networking authentication protocol based on public key technology. Planned versions of Kerberos will be able to be interoperable with PKC-type authentication and will be combined and integrated with PKC functionality, too. However, given the availability of UNIX-based PKC systems, purely secret key compatible Kerberos is not the best choice for heterogeneous, large-scale distributed environments.

Secret key Kerberos is useful in some contexts, such as local area networks. It will have a wider role as a part of larger security architectures, such as IPv6. IPv6 can authenticate with secret keys, and it can use Kerberos as a good method for distributing secret keys.

Meanwhile, PKC, or its analogs, is being implemented on the Internet with applications such as mail and Secure Socket Layer (SSL). PKC will be the basis for secure commercial transactions on the Internet.

I will examine both Kerberos and PKC, pointing out their relative strengths, and the generic interface that will interoperate them both.

Private key versus public key encryption

The first hint that networking could be made secure was the proposal of DES in 1975 by IBM. DES is a single-key, or secret or symmetric key, encryption algorithm, called *private key encryption*. A single large random number, or secret key, is used to both encrypt and decrypt text. *Encryption* is scrambling readable text into seemingly random bits, and *decryption* is descrambling them back to their original text.

Attempts were made to field various secure networking architectures based on secret key technology (e.g., Kerberos or secure NFS). They were limited by problems such as how to securely manage the storage and distribution of the secret keys. To decrypt encrypted data, the recipient must get the secret key that the sender used to encrypt it. However, it's a problem to secretly send the secret key. Key servers were attempted but raised too many doubts about trusting them. Problems persisted with the general purpose use of encryption.

In 1976, an MIT mathematical lightning bolt struck: RSA, or public key, encryption. RSA is an encryption algorithm that uses two encryption keys, one of which actually can be made public. This obviates the need to transmit secret keys and can be used to provide privacy, authentication, data integrity, and nonrepudiation (the sender can't deny that he or she sent the message to the recipient).

Kerberos was the first security architecture for client/server systems. Its primary mode is to authenticate clients to servers for a session, and it is the basis of most designs.

Kerberos

Kerberos is a server of secret keys that initialize login processes and authenticate clients to servers. It initializes login processes with a login session user secret key that their clients use to authenticate themselves to servers. Kerberos uses the secret key to encrypt the messages that it sends to users. During requests, once it authenticates users, it gives them secret keys for server/client sessions that they use to authenticate themselves to network servers, such as for rlogin service.

Kerberos keeps the user login session keys encrypted with password storage keys that are derived from the user passwords. However, it doesn't keep user passwords. It derives the password keys again to verify the users' passwords. However, it does keep the users' login session keys, which is its major vulnerability. If Kerberos is violated, all users lose privilege and can be impersonated. Because of that, Kerberos servers must be given ultra-security. Under Secure UNIX, that might be much easier to provide, but it still involves too high of a cost in the case of a lapse. It also is vulnerable to denial of service problems if the centralized facility fails.

Kerberos (and other client/server authentication systems) doesn't replace, or lessen the need for the quality of, passwords. Passwords still are needed for the initial authentication at the system-entry place. They are how users get issued their secret keys for presentation to distributed checkpoints.

Kerberos protocols use timestamps on their protocol exchanges to prevent replays of stolen or copied old messages. This requires that the network be synchronized to some extent.

Keys are installed during login (or for service use) in the form of a *ticket* by the Kerberos *ticket granting service*. Tickets include a timestamp, duration, and key and are transmitted and cached in encrypted form. Kerberos encrypts server session tickets with the user login session key and again by a user password hash before it sends it to the users.

While doing client/server authentication, Kerberos creates a ticket for the server after it receives a timestamped client request. The timestamp is encrypted with the client login key, which authenticates the client to Kerberos.

Kerberos gives the client a ticket that is encrypted with the secret key of the server that Kerberos knows. It sends the server ticket, server session key, another timestamp, and duration (all encrypted with the user login session key) to the client.

The client verifies the timestamp and sends the server ticket with another timestamp encrypted by the server session key to the server. The server authenticates the client by decrypting the timestamp (known as the *authenticator*) with the server session key that it pulls from the ticket after decrypting it with its server key. Optionally, the same method can be used to authenticate the server to the client. After checking the timestamp, the server returns the timestamp plus one to the client.

Kerberos allows distributed Kerberos servers to be accessible by use of the same mechanism. Local users are known as the *realm*, and Kerberos servers from other realms are registered with the local realm Kerberos in the same way that servers are.

Kerberos methods established the basis of distributed authentication in client/server systems, many of which were carried forth in public key cryptography.

The distributed nature of these systems required that, in addition to the initial system-entry authentication, a user security "credential" be presented to distributed authenticators, such as file servers. This ensured that impersonators or spoofers that entered the system by circumventing a legitimate login were blocked.

Kerberos did this by tickets, which held encrypted session keys that were hashed using the user's password. (A *hash* is a one-way transform. With the input value, such as a password, it is possible to verify by rehashing the input that the ticket is a hash of the same input).

These credentials are bound to the user's login session when he or she logs in. They then can be verified as security credentials when the user clients present them to servers.

Kerberos tickets are a way to distribute secret keys, aside from the authentication function. Newer Kerberos can use public key methods to do authentication, while doing the rest of the functions, such as ticket service. Likewise, other protocols, such as Internet SSL or IPv6, can draw on Kerberos for some of its functionality, such as secret-key distribution.

The problem with secret-key authentication systems on the large scale is the dependence on a centralized, trusted authority that must protect users' secret data or cause massive security failure. Besides all of the usual drawbacks of a fixed- capacity single point of failure, there's the distributed and security aspects. To use Kerberos, your account or your realm must be registered on it by the Kerberos or system administrator. That might be feasible for the local user network; however, for widely distributed network users, that can be a severe restriction. Kerberos also deals only with the client/server session.

Public key cryptography

There is a better way. Authentication can be based on public key technology. It solves the problems with secret key systems in that it is suited for distributed systems and not vulnerable to security lapse. Public key cryptography (PKC) based systems are used to do secure bootstrapping, peer-to-peer authentication, as well as the client/server session. (See Figure 7.1.)

PKC systems, such as RSA, work by using separate keys to either encrypt or decrypt text when appropriate. One key is called the private key, and the other is the public key. Each set of keys is unique (i.e., for each private key, there is only one matching public key and vice-versa).

PKC servers keep users public keys, not their secret keys. Their jobs are to provide proof that users own their public keys. Because no secret information is kept on them, the worst case in a security failure is that the source of a message might become confused, but no loss of privacy could result because only owners of private keys can decrypt messages meant for them. Distributed users need not be registered on the local machine. They only need to certify that their public key belongs to them.

The two keys are used to send encrypted text in the following manner. The senders and recipients both derive their own public and private keys.

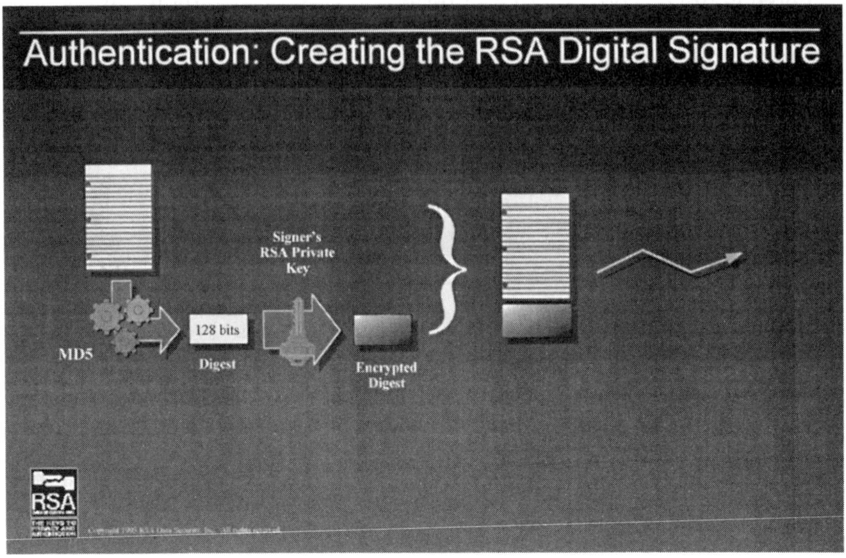

Figure 7.1 Digital signatures.

The public keys can be transmitted to recipients, managed by a third party or server, or posted on a public built-in board.

To send private messages, the sender uses the recipient's public key to encrypt messages, and the recipient uses his or her private key to decrypt them. Thus, the only party that can access the message is the holder of the private key. Gone is the problem of how to secretly transmit the secret key.

However, it is possible that, because the public key might be well-known, a number of senders might use it to send messages to the recipient. The sender provides proof to the recipient of his or her identity (authentication) by encrypting the message with his or her private key, known as a *digital signature*.

If the sender wanted both privacy and authentication, he or she would first encrypt with the recipient's public key, then with his or her private key.

In the case where the sender chose both privacy and authentication, the recipient first uses the sender's public key to decrypt the message, which proves that it came from the sender. Because each key pair is unique, the fact that the public key works proves that it came from the sender. To be more precise, what's proved is that the sender has the private key that corresponds to the public key that the receiver used to decrypt his or her message.

The recipient then uses his or her private key to decrypt the messages, ensuring that the message was received confidentially, because only he or she owns his or her private key. Thus, public key is a brilliant scheme for networking privacy and authentication.

The only thing lacking in the previous scheme is the recipient's proof that the sender sent the message (nonrepudiation)—the proof that a public key used to verify the digital signature belongs to the sender. This could be accomplished in a trustworthy manner by well-known third parties (certificate authorities), who certify the identity of public key holders.

Certificates bind the identity of user to his or her public key. They can be part of a user's credentials and can be transmitted along with messages. Certificates are encrypted with the private key of the certificate authorities.

The final assurance that you can gain from public key methods is data integrity. If you generate a message digest or cryptographic checksum, such as MD4, and include it with your message, you can use it to ensure that the message wasn't modified (i.e., message integrity).

Various public key methods are in the process of being embedded into worldwide network architectures, both as applications and at the lower networking protocol levels.

PKC installs private keys in user logins and provides public key certificates that certify that users own their public keys. No secret information is kept by PKC—no passwords or private or secret keys. Only users know their private keys; they authenticate themselves by proving that they know their private keys, not by giving them away.

At login, PKC systems install a private key in the user login process, maintaining its corresponding public key, which is encrypted by a hash of the user password in a certificate database.

It is essential to note that the PKC server doesn't keep the user's private key for him or her. It installs it as part of the user's initial account and keeps only the public key in its certificate database. The private key is known and kept by the user.

The protocol uses a host-supplied *nonce* (random number) as the encryption key to distribute the private keys, and it installs public key certificates in the host. When the login session ends, processes that contain the public key certificates and the private keys are discarded.

Just as Kerberos does, PKC systems authenticate clients to servers for a session of service use. Clients send session keys (secret keys for encrypting during a session) to servers by using the servers public key for privacy.

Clients also can allow the server to delegate, or establish sessions for them on other servers. They send a delegation key in a ticket. This key is used to allow servers to use other servers in the name of the client. The ticket and the public key certificate are sent to the server encrypted by the client private key. Clients can send the delegation, public, or private key to the server, depending on whether they want to delegate. The client sends a session key to the server with the server's public key. The server returns a nonce, encrypted by the session key. (See Figure 7.2.)

No central secret key server is needed. Remote users can be authenticated merely by proving that they know their private keys and that they are the owners of their public keys. They need not have an entry in the local PKC server, unlike secret key systems, which would have to have users registered and login or have an inter-realm server for them.

The only requirement is verification of the public key certificate. To do that, public key systems use the concept of a trusted certificate authority (CA). It doesn't need to be centralized. Users have it installed with their login credentials. It specifies which PKC server it uses. Remote trusted authorities should be registered with the local PKC.

The CA is part of a CCITT standard, X.509, or directory service. It is an essential component of distributed security, as it prevents masqueraders. The users' public keys are matched to their identities in it.

CAs are managed with chains. The local CA might have other CAs' certificates in it. Because the CA is a repository of information that is used to determine the trustworthiness of users, it is something that each organization has to carefully manage for itself, because the organization is the best judge of who to trust.

Trust is related to the organizations that are dealt with. They might be a remote office of the same organization, a publicly trusted authority, or some other organization. In each case, the policy enforcement, the use of Secure UNIX, and other factors must determine how much trust can be placed in their certificates.

PKC keeps certificates for the servers' public keys, encrypted with the private key of the clients. Public key encryption algorithms have the disadvantage of being slower to compute (i.e., to use to encrypt and decrypt) than DES. This disadvantage can be avoided by using public key cryptography (PKC) techniques to compute only the minimum data, such as

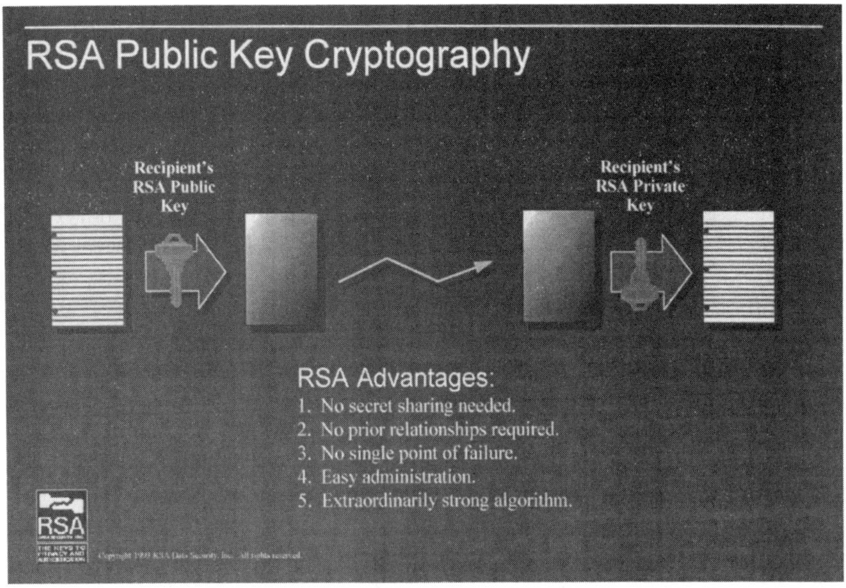

Figure 7.2 Public key.

the secret keys, and not the message text, which is encrypted by DES. (See Figure 7.3.)

Sender (A)		Receiver (B)		Service type
Digest	= f (MSG, Time) (MSG, Digest, time) →	Digest	= f (MSG,Time) (Digest received = computed?)	Nonreplay Integrity
Message encrypted	= f (MSG, Public key B) →	MSG	= f (MSG_encrypted, private key B)	Privacy
Digtal Signature A	= f (ID, Private key A, nonce) (ID & nonce encrypted, ID) →	ID	= f (DS & nonce, Public key A) (ID Received = computed?)	Authentication (Digital signature) Nonreplay
DSA signed by third party	= f (DS, Trusted Certificate →	DSA	= f (CERT, Trusted public key) (then authenticate DSA as above)	Nonrepudiation
Reverse nonrepudiation of origin (as above)	←	Receipt	= f (Timestamp, digest or copy of MSG)	Nonrepudiation of delivery

Key:

ICV: Integrity check value (ICVR = received; ICVC = computed)
MSG: Message
SN: Sequence number
PUB: Public Key
ID: Identifier (IDR = received; IDC = computed)
PRIV: Private Key
DS: Digital signature
CERT: Certificate
TP: Third party
DR: Digital receipt

Figure 7.3 Digit encryption protocols.

Security-enhanced Protocols

Before I proceed, I'd like to address a dilemma that's been urgently considered these last few years regarding public key technology. With such a tantalizing utility at hand, you might wonder why it isn't ready now. Well, there's been a hitch having to do with standardization and, some speculate, with other issues, such as national security, law enforcement, and the U.S. global competitive stance.

Rather than agree to standardize on RSA, NIST (the National Institute of Standards and Technology) has proposed another public key encryption algorithm, which is called Digital Signature (DSS). RSA already has momentum in Europe and, for commercial products, domestically. It's a *de facto* standard in that sense.

One problem with RSA is that, for national security reasons, vendors can't export DES-based systems, which provide the privacy of messages in some RSA-based protocols. Also, at this time, DSS doesn't include a private key algorithm, which means that it lacks privacy (it doesn't encrypt the message text). NIST has implied that an exportable private key algorithm will be offered for use with it sometime soon.

Another problem with DSS is a trust issue. Although there's no rigorous mathematical proof, there seems to be more trust out there that RSA has no "trap door" in it than there is for DSS. The trap door is a built-in (by the algorithm developers) method to decrypt.

The aforementioned considerations aside, it is clearly in the economic interests of the U.S., and in the technological interests of all users, that this matter be resolved with the highest urgency and priority.

Despite the confusion, the Internet is researching and planning the deployment of PKC technology using the *de facto* standards, as I now will describe.

Privacy enhanced mail

The Internet has a secure version of mail called *privacy enhanced mail*, which includes RSA, DES, MD4, and a CCITT standard X.509 PKC public key server for certifying. It puts the encryption keys, the message digest, and the certificate for the public keys in its message header. The message itself is encrypted with a DES key. The DES key, the certificate of the sender's public key (encrypted with the private key of the certifier), and the message digest are placed in the message header and encrypted with the public key of the recipient, then again by the private key of the sender. The header also has the sender and receiver identifier.

MAXSIX

Secure UNIX networking protocol has labels and other security attributes that are part of connections. The label of the connection and the data carried by it are related by the label laws.

Other security attributes of secure connections are the information label, audit identifier (ID), audit mask, terminal ID, user ID, group ID, other groups, processes ID, privileges, and the session ID. Each of these will be described in this section. (See Figure 7.4.)

During connection establishment, if a label isn't presented, you know that the remote system isn't secure. The network interface will label the connection with a low label that would restrict its access rights by the label laws. If you take this precaution, you can network with secure and insecure systems alike.

Thus, the connection-establishment phase (carried out by the transport protocol) relates the authentication strength to the maximum label allowed for the connection. Authentication methods can be rated by trustworthiness: public key encryption would be the highest with nonencrypted, nonlabeled the lowest.

If you've connected with a secure remote system, you know it because it has a label in its protocol and is strongly authenticated. If the remote system is a clone of your TIB, it has the same label names and meanings as at your site. That is a possibility if the remote site is a branch of your organization.

If you want to communicate with a different organization, you can translate its labels into yours.

The new secure networking protocol with user security attributes in the transport networking level is one of the main new features that Secure UNIX networking is based on.

Secure networking functionality is largely the same as that of pre-Secure UNIX remote login, mount, and file transfer. In those, users first would login to the remote system, then get a UNIX shell, a service shell (such as file transfer), or a remote mount. However, this was done with a dangerous lack of accountability in many aspects.

One problem was the accountability of callers after they accessed the remote system. From the remote, or called, system perspective, no matter how well the information access was managed on it, once the bits flowed out the wire, for all you knew they then were flowing across the Times Square teletyper.

Also, the accountability of the network servers was low regarding who was using it. Servers would execute subprocesses on the client's (calling user's) behalf without imparting to them the user's identity. So, once a user got onto a remote system, his or her activities were virtually anonymous.

To solve this problem, Secure network connections include a user identifier (uid). The presence of a uid and its accompanying data means that the remote system is a TIB, it has properly authenticated the users, and you can allow users to login or use system services with all of the TIB protections afforded local users. You know that client users are operating within a TIB,

Label
Information label
Effective privileges
Login user ID
UID, GIDs
User ID
Group ID
Groups
Process ID
ACL

Figure 7.4 Secure Unix networking protocol: MAXSIX connection attribute data can be embedded into protocol headers.

and any information that is sent to them will safely arrive and get the same protections that it gets locally.

The uid allows you to afford the same protections and status on the server environment as on the client. Clients that call in, say with rlogin, will execute with their identities and security attributes that they had at the time that they made the call on the originating system.

Many of the notably non-Secure, but highly popular, systems—such as rlogin (or r*), trusted hosts, NFS, and NIS—will be redeemed with these new labeled, identification and authentication enhanced protocols. Their major weakness was a lack of authentication capacity.

The servers invoke services, command processes, or shells on the remote user's behalf with full accountability and audit, as though the user had logged on locally.

Along with the uid, the label is included in the connection protocol. It is the label that the client process had when it made the call.

Connections are labeled. When clients request connections, the clients are at a label. The client label is made known over the network to the server. If the server will provide it, the connection is made at that label.

All labeled resources are related by the label laws. Information labeled higher than the connection can't be transmitted over it, so important files can't "walk" out over the network.

Secure connections supply information labels in the protocol, referring to data that is being transmitted over it.

The *audit ID* (also called *login ID*) is the identifier given to users when they initially login onto a networked environment. No matter whether they continue to login to subsequent hosts, their audit ID is fixed and is propagated to each new connection.

The audit ID is used to record the course of remote logins from host to host. Audit records from servers will record the course so that such activity can be reconstructed networkwide. The audit ID also is important authentication data because it refers to the host on which the user was originally, and perhaps most thoroughly, authenticated.

The Secure connection also has users' audit event list or mask (which contains the events that they are configured to audited for), the terminal ID of the login terminal, user and group ID, process ID, and privileges. The session ID is used to identify events of a particular network service call, such as a rlogin call.

Not only do networks have label lists, so also do hosts. When servers receive connection requests at a label from remote hosts, the connection is allowed by the host's label list or the servers rejects the connection.

Servers can handle connections at different labels so that they accommodate clients at different labels. They are trusted processes—processes that run with privilege. They first determine whether the connection request is within the host label list. If so, the client logs in. Then, the server will create a child server at the label of the connection.

The server subprocess is created at the label of the client (and connetion). It thenceforth is subject to the label laws. All of the resources of the TIB are labeled including filesystems, files, devices, and other user processes, and they are compared to the subprocess label for access control.

The client user must have a login account on the server machine with a label list that includes the label of the call. The server network device has a label list that also must include the call label. If not, the server won't establish the connection.

NFS, Rlogin, and NIS using MAXSIX

Secure networks are similar to pre-Secure networks in that they are based on a client/server architecture. Some machines, called *servers*, provide a service to users on remote machines, called *clients*. When clients are using servers, they have established a connection with it. User clients can open connections much as they do files (i.e., they can call the remote machine). Services include file transfer, remote login, or mount.

To explore the impact of labeled connections, I'll see how they will affect typical UNIX networking services, such as NFS or NIS.

Pre-Secure NFS allows users to mount filesystems on remote machines. It uses a system database file, etc/exports, which specifies which hosts can mount each filesystem listed. Pre-Secure versions also specified which hosts could have root access to the filesystems.

The salient new feature of Secure networking is the inclusion of a user identifier, label, and other credentials in the low-level protocol. The label is transmitted from the users current label. The significance of this is that operations, such as remote mounting, will be subject to the label laws.

Pre-Secure UNIX NFS relied on the export host file to control access to filesystems. A typographical error could leave the system wide open. It was up to the administrator to define the access that hosts and users were allowed with enough precision. Typically, access control was specified only to the level of hosts rather than of users.

With label checking, every attempt to mount the filesystem is verified against the individual user's access rights, regardless of what's in the host's database. That is, client hosts might be allowed to mount a filesystem according to the exports file, but only if they first have access according to the label laws. The label of the connection, which is in effect the label of the user client, is compared to the label of the filesystem for access control.

So the authorization protection accorded even the pre-Secure host access is far beyond what is provided by the export file. In fact, label protection will supersede it.

NIS is an authentication method that uses a shared facility for managing password and group files on a network with a client/server architecture. A server keeps all of the password and group files for the machines in a local environment for the purpose of simplifying their administration.

Pre-Secure UNIX NIS is a security disaster. The first thing SATAN or ISS (the security penetration testing programs) do is look for NIS, because its simple to spoof it into giving the password file.

An NIS client is a workstation that is using the server whenever it authenticates a user during login. It is configured to use the server by having a special entry in its password file that is preceded by a plus sign. NIS group authentication takes place similarly. Some users on a workstation can be authenticated on it, with all others done by NIS.

Secure versions of NIS perform label checks on client requests, ensuring that the client label is higher than or equal to the server password file. The response to the request is returned at the lowest user label that all users can read. NIS systems also handle printer and host information.

In consequence, only higher-labeled connections will be able to use NIS, which would allow network firewalls to separate user password information from low-labeled users.

Users that call into the gateway on nontrusted networks will be confined to logging onto the gateway only (as opposed to using the NIS server, which is a separate machine). I'll discuss gateways more in the following section.

NIS clients have password files with asterisks in their password fields for some system accounts, but all user entries are on the server.

NIS users can change their passwords by using the `passwd` program that they can run from the trusted path. Administrators can change passwords through the administrative interface.

Auditing will monitor all elements of the NIS system, including the trusted processes (NIS daemons) that the system runs and the password and group files on the client and servers. These processes include privileges to override network labels, to use privileged ports, or to set processes labels.

NIS can be securely implemented on a secure network—usually one that is local with high-labeled connections. When the environment includes less secure hosts or networks, other facilities are needed to administer password files that are used on large, less secure networks.

Authentication on LANs either requires accounts on individual LAN hosts or will make use of a facility to provide central administration of the password and group files, such as NIS (Yellow Pages). NIS can allow users to log in to hosts on a LAN without requiring that they have password file entries on them.

Using pre-Secure rlogin, the "trusted host" facility allows users to obtain a login session or execute a shell on a remote system via `rlogin` or `rsh` without having to enter a password. The hosts allowed were listed in the system database file /etc/hosts.equiv. Users must have the same identifier on the local and remote host, and access could be further restricted to specific users and hosts. Specifying a plus for the host name would allow all hosts to be trusted hosts.

Clients with Secure connections with high labels already are authenticated by the client host and by the networking protocol. When they `rlogin`, they log in and must have accounts on the remote host.

Servers that run at one label need not have privilege and are kept in low-label directories where users can't create executables. These are servers that are programmed by users, rather than being part of the TIB system software. Because they might allow data transfer without login, they are kept in "miscellaneous junk" directories.

Secure Socket Layer

Internet engineers are researching and soon planning to deploy a secure TCP protocol called Secure Socket Layer (SSL). Secure versions of Web browsers such as Netscape are based on it, and they can be used just like a socket by any TCP protocol-based process. They provide all of the functions that I described in the "Public key cryptography" section "built-in" to the TCP interface.

As such, they will use PKC methods to provide a process-to-process transport level supplied authentication, privacy, and integrity.

Clients authenticate servers by the following. They exchange their PKC certificates (which bind their names to their public keys) and challenge data. The challenge works the same as password/challenge response. In this case, the client sends a random challenge value to the server. The server encrypts the random value with its private key and returns it. If the client can resolve the challenge value with the public key in the server's certificate that proves that the server knew its private key.

Next master keys are exchanged that can be used to make multiple shared secret session keys for privacy.

Integrity is ensured by inclusion of a message digest that is a hash of the message and other information, such as a sequence number and a secret value. The extra information ensures that the digest hasn't been rehashed on an altered message.

SSL will employ option negotiation to interoperate with systems of varied levels and types of security features. Some of the options that it negotiates are mutual (for client to server and server to client) authentication, type symmetric key or key token used (tokens are keys exchanged and used in encrypted forms), type of message digest used, or certificate format or authority.

Internet engineers are working like beavers on espresso to solve the problem of Internet security. One of the issues that they're working out is the certificate authority. The X.509 version hasn't been implemented too widely. Some vendors, such as Northern Telecom's Entrust PKC libraries, allow organizations to manage their own certificates. Internet certificate management is under development, primarily in the form of the IKMP, or key data in secure DNS. Good solutions will allow interim systems and flexible negotiation.

A typical user of PKC might be a software vendor that will allow their users to generate their key pairs for their binaries of their products, keep their private keys, and register their public keys in a choice of certificate formats, management schemes, and authorities. The existing authorities are RSA, PEM, DNS, and PGP. (See Figures 7.5 and 7.6.)

IPv6

Another security protocol under research and development on the Internet is the new IP version 6, which also is known as *IP tunneling*. Tunneling is the encapsulation of IP or TCP packets in another IP envelope. The encapsulated packet will be encrypted.

IPv6 will provide privacy, authentication, and integrity, all with extensive option negotiation.

It will use a secret key in its header (Authentication Header) for authentication and integrity only. If privacy also is required, encapsulation will be

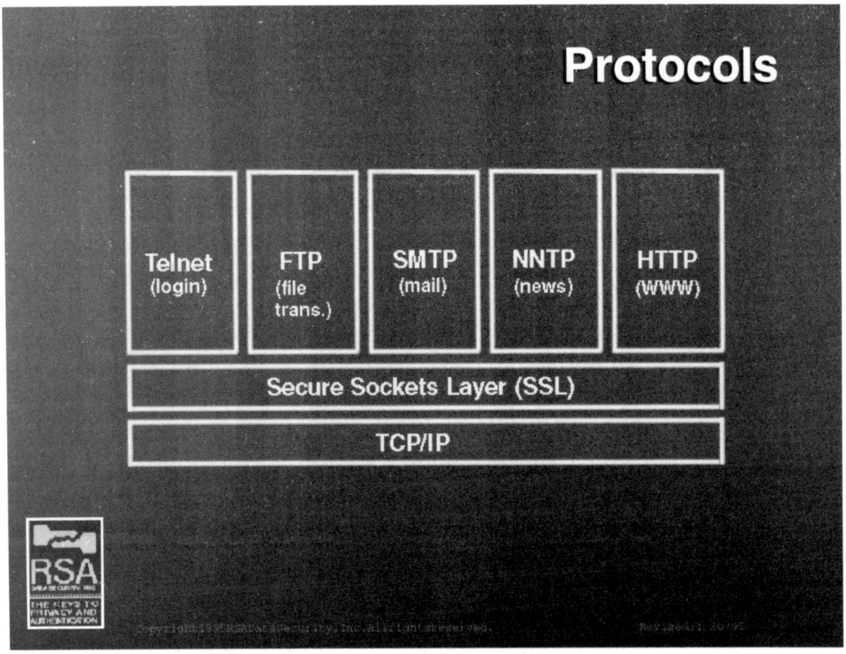

Figure 7.5 SSL.

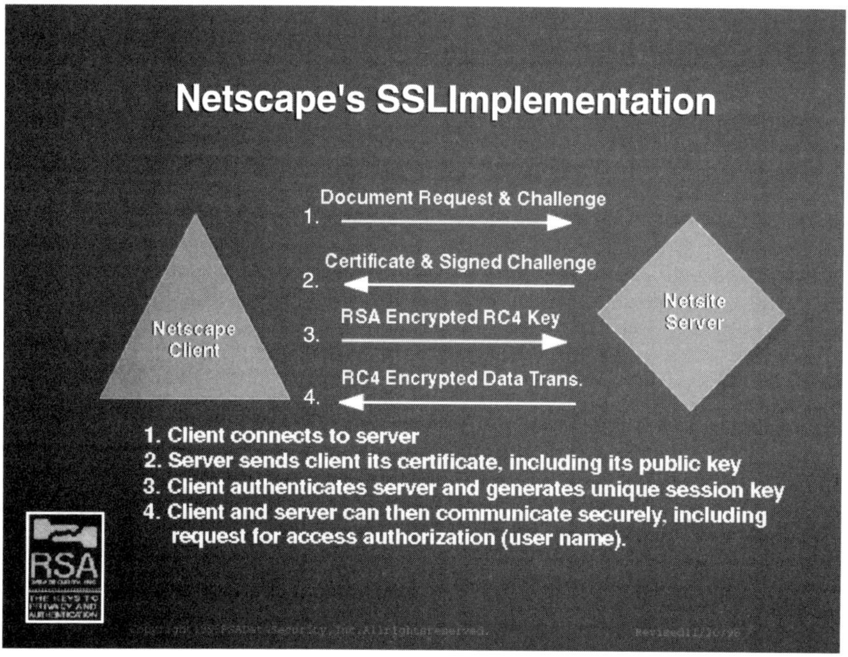

Figure 7.6 Netscape SSL.

used rather than the Authentication Header. The two modes can be combined to provide the previous services and nonrepudiation as well.

The Authentication Header provides assurance that the source, destination, transport protocol, and port number in the protocol header are secure. These values are critical and are examined by firewall gateways and screening routers, as I will discuss soon.

The Header also can be the basis of Secure UNIX MAC labels, as the interface can map the different keys for each header to a MAC label.

Secure HTTP

Another secure protocol under development is the Secure HTTP. It again applies public key technology to provide privacy, authentication, integrity, and nonrepudiation. It will be used by Web servers and browsers.

OSI

The OSI Security Architecture specifies embedding public key methods into the transport- and session-level protocols to perform authentication, privilege, and message integrity. Other features include timestamping, clock synchronization, duration, and routing in the protocol to prevent replay of authentication data or other forgery, routing control to maximize security, encryption key provision and checking, and password servers.

Distributed TIBs

This section will tie together the new systems available today and envision how they will be applied to provide distributed security.

With labeled connections on the local area networks and with the integration of public key encryption into the wide area networks, secure networking is here today and becoming more capable of supporting high-labeled connections over the wide area in the next few years.

I'll discuss some likely scenarios of distributed Secure communications, trusted LANs, distributed trusted LANs, distributed but different Secure organizations, and network firewall gateways.

The strategy that I'll follow is to place the most precious resources into a secure logical area, or security perimeter, then widen and distribute access to them in a controlled and trusted manner. I'll start with a closed TIB on a LAN, then build on it by adding networked connection and insecure system interfaces, showing how security can be maintained.

Inside the security perimeter

There usually are certain resources, perhaps some database servers or other transaction processing facilities, that are an organization's major information repository. Any security incident is bad, but unauthorized use, theft, or vandalization of these can be fatal catastrophes. I'll call these the organization's core information assets, or core.

Now imagine drawing a circle around the core; this is the *security perimeter*. Inside it are the users that are authorized to access it, who are accountable for its use. There might be Secure local area networks (LANs) with a closed system of Secure UNIX systems on a network media. I use that as an example of an initial departure point for a more distributed TIB.

The users are all known members of the organization, the hosts are located in proximity, there is physical access restrictions of some kind, and the hosts are all Secure UNIX systems used with the organizational security policies described in this book. The system is closed in the sense that there is no insecure dial-in, public data carrier, PCs or PC LAN, mainframe, or any other insecure interfaces.

In such an environment, there'd be trustworthy high-labeled connections. Secure networking protocols, such as CIPSO, assert the client users' security attributes to remote service providers, and they establish high-labeled trusted connections. Confidential data then can be safely communicated. You know that authentication of the client user, implicit in the attributes presented, is reliable and that the connection isn't being spoofed, tapped, or tampered with. Such an environment also might use a distributed authentication service, such as NIS (Yellow Pages).

That model might be used as the base of the trusted logical area. It has digitally authenticated processes and users, auditing, and policy enforcement.

Authorized use of the core resources also is assured by the use of network screening routers and firewall gateways. I'll discuss those soon. They can be used within organizations, not only as the interface to the outside world but in front of the core resources to create trusted subnets within the internal networks.

A typical large organization might have PC LANs, mainframes, minicomputers, UNIX workstations and database servers, and wide area (WAN) connections on an internal network.

The users of the local workstations and PCs are the trusted internal users. They might be application users, administrators, operators, or developers. The users coming in over the WAN might not be allowed as much access as internal users, but they might allowed some access, say to an Internet Web page.

The basic policies enforced in this case would be that only trusted users can have privileged access to core resources and that external users can not access internal resources except for those restricted for unprivileged use (such as public Web pages or read-only access).

To create the internal subnets, screening routers and firewalls would be used to enforce some basic policies. Connections to the core resources would be allowed only from internal PC and workstation LANs. Exception might be made for an application of appropriate privilege (read-only or restricted access) on a particular port. Connections to the internal LANs, or those from the outside, might be blocked.

Untrusted connections in to the security perimeter

The next step in expanding the security perimeter is to widen access to wide area networks and insecure systems. The problem with that is the admittance of unauthenticated users and strangers from non-Secure hosts and networks.

The Secure UNIX solution to the problem is that it's okay to connect with untrusted networks as long as the fact that they are not secure is considered during access decisions to all resources that they try to access. As long as you can tell which users have been well authenticated and which haven't, you can restrict the access of the strangers.

Secure UNIX offers a way to guarantee this: the MAC label laws. Network connections that come from poorly authenticated users will have a label that reflects that and will deny them access to secured resources.

The same applies to network connections that are insecure in other ways besides poor authentication. They might be carried over lines that are subject to eavesdropping and in need of encryption.

Using a Secure UNIX system as a network firewall gateway, you can network with Secure and non-Secure connections in the same manner. Non-Secure clients that attempt to establish calls to the gateway will present an untrustworthy networking protocol that lacks security attributes to the gateway, and it will "stamp" the protocol with a low label that reflects its untrustworthy source. Any use of your system will be restricted and confined by that label, which will be on any server-invoked processes or login shells and will control which directories, devices, and files they can access. (See Figure 7.7.)

Pre-Secure Internet gateway strategies rely on restricting services and port usage, preventing access to local user databases (such as /etc/password), and enhanced auditing and authentication. They include Internet firewalls and screening routers, which I'll now briefly review.

Screening routers use a rule set to screen packets. They are good at blocking unwanted ones. The decisions in the rules are based on the IP header: source and destination address, whether the packet is inbound or outbound, which router interface (inside or outside), the source and destination port (which might determine the type of service), and the protocol bits (used to screen TCP connection requests).

Firewalls are at the application level; they make decisions based on application-level events and data. They are bastions; they separate the IP address space of the internal and external networks.

Firewalls use two types of application types: socks servers or proxies. Socks applications allow internal users to connect outside the firewall without logging onto it, and proxies require that users do.

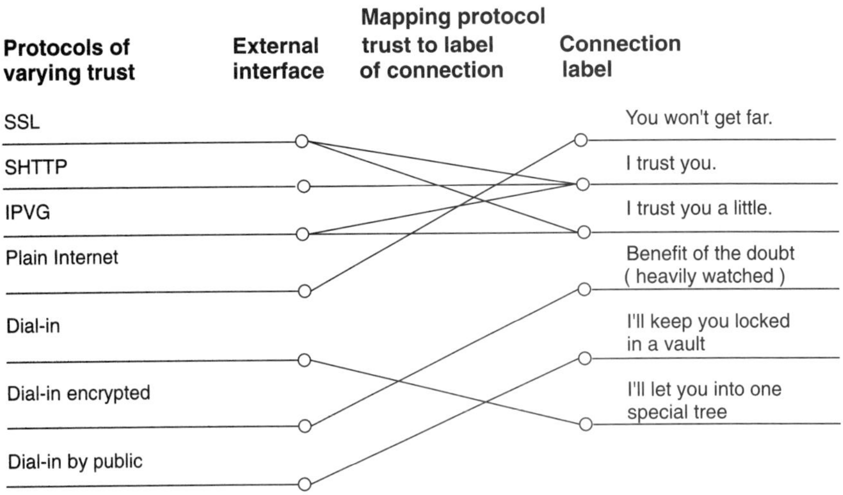

Figure 7.7 Secure Unix firewall.

In any case, the function of the firewall is to make decisions on what type of application use is allowed (such as the need for digital authentication or not), to hide internal information (such as user accounts or addresses), and to serve as the sole and highly secured and monitored entry point for wide area or untrusted networks.

Firewalls do authentication of WAN users. As such, they are where the new security-enhanced protocols will reside. They also will be based on Secure UNIX systems to project security credentials into the TIB using MAC label based connections.

A single SLIP or PPP line can entirely subvert a firewall. To assure the effectiveness of a firewall, disallow those "back doors" and make the firewall the sole interface to the Internet.

Current firewalls provide restricted environments and shells to external users after digitally authenticating them with smartcards. One of their jobs is to determine how to authenticate users depending on whether they are internal or external.

Secure UNIX firewalls digitally authenticate with PKC technology embedded into the new Internet protocols, such as IPv6 and SSL.

Screening routers that use IPv6 have cryptographic assurance that IP header data, such as addresses, are authentic. That limits IP spoofing, which is a major threat today.

Firewalls will establish security credentials for users, including their key certificates, and then will perform an essential TIB function: They are the interface that will assign the MAC label to the connection. The user's method of system entry and the trustedness of the network and authentication that they had will be a part their networking connection and carried throughout the TIB by the internal labeled protocols, such as CIPSO.

Because CIPSO will carry the authenticated user identity to networked facilities—such as NFS, servers, and hosts—the access firewalling is assured systemwide beyond the firewall. All of these methods are applicable to a firewall gateway that is implemented on a Secure UNIX system. In addition, it would inherently assert an access firewall.

The gateway's job as an authentication point would be to rate incoming user connections on the basis of their authentication strength. It is the site of digital authentication service, preferably public key.

The authentication services that gateways provide will take advantage of authentication data carried in the protocols of wide area networks. The gateway might implement a network-layer protocol that is a standard, at least within the organization, such as public key. It also might take advantage of services that will be provided by the network, such as the Internet, perhaps at lower network layers.

Connections are rated by factors such as the network security and authentication strength of the connection. The labels that Secure gateways give to connections can include a lot of information regarding how the connection was made. The categories section of the label can finely specify what the connection can access. The categories could relay such factors as the authentication method used, whether the data carried is encrypted, whether the host is trusted, etc. (See Figure 7.8.)

Here's the key difference with a Secure UNIX gateway. Once the connection is made, it gets a label, whether or not the protocol carried a label when it came into the gateway. An unlabeled caller will be assigned a label when he or she enters the gateway. This label will reflect its insecure source.

Non-Secure systems interfaced by Secure UNIX network firewall gateways can include mainframes, PCs, PC LANs, non-Secure UNIX systems, dial-up hosts or terminals, etc., as well any non-Secure networks such as the Internet, Public Data Networks (such as telnet), or private X.25 or SNA networks.

As I've previously said, wide area high-labeled connections over the Internet or X.25 public data networks are near widespread availability with the introduction of public key cryptographic technologies.

Connecting to other TIBs

Assuming that the capacity for Secure high-labeled wide-area communications is available, the next scenario is that you then might create a distributed network among remote offices of your same organization. Secure connections on the gateway would network multiple trusted LAN environments or distributed standalone Secure systems. All of which would form one distributed TIB. Such a system would have some form of shared, or at least jointly administered, authentication and a shared label database.

The authentication would take either one repeated on the separate LANs, each with their own NIS system. They could share a central NIS-type authentication, or each local site might communicate with the other sites during authentication. In this case, NIS would be a second level of authentication because the public key method embedded in the protocol is a form of authentication.

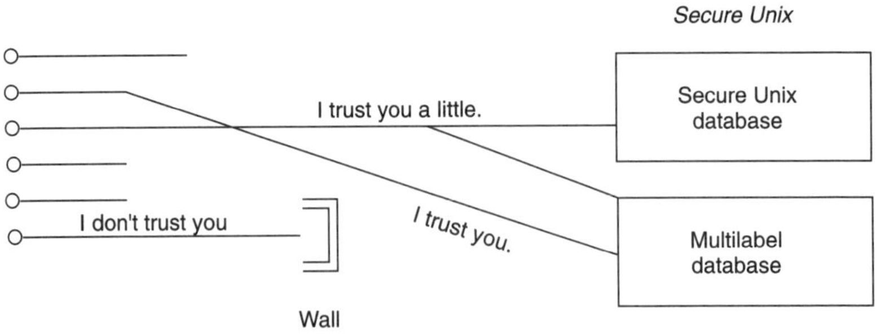

Figure 7.8 TIVs with Secure Unix firewalls.

The other aspect of this distributed TIB is that it uses the same label database throughout. The label access control is performed by using the same interpretations of TIB security protections, as well as using identical labels for all similar resources for all of the distribute LAN TIBs.

If communicating with another secure organization but with a different TIB, the call has a label, but you need a way to correlate its to yours so that you can give it equivalent treatment in terms of monitoring effort, exclusivity, or whatever your labels mean to you. Likewise, you expect the remote organization to treat your information as you do.

The way that is done is by conference. Organizations get to together and agree on a common labeling convention. That agreement is coded into the communications protocol so that you can translate labels between organizations by referring to the labeling code. You might have multiple labeling codes in use for different connections.

It isn't necessary that labels be identically named among these organizations, as long as there's agreement by all parties on how the labels will be treated and that the intent of the label is carried out.

Labels have many possible meanings. They are an access control method; they control which users, or classes of users, have access to information. They also can determine how closely monitored or guarded information labeled with it is or any number of other implications. They can be arrayed on an ordered scale or be part of a random matrix.

So it is with a convention among differing TIBs. They are highly custom to the group's needs. If it is important that some data be closely monitored, all parties must assure that the label that they're respectively mapping to is sufficiently closely guarded to satisfy everyone's requirements. If two labels are ordered relative to classes of users that they grant access to, these organizations must have correlated these users into the same, or acceptably analogous, classes in regard to their ordered relationship.

Whole networks are labeled; that is, they provide connections within label lists or at single labels. It is the job of the network administrator to ensure that systems are configured to match interface port labels to the corresponding networks labels. The networking software chooses the route with respect to the label.

Secure networking protocols provide the mapping function in their upper layers. When you interface users over an untrusted wide area network or when the local area network includes a non-Secure machine, you cannot trust the users' labels, as their connections might be spoofed or tapped. Wide area network service providers might not provide enough security in terms of encryption, physical access protection, electromagnetic shielding, etc. to qualify to provide a labeled service.

During connection establishment, if a label isn't presented, you know that the remote system isn't secure. You label the connection with a low label that would restrict its access rights by the label laws.

If you take these precautions, you can network with Secure and non-Secure systems at once. By distinguishing with care, you "defuse" any potential hacker or bug-ridden code that you receive, keeping it at a low label.

If there's a non-Secure machine on the LAN, there would be a thousand reasons to doubt the identity of the user attempting the remote operation.

Yet, you still need to authenticate users on "mixed" networks. To do this, you use a Secure network gateway, which acts as a firewall. It will be the sole interface of unlabeled network communication and non-Secure hosts. It maintains a separate password database file for authenticating unlabeled users.

Secure UNIX networking includes a label for the connection and the data that is sent over it. If there isn't a label, you know that the remote system isn't secure. You label the connection with a low label and put anything received from it in a "miscellaneous junk" directory, where upgrading isn't allowed and where nothing has execute permission. Only miscellaneous junk could be sent out over it too, because it's at a low label.

Therefore, two types of Secure networking will take place: labeled and unlabeled. Networking protocols that use encryption, etc., and that can provide authentication and privilege over a wide area network will be labeled so that they will come into the network and be as trusted as the local LAN hosts. Unlabeled connections will come on with their restricted access powers via the gateway.

When unlabeled users attempt to connect, the interface will stamp their connection with the lowest user label and authenticate them with a separate password file from the trusted users.

The separation of the password files is part of the shielding of trusted systems by a network firewall. Information about it isn't available to unlabeled users once they log onto the gateway. Any services that they request from it are strictly controlled by the label laws. For example, if they try to log onto a trusted machine from the gateway, they might find that their label isn't high enough to do that. The trusted machines have labels and won't accept a connection if the users' labels are too low.

Non-Secure network gateways, or interfaces to pre-Secure UNIX machines or other non-Secure machines, are implemented on Secure UNIX machines. The password file on them includes only users that login from them, and they must login at a low label. As on all Secure UNIX systems, the publicly available /etc/password has no passwords in it. They are kept in a system private version or "shadow" password file.

So the "real" password file is kept well insulated from the outside world. No longer can hackers use it to guess passwords, either by taking quick guesses or by automation, perhaps after mailing to themselves.

The gateway handles non-Secure hosts that dial-in or are on the LAN.

Level Network Initialization

Networking security begins during system initialization. To initialize trusted networking services, two chores are necessary. First, similar to a trusted path, trusted network startup processes will kill any processes that are lurking about the well-known networking ports. Next, it will use digital authentication (public key, most likely) to authenticate the networking processes before it starts them.

Secure system initialization is a key step in creating and maintaining a TIB. Building the secure logical area begins with authenticating not just the users but also the proceeding infrastructure. In this case, the networking servers are authenticated, and Trojan horse spoofers are prevented. As long as there is a keep-alive mechanism on servers, such as inetd or ftp, it is assured that the trusted server is servicing the port.

The keep-alive mechanism would likely be a signal to the network initialization processes on a regular period and when the server is killed. Other systems, such as audit and administrative security programs, would detect its death and the attempted unauthorized replacement. Ports are single open exclusive. These measures would prevent a spoofer (Trojan horse)—a program that pretend to be another program.

The use of a public key to authenticate servers (as opposed to a local database of cryptographic checksums, such as the administrative security programs use) is necessary to trust distributed servers. That way, the same certificate-based trust mechanism used for users is integrated with user authentication.

Certification of Networking Products

This section is for those readers who are concerned with NCSC certification of their systems.

As a warning that applies to networking and many other major applications (depending on what your particular computing environment is), not all systems have gone through the NCSC certification processes fully integrated with the applications that you need and want.

Application vendors are hard at work creating Secure versions of their products that hopefully are going, or will soon go, through certification. It might be the case then that, as an interim security solution, you might use some "almost" certified applications.

Machine vendors will offer the choice. If you must have the assurance of using only certified systems, you will have to settle, at least for a while, for less diversity and options in terms of what applications they can provide.

If you can live with noncertified products, you still will get a very secure machine. Of course, most of us will use noncertified products because we won't give up all of the great applications, such as the Internet or Usenet.

Yet, learning how to deal with the concern is essential; it's the "real world." It is better to have the vendors develop strategies for safe interfaces to non-Secure systems and let users use the uncertified products in that context.

So it is that presently, for example, uucp isn't available as part of a certified environment. However, you can get a certified system that vendors configure with uucp integrated into a low-labeled directory where it is safe and controlled to use for activities such as getting a Usenet newsgroup.

In any case, the result is that, for now and the near future, you might not be able to have the assurance that all of the systems and applications that you need to use have gone through the formal certification processes at the NCSC. This should not deter you from using the state of the art, as it's a much more secure environment than pre-Secure UNIX.

Databases

On a Secure computer, database-management systems offer file management that takes full advantage of the new Secure UNIX features.

In general, a Secure database is closely integrated with Secure UNIX in that it doesn't redo work that UNIX does. It lets UNIX do login and doesn't deal with passwords, although it might do some checking that the user is listed in the database to use it. It also uses the Secure UNIX labeling system and doesn't have separate labels. Many of the privileges that it uses are the system-wide privileges. It uses the same audit system as the rest of the TIB, and system administrators administrate it.

However, there are some extra features that it provides to UNIX. UNIX distributed systems, such as databases, are based on a client/server design. This means that a process is handling requests to files from many users. So, there is an auditing requirement put on the database to track user file access, because it is the process actually doing the file access on behalf of many users. Yet you need to have accountability on the user level.

Another new feature is that some databases mix data of different labels in the same file. Ordinarily, Secure UNIX keeps files that contain data at the label of the file. Secure databases have gone further; they manage files with data that is at the file label or lower. Each row of the database file is labeled.

The database does its own label checking for user database requests. From UNIX, the database gets the label of the user making the database request and compares it to the label of the requested row to allow access by the label laws.

This is a job that otherwise is done by Secure UNIX, so only the most reliable commercial products should be allowed to do it. The database will have privilege to do things such as lower the label of information, so it must be highly trusted software.

Mixing levels in a file also is a very complicated task and will incur auditing overhead that perhaps might tend to be heavy. If adequate auditing is difficult, avoid this approach. The database can be confined to users and data at a single level, without using files with data of mixed labels. In any case, it is a good idea to hold usage of mixed files to a minimum.

Secure databases also provide access control lists for all files that they maintain, including data, data format descriptions, or processes. They use the "grant and revoke" commands for access control. (See Figure 7.9.)

X Window

Pre-Secure X Window was written with the "open" philosophy (and the security problems) of pre-Secure UNIX, but X in particular was a spoofer's paradise. It allowed anyone to get a window on any terminal or tap into keyboard input, using the power of high-tech graphics, too.

X basics

First, a little about X Window. X Window is a software system that provides an application windowing environment on graphical terminals. Software-wise, it consists of an X server, an X window manager client, and the X application interface, including Xlibrary, XToolkit, and a few widget sets.

X applications, called *clients*, communicate with the server via the application interface libraries. The clients work with the server to lay out their windows into graphical zones, which are hooked back into the application code. Keyboard and pointer actions on these areas branch to it.

The window manager is a special X client that manages interactions among multiple windows, such as their overlapping (overlaying), and the

Figure 7.9 Multilabel databases.

moving of text (cut and paste). When text is cut, it is stored in a paste buffer, which can be pasted into another window. Windows and icons can be dragged onto and cover each other. (See Figure 7.10.)

Secure X

Secure X treats icons, windows, and paste buffers as labeled objects. As such, they interact subject to the label laws. Each window has its label displayed on top. There are other labels associated with windows. Each has an input label, which is a label for input from the keyboard and mouse, and a data description.

X Window uses a system of multiple windows on a screen. The users must choose which window their keyboard and pointer input refer to, which is called the *input focus*. To make things clear, it is a good idea to make it a default that users explicitly choose input focus by clicking the mouse on the window.

Trusted path from Secure X

Secure X has a graphical means to have a trusted path. A trusted path is a guarantee to users that, when they need to invoke an operating system service or command, they aren't invoking a fake and that communications (such as terminal input) are held privately between the user and the operating system—nobody is "tapping the line."

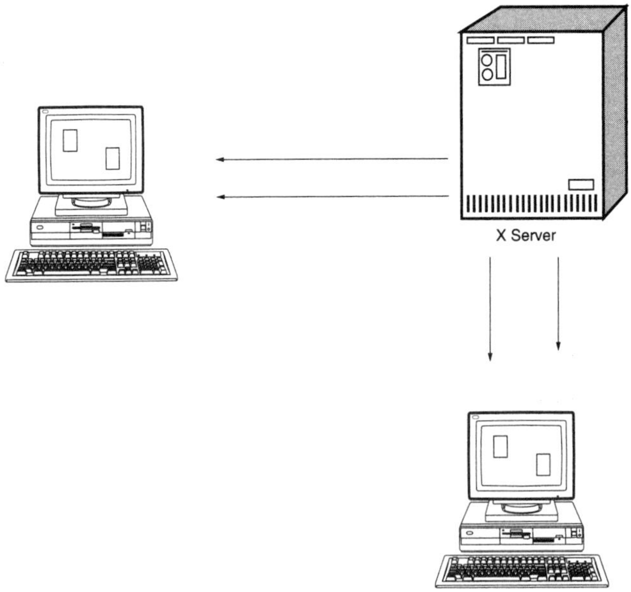

Figure 7.10 The X Server manages objects on screens.

One of the most conspicuous new features of Secure X is a trusted path window that is glued on the display. It can't be overlaid. Whenever users need system services provided by the operating system, they invoke the trusted path menu by clicking the mouse on the window.

The trusted path menu provides functions such as those that change password, session label, default processes label, session maximum label, or labels on files. The connection menu also is how you login, logout, and lock your screens. These require a trusted path because, otherwise, you might be executing an impostor, possibly with your privileges, that's stealing your confidential data.

The menu also is how you change values that are specific to each window—such as the keyboard input label, window label, and data description—and how you clear windows.

The trusted path menu also is the systems administration interface. To execute programs with privilege, users have to be listed as entitled to use sets of commands with privileges specified for each that are needed to do systems administrative tasks. The only way to invoke programs with privileges is through the trusted path menu.

Some administrator commands involve managing access to X (such as X ACL), authentication of hosts, and X-specific privileges. Others control cut-and-paste operations between labeled windows.

Other times that you must have a trusted path is during login or when reauthenticating after screen lock. Here, the login screen is the only screen that doesn't have window dressing and the label.

Because the only way to actually login is via the trusted path, even a fake login program couldn't log a user in.

The trusted path window can't be overlaid. The significance of this is that a fake process can't hide on it. A display of status regarding activity on the screen—such as an indication of when the trusted path is in play and the input and window label of the window that has the input focus—is in the connection window. (See Figure 7.11.)

Another security problem of pre-Secure X is that clients can perform keyboard grabs and get input focus, with the result that the recipient of keyboard input might be a thief or a snoop. On some systems, keyboard grabbing might be indicated on the trusted path window state indicator, and the user is relied upon to spot trouble.

Keyboard grabs should never occur within a trusted path.

The trusted path menu should be available not only from the secure window, but also via a single keystroke. This is insurance against a pointer-grabbing client that is blocking pointer access to the trusted path window. This way, runaway or malicious applications can be killed by administrators, preventing an availability problem.

To ensure that there are no fakes inserted, the functions executed from the trusted path menu should never be bound to a key, as the whole menu

Windows can be dragged onto, or overlay, each other.

The Trusted Path can't be overlayed.

Figure 7.11 The Trusted Path.

is. The menu shouldn't have any cascade menus added, because menus can be overridden by resource files in users' home directories.

However, the trusted path menu, along with its label options cascade menu, is kept in the system X application resource file, not in home directories. It won't allow users to override it. On most Motif systems, that file is /usr/library/X11/system.mwmrc. Any attempted trusted path menu in the home directory, ~.mwmrc, will not be used by Secure X.

Secure X Window

Secure X Window enforces the label laws, so users' labels are compared to the labels of all data and other system resources to determine if access is allowed. The users in this case are X clients, the windows on the screen that can be shells, or application programs running at their respective labels.

Windows and covert channels

Covert channels are the disclosure of information that subverts the label laws. It is a problem in Secure X that might have more than one labeled window on a screen.

The windows inherited their labels from the user that spawned them. Cut and paste between windows must conform to the label laws. Users are presented with a verification prompt where they must explicitly request the transfer of data between windows at different labels.

The prompt is required to prevent a covert channel problem. The covert channel here is the use of pasting data to a lower label to convey information implicit in the act of pasting. In other words, the pasting process sends an X event to windows, and that can be used as a signal. One of the main reasons for the interactive prompt is to impede the speed of the pasting transaction to limit the covert channel threat. (See Figure 7.12.)

The prompt also serves as a check that the user isn't making a mistake and pasting to a wrong-labeled window. To transfer information to a different label, users require privilege.

Pasting from a labeled window must be done to a higher or equal labeled window, you are "writing" to it. One needs privilege to paste to a window with a different label. Cutting (reading) and pasting (writing) to different labels involves X events and can be used as covert channels, so requiring privilege restricts it, and abuse would show up on the audit.

Another covert channel that menaces Secure X is from the expose event. When a window is dragged off another, X sends an expose event to the window that was on the bottom. That can be used to signal it. The only way to avoid the threat is to use workstation hardware, called *backing store*, that can be used to store images so that clients don't have to redraw themselves when exposed. This hardware usually is found on some high-end machines.

Labeled X Objects

Keyboards and pointers also are labeled. Windows and icons each have an input label, and they check that the label of keyboard and pointer

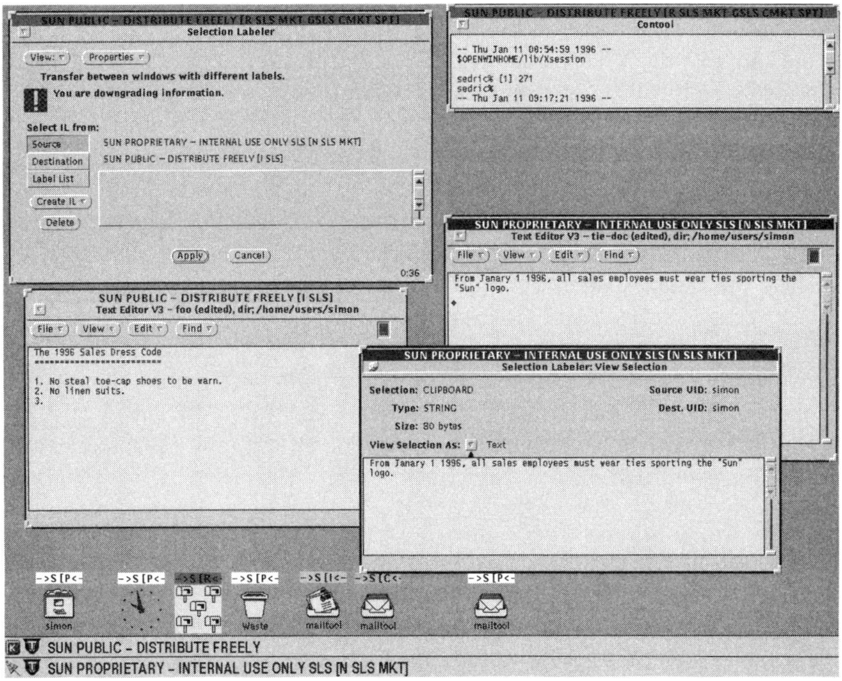

Figure 7.12 Cut and paste with Secure X Window.

input conforms to the label laws. In this way, users can label their client windows to ensure that only particular users or workstations can get their window's focus.

That is particularly important given that X applications can grab input focus, conceivably without the knowledge of the user, who is busy typing away. It is possible to label your windows to prevent that by the label laws.

Any keyboard input allowed will be entered at the label of the keyboard.

The input label also determines which icons can be opened or dragged by which users' mouse pointer.

Some tools, such as a file manager, manage icons that are dragged in and out of them. The tool label must be higher than or equal to the label of the icon to drag the icon in. Tools that make image files from windows are similarly related to the imaged window.

Pop-up windows, which don't have the usual window dressings, aren't labeled. They really are not windows, as they aren't managed by the window manager. They typically serve as one-time reminders, such as status dialog boxes.

X, authentication, and access control

X is a distributed system; clients can be distributed among windows and workstations. The conjunction of X Window and its client applications takes place between the X Server processes and client interface code that "open" the X connection. That moment also is the time to authenticate the client to the server.

Authentication can take place at the host or the host-and-user identifier. Network password servers, such as Kerberos, can be called.

Secure X uses the access management methods of UNIX. The server can maintain ACL with host or user identifiers.

Window managers keep track of which terminals they serve. Clients on other workstations will not have access.

For programs executed via the trusted path, they are verified with a magic number that is a resource of X, against magic numbers in the processes environment.

Role names can be kept in an X resource to prevent multiple instances of administrative programs.

Information labels

Windows also have information labels. Information labels are entirely different from MAC Labels. They serve as descriptive information and are used as markings on print-outs. They aren't used for access control.

When data with different information labels is combined by a cut-and-paste, the labels are combined to show the combination of both labels. This combination sometimes takes place by the relationships laid out in the label-encoding files.

Label encodings lay out how information labels will change when information from one file is combined with another or when information status changes.

Chapter

8

Administrative Security

Administrative security involves the tasks that administrators must perform to keep their systems secure. Much of them are the same practices as those of pre-Secure UNIX, such as regular backups. Administrative security also includes the interface to the new Secure Unix features that administrators use to control and maintain their systems.

It is by administrative security that the confirmed integrity and managed resources policies are carried out. Confirmed integrity is the persistent confirmation that the integrity of the system hasn't been broken, either in the past or present. Managed resources is the policy that prevents availability losses by limiting resource consumption.

The confirmed integrity policy is laid out by running consistency-checking programs, Secure recovery processes, and Secure backup. Integrity assurance also has to involve every stage in the manufacture, delivery, installation, and operation of a system. These stages include system delivery, generation, installation, configuration, maintenance, recovery, hardware, backup, start-up, ease of use, physical security, self test, user and administrative documentation, flaw fixing, and revision upgrading.

The other aspect of integrity comes by the proper application of the Secure features that I've described in this book by using the administrative interface to control authentication, access control, audit, etc.

The managed resources policy is administered by limiting the consumption of user and system resources, such as disk space, memory, and CPU capacity.

Consistency Checking

Administrators run programs called consistency- or integrity-checking programs that regularly comb the system software for evidence of corruption, inconsistency in its operating state, improper security attributes, user policy mistakes, and other inconsistencies that might indicate or threaten a loss of system integrity.

The integrity of the SIB resources is maintained within Secure UNIX systems by all of the many tools, methods, built-in systems, and vigilance described in this book. It seems almost embarrassing that, after all that, it still is prudent to use the security method called consistency checking that might detect a problem that has slipped through the many defenses and already might have done harm. However, the likelihood is that it might detect a normal action that was taken and was not logged or processed properly by the administrators.

Consistency checking means verifying that the operating system files and commands, especially those that enforce security, are consistent with your stored descriptions of them and with how they should be formatted and interrelated. In this way, you ensure that they haven't been tampered with or otherwise damaged.

Although almost any problem that it uncovers should have been handled by the audit alarm detector system, there are some jobs that only it does, such as terminal lock on ASCII terminals. It operates independent of the audit system but can communicate its actions to the audit detector by generating audit events.

Consistency-checking Functions

There are five types of consistency checking. Three types of consistency checks are primarily for system files: system file attribute consistency, internal consistency, and basic access precision consistency. System processes are checked for attribute consistency. Finally, user files, and some user activity, also are checked to ensure user policy consistency. User files include startup files, such as ".exrc" or ".profile."

File-attribute Checking

File attribute consistency checking is done by building and maintaining current system file attribute descriptive data, possibly via a database management system, that might include sizes, CRCs, and security attributes, such as owners, file type, labels, ACLs, and privileges. (See Figure 8.1.)

The descriptive data should be created when the system is first installed, and it must be updated whenever the system is reconfigured. If an administrator forgets to update the descriptive data after installing some new command, the consistency check will fail.

The file attribute consistency check compares the attributes of the system files to those in the attributes description file. Any discrepancy is a time-zero alarm. Exceptions include some writable system files—such as utmp, wtmp, and acct—whose sizes vary.

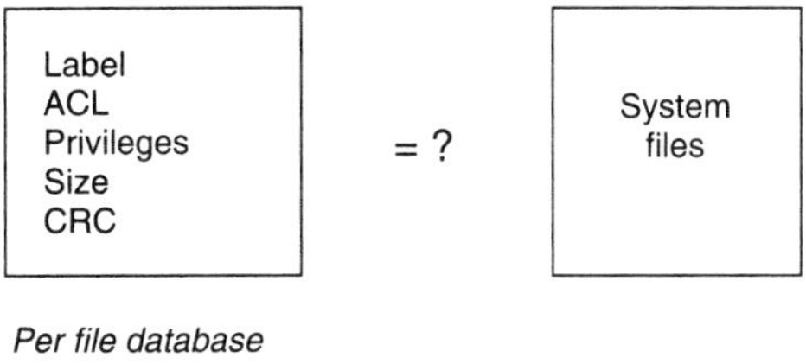

Figure 8.1 Compare consistency of system file attributes.

It also is important that any files found that are not in the description file are disallowed. Finding some junk file planted in the system directories is impossible for numerous reasons. Nonetheless, you want check to make sure its not there.

Attribute Checking of CRC

One of the attribute descriptions is a CRC. A *CRC* is a number derived by a mathematical operation on the bits that compose a file. The CRC derivation for a file is the same each time that it is derived. By comparing the previous and current CRCs of a file, you can determine whether the file has been modified since the previous time that the CRC was derived. (See Figure 8.2.)

CRC checks can detect hardware failures, either in memory or disk drives, that have corrupted our system software. It is unlikely that these kinds of problems would have escaped detection by other system facilities, such as built-in hardware error detection and system software, but stranger things have happened.

A CRC discrepancy also might indicate that the file has been corrupted because of tampering. This clearly should have set off the alarm detector.

The most likely cause of all is administrative activity, such as a system reconfiguration by an administrator who failed to update the system consistency database or some accidental change by an administrator to system files. Either should have showed up on the audit log; however, it might have been passed as legitimate activity.

Internal Consistency Checking

Another consistency check is the internal consistency. It verifies that the system security databases, such as the label files, both conform to their expected format and are consistent among themselves, such as having labels that are in the labels file. (It includes checking the files' labels themselves.)

The password file, or (NIS) yellow pages password file, is checked for null passwords, the proper number of fields, duplicate identifiers, nonnumeric gids (group identifier numbers), blank lines, and non-alphanumeric identifiers.

Group files are checked for passwords, the proper number of files, duplicated users in groups, blank lines, or duplicate group identifiers.

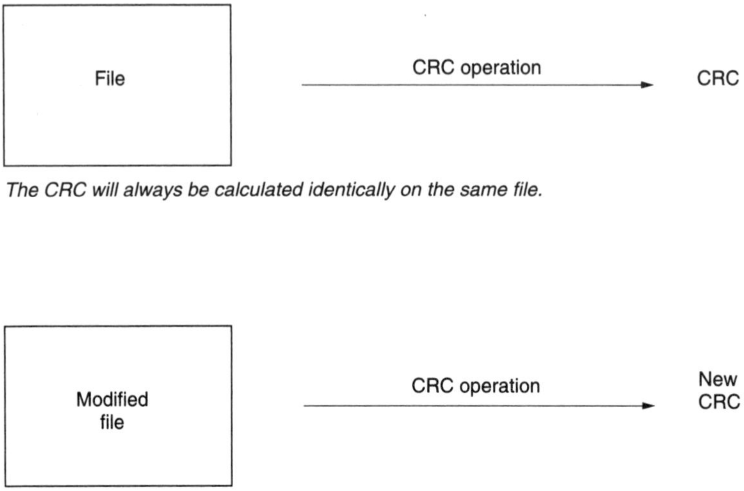

The CRC will always be calculated identically on the same file.

Modifying the file will change the CRC.

Figure 8.2 CRC operations.

Consistency checks are done as often as can be accommodated by system processing power. That might be by `cron` at 3:00 A.M. or running as a system daemon and privileged process at all times. Hopefully, especially as hardware gets souped up, it'll be the latter, running at all times, perhaps running all of the checks at the same time.

Consistency checking is similar in purpose to audit alarm detection; however, it doesn't involve audit event analysis. Many of the problems that it checks for should have been detected by the audit detector. If a problem is found, response urgency is classified on the same timescale as audit alarms and consists of the same kind of process.

However, it has value as a separate and redundant detector to the alarm detector based on audit. As such, it should be managed by, report to, and be carried out by an administrator separate from the secure auditor. Its consistency alarms should be sent to these administrators via an independent system that includes the process that detects them, the terminals or beepers that display it, as well as the people that are responsible for it.

However, it also can communicate with the audit detector by generating audit events.

In general, if there are problems that are detected by consistency checkers that alarm detectors missed, it suggests that the audit system has experienced a failure. It might be that a time when the audit system was down was exploited somehow, that a mistake was made by an administrator then, or that audit was shut off and evidence of that was covered up.

Because the auditor is the only administrator that can control the audit system and you configure secure systems to shutdown if the audit system is otherwise interrupted, it is hard to imagine how problems can slip by it. Even if an auditor has shut down audit, he or she doesn't have the privileges required to affect the system beyond audit.

One possibility is that, in a time of repeated failures of the audit system, a decision might have been made to run without auditing. A Secure UNIX organization wouldn't make that mistake.

User File Consistency Check

The third consistency check is on the users' files (as opposed to the system's files). You cannot compare users' files to a descriptive database because users can modify their files at will. However, there are some policies that you have set that you can use to check the users' files for consistency.

The policies cover what users can do with their files. They might be allowed by UNIX to do certain things, such as giving the world access to their files, but that might not be allowed by the organization's policies.

User policy consistency checking examines the files in users' home directories. In part, the checking depends on what your organizational security policies are.

A policy described in this book states not only that there should be default ACL on directory and file creation for users, but also that users cannot open the ACL beyond the default setting. User file policy consistency checking can examine user files for this.

Another way that ACL policy in effect can be undermined is by the use of setuid files. If a user creates a setuid file, it provides a way for any user that executes it to have the executable owner's identity. (Setuid is regulated by privilege.)

Setuid programs are dangerous to the owners files. For example, if its output file can be redirected, it can be used by whoever executes it to destroy all of the owner's files, even if his or her ACL is set to owner only.

The policy checker would protest any setuid files in users' accounts. There can be no world-writable or shell setuid files. There also must not be any .rhosts files, which are used by nfs. (See Figure 8.3.)

Other user directory policy checks include no special device files.

All home directories must not be world writable, neither should the home files: .profile, .login, .cshrc, .kshrc, .tcshr, .crhost, etc.

Idle-session Checking

I now come to a function that is the exclusive job of user policy checking and that is not redundant to the alarm detector. That function solves the problem of an idle terminal during a user session on character-based terminals, which necessitates reauthenticating the connection after the logged-in user

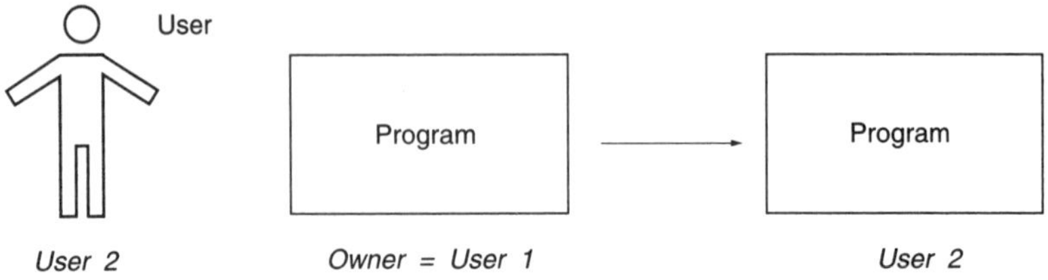

Non-setuid: File runs with the user's identity although owned by another user.

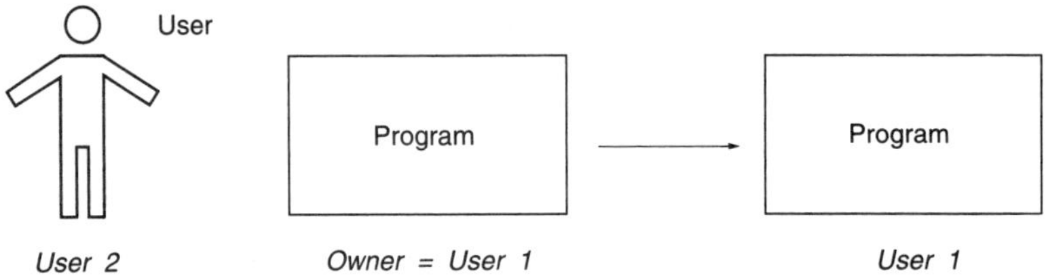

Setuid: File runs with file owner's identity although executed by another user.

Figure 8.3 Setuid.

hasn't typed for awhile. Secure X Window on graphical terminals handles idleness for you by enforcing reauthentication with terminal lock. (See the "X Window" section in chapter 7.)

Not all workstations will have X Window. For those that don't, terminal lock is the job of the policy consistency checker. It checks with the `who` or `w` command and keeps count of how long it has been since logged-in users typed on their terminals. If the terminal has been idle too long (say, 15 minutes), the checker either locks the user's terminal and demands relogin or kills the user's session altogether, depending on the operating system facilities available (terminal disabling, authentication command interface, etc.).

System-process Consistency Checking

Fourth, you check the consistency of the system processes, or daemons, with a list of them, their privileges, uids, setuid, etc. They, and only they, must be running, such as /etc, /etc/init, cron, syncd, qdaemon, etc. Other resources, such as disk usage, can be monitored.

There are some functions of the consistency checker that are redundant to the alarm detector.

When you first install a secure system, you build the file attribute descriptive database. Consistency checkers will check the existing system against the attribute description files. If an administrator incorrectly modifies the system and then regenerates the attributes descriptions with the incorrect attributes, then the checker is corrupted and useless.

That is why the initial attribute database must never be modified. It always is used in its initial state to serve as a regression test. If there are any changes to the basic installed system, the changes should go into a *delta file*. Additions to the installed system should be described in a separate attribute database. Consistency checking programs first should check files against the base description file, then against the deltas.

One advantage of using a certified product, or at least one from a vendor that is committed to certification processes and is concerned about providing secure products, is that the base attribute might be offered at distribution time.

As a final measure of protection against the previously mentioned corruption of the attribute database, you should run some basic checks on the existing system to make sure that it is consistent with some general access precision guidelines, mainly ensuring that there isn't any excessively permissive write permissions on system files.

Tests include checking system files to ensure that they don't have world write or read access. Devices that service filesystems must not have world read or write access. There mustn't be any world writable or shell setuid files.

All of the paths and files in /etc/rc/* or /usr/library/crontab must not be world writable.

The ftp directory permissions and ownership must not be world writable and owned by ftp users.

Integrity

The integrity of the system includes hardware integrity. Most hardware tests are run during start-up or as a standalone loadable program. However, whenever possible, self check and diagnostics should be part of the consistency checking programs.

Confirmed integrity also includes Secure methods of backup. Secure UNIX backup media have security attributes—such as labels, privileges, ACL, and others—that ensure that the information on them is subject to the same access controls that the filesystems are.

A weakness of pretrusted UNIX was that, once information was backed up to a tape archive, it could be restored by any user. The only access control was on the ability to create the archive. Once the archive was created, it could be restored by whoever had it in their hands. Another problem was that backup programs ran setuid to root, so users could get control of the backup device, eroding accountability and relying on the unsafe root mechanism.

Secure UNIX creates archives that preserve the files' labeling, ACLs, and privileges. Archives cannot be restored unless the user has label and ACL access to the files in it or has administrative privilege. So, information on removable media, such as floppies, now is subject to the same access controls that the rest of the filesystems and SIB are. Indeed, it becomes a part of the SIB.

Secure UNIX has created secure versions of the familiar UNIX archivers: cpio and volcopy. Secure cpio allows users to make backups of or to restore selected files at a specified label or label list. Volcopy is for copying whole filesystems. Some systems have the pretrusted versions of the archivers for administrative use only.

To do backups, nonprivileged users must make a request for use of the backup device. The devices granted will have the user as the owner and have the user's group as the group, making accountability by audit possible. They also inherit the current label of the requesting user, so all information carried by them must be at that label or the operation will fail.

Backup devices, such as tape drives, are initialized with a label range within which users can request it at. Device label lists also must match the labels of the files being backed up. For Secure cpio, the device range must include within it the user label.

User device requests allow unprivileged users to use system devices. Devices can have lists of users that are permitted to use them. Requests protect system-only devices from unintended use by users and ensure that label changes are permitted. By default, using a device requires privilege, and some devices are privileged use only. Login automatically requests terminals for users. When users logout, their devices are returned to the system and to privileged use.

All files restored by an unprivileged user will be restored at the user's current label, be owned by them, and belong to his or her current group. The files will have the same ACL as they were backed up with, except for any permissions masked off by the umask. Setuid bits are cleared in all cases.

Using an administrative interface, administrators can use archiving tools with privilege. Files can be restored with their original owners, group, level, permissions, and ACLs, or these can be changed on restore.

If file levels, owners, or groups have been deleted since the archive was created, they can't be restored unless the command is evoked with mapping information on its command line or via a table. Files with ACL users or groups that have been deleted can be restored, but they will need to have their ACLs adjusted.

Some Secure versions of cpio restrict the level ranges that they accept as command-line input to exclude system level files. Secure cpio is used to do backups by operators who lack administrator privileges.

Secure volcopy must run with privilege. It backs up entire filesystems, without the option to make selections of files within it. When copying from disk to tape, it stores the system name and information on system level files, which it verifies on restore. If an archive contains a level that has been deleted from a system, the archive must be fixed when it's restored.

The errors generated by such inconsistencies as missing levels of an archive constitute an auditable event. When the errors are fixed, they must be reconciled against the audit trail.

Pre-Secure cpio is included for backward-compatibility to non-Secure systems. It can handle security attributes and multilevel directories. In the wrong hands, it constitutes a security menace and must be audited.

Integrity Checking

Confirmed integrity also includes Secure methods of system recovery. The procedure does checks of the security data files, system software, and filesystems, taking into account the unique requirements of Secure UNIX.

Systems crashes, power outages, or any other times that systems unexpectedly go down require administrators to ensure that the integrity of the system hasn't been compromised, either by damaged hardware or by intruders seeking to make use of system vulnerability at those chaotic times.

The best insurance against loss due to identifiers of this sort is a timely backup. This method isn't news to any DPers. It is as true on Secure environments as it is elsewhere. Make a thorough, timely backup routine a persistent certainty. This is especially needed if a hard disk fails or is corrupted.

The first duty after a system failure is to bring the system to a single-user state and check that the filesystem is corrected for any data in a disk buffer cache that was lost. This also ensures that no serious damage was done. Any damaged files should be restored.

If your Secure system uses its own database management system, the consistency of its database records and indexing should be checked, and any necessary repairs or restorations should be made. A system's ACLs, labels, and other data can be maintained under this. Some vendors supply routines to perform the task.

Next, the labeling of each directory and file must be checked for validity in the system label database. For directories, each subdirectory must have a higher label than its parent. If labels are corrupted, they can be interactively set or default to the lowest possible label in the context of its subdirectories or parent. Directories can't have wildcard labels. File labels must be higher than the label of the directory that they're in.

For CMW-type systems, information labels must be valid and must be a lower label that the file label.

Multilabel directories are for /tmp and spooler directories, such as mail. They are accessed by users with different labels, and they have different labels, even though they appear to the users to have the same name. In reality, they are a directory tree with subdirectories of different labels.

They are temporary directories. Some systems delete them whenever the system reboots; others have facilities to verify them.

Finally, the integrity checkers must be run to check the system security file and cross check the authorization files.

Confirmed integrity is based on active, persistent confirmation of integrity at every stage of the system life-cycle.

Integrity Life-cycle

A system life-cycle consists of distribution, installation, generation, configuration, and maintenance.

Distribution is the delivery of the system from the supplier to the user organization. It is necessary to have a method in place that confirms that the system hardware and software has been received as it was sent from the supplier. Physically, that might entail use of shrink wrapping and other "one-time" cargo wrapping and certified manifests with detailed serial numbers and barcodes. Check all parts carefully against the documentation and for signs of tampering. Software can be verified by use of a CRC or cryptographic checksum.

Installation is the transfer of the system software from its delivery media onto the system media. Filesystems are created, and the software is copied into them.

System generation is the compilation and linking of the system software from system binaries and source files.

Configuration is the set up of a system according to its devices, memory, user process limits, etc.

For installation, generation, and configuration, manufacturers must supply automated processes in the form of shell scripts and make files, as well as full documentation on the processes and any configurable options.

Maintenance is the latter stage of the life-cycle. It implies not only maintaining the original system, but also the capacity to accept revisions, updates, and additional products. Any change must be reflected in all records and online description files regarding the system components.

Maintenance revision requires an automated facility for handling revisions, such as sccs (source-code control system). The facility must use numbered versions, including completely documented and verifiable components. The process is called *configuration management*. The same system should be used for the initial system generation.

Users and administrators should be provided with complete documentation on the use of all features.

Integrity Interface

Another integrity need is for logical protection of the system software. That refers to the separation of user and system address space. Only privileged users can use the administrative interface to have system access. All user parameters are validated by address, value, or permissions.

Physically, integrity can be ensured by tampering, theft, wiretap, jamming, water, fire, vibration, impact, or emanation protection. Some systems, known as Tempest, provide extra-heavy-duty physical protections, particularly against emanations and physical stress.

Hardware integrity requires self check and diagnostics, run by the consistency checking program as is possible. Other tests are on power-up or are loadable.

TIB Integrity

The final aspect of the assurance of integrity is the implementation of a Trusted Information Base (TIB) based on all of the Secure UNIX features in this book by using their administrative interface. To maintain your organization's information security, Secure UNIX must be put to use to keep its own integrity.

That means that the administrative interface must be used to configure, generate, and install the system; do recovery and maintenance; create user accounts and groups; assign security attributes to users and the system, including ACLs, labels, privileges, authentication, system entry, session management, resource quotas, and audit control; and operation and analysis. Maintenance mode, or the single-user state, is used for system installation, recovery, and startup; initializing administrative roles and privileges; the system-entry requirements; and the authentication method and formats.

Other jobs that are done from the administrative interface include enabling and disabling devices and accounts; mount; backup; setting password aging and format, maximum allowed sessions, session schedules, and inactive-session time limit; listing user attributes; and defining user label lists, authentication methods, failed login limit for a terminal or user, and consistency checking programs. Preferably, the interface can be centralized when used to control a distributed environment.

The interface also is used for operations such as device enabling, mount, backup, and other routine tasks.

To prevent mistakes, the interface must be easy to use. It must provide defaults whenever appropriate. Defaults must be in place for the values of system attributes. An application interface specification should be available for administrative programmers.

The policy of managed resources counters threats to the goal of system availability caused by excessive use of system resources. Resources, such as file space, are managed by limiting the amount of them that each user can use.

Availability is system readiness—its readiness to do the work that users need done. That includes system readiness to allow users to login, to access their files, and to use system services, such as printing and networking, all with normal system response times and throughput. For example, a user might attack system availability by spawning too many processes, causing a loss of system throughput due to procedure overhead.

Protecting system availability includes limiting user process creation, file space and memory usage, login sessions, and process size.

Some limits are configured during system generation by the configuration source files. Others can be restricted by a quota system provided by some UNIX systems.

Some systems can enforce resource limits by the consistency checking programs, which could be polling the system statistics to determine the extent of user resource use.

Chapter

9

TIBs in 2001

Remember HAL, the treacherous computer from the movie *2001*? Well, he's just a pussycat compared to PAL, the guy that you trust who's been losing big at the casinos that are popping up all over. The insider is the greatest threat, and now more than ever, in this struggling-to-adjust society, you must do more to verify the trust that you give.

How about Aldrich Ames, the CIA mole? He had access to crucial state secrets but was selling them to our enemies. The CIA trusted him and didn't detect his activities until great damage had been done. Organizational policies were lacking to counterweigh the trust given to any individual.

However deep the damage, there will always be a CIA. The same cannot be said for commercial organizations—even the large and powerful. No one would have believed that Baring Bank would be ruined and auctioned off and have its directors fired or that Daiwa Bank would be shut down because of unauthorized transactions or fraudulent executives covering losses.

We live in an exciting age in human history where computers are fulfilling the promise of the "Global Village," including commerce. Yet some villagers are sophisticated thieves, spies, and saboteurs that find and test us as soon as we say "Hello, world."

Computer networks have created a democracy. There are no longer venerable institutions, such as universities, to "know" who we primarily are dealing with. Malicious and trustable users share highways; no troopers, speed limits, licenses, or plates.

Just as this book went to press, the federal government warned that the powers of networks could cause massive damage before detected and destabilize world economic systems.

In the movie *2001*, a flying slab saved the world. In the year 2001, you have to be prepared for a dangerous world wherein you must organize and protect yourself.

The Trusted Information Base

When I contemplated this book, I wanted to identify some security guidelines that could be easily put to use. Yet, rather than compile technical details of current systems that are poorly equipped for security, I sought to envision the security architectures of the near future and how organizations can begin to put in place policies and infrastructure for them. That way, they will not only make the best of the current systems but will rapidly be able to absorb new and better solutions when they come online.

There's a new breed of UNIX fortified for security: Secure UNIX. It typically runs on ordinary workstation hardware, but it is a new version of UNIX system software that not only has cured the security ills of pre-Secure UNIX, but also has added many powerful new security features.

To be secure though, an organization also must put in place policies governing Secure system use. Security policy involves mandatory organizational rules about use of the system, administrative coordination, and how to respond to events, which takes resources of staff work and facilities.

If an organization uses Secure UNIX properly, its systems are said to be *trusted*; they've achieved a degree of assurance that they are secure. If the organization has followed the methods and put in place the policies described in this book, it is said that it manages its information within a *Trusted Information Base* (*TIB*).

Policies

I'd like to state in plain words what must be put into practice to be secure. Pre-Secure UNIX lacked it, so there is a need to spell it out.

In brief:

- Determine what your organization's legitimate system activity is (Policy Statement).
- Precisely configure access control according to the policy (Precise Access).
- Log the activity, and confirm that it is authorized (Confirmed Authorization).
- Check the soundness of system software (Confirmed Integrity).
- Put limits on resource usage, and prevent overuse (Precise Usage).

Pre-Secure UNIX lacked the facilities, both access control and auditing, to put these into practice. Now, with Secure UNIX, these basic practices can be fully implemented. Just in time too, because regulators are demanding it.

With Secure UNIX, you can:

- Decide what the most critical resources are: file servers, databases, etc.
- Configure ACLs and MAC labels to reflect classifications.
- Decide what activity is most important to log, and log it.
- Analyze the activity log, and confirm that it is authorized.
- Alarm suspicious activity as it occurs.
- Check that the underlying system software is consistent on a regular basis.
- Make all activity accountable to a user.
- Make all activity conditional on a credentials check.
- Monitor resource usage and have per user limits.

Policy guidelines

I have described four policy guidelines: CAP, PAP, CIP, and PUP.

CAP *Confirmed authorization policy* (*CAP*) is confirming that critical activity is authorized. CAP is essential; without this capacity, you can't know whether a system is secure. Another benefit of it is deterrence. If crooks knew they'd be detected and possibly tracked down and arrested, many of them would prefer to stay "honest."

Maintaining authorization requires these basic steps:

1. Knowing what's going on: What files are being accessed and by whom, what commands are given with what privileges, etc.
2. Judging whether what occurred is authorized: Whether the users are who they say they are, whether what they're doing and the data that they're accessing is permitted by the organization, etc.
3. Being ready to respond if what's going on isn't authorized: To kill the login session, lock an account (thereby prohibiting logins), make follow up inquires, etc.

PAP *Precise access policy* (*PAP*) is using all system facilities to ensure that access is allocated on an as-needed basis. PAP is necessary to have the ability to define what activity is authorized. If all users are lumped into a group that has file access, yet you don't want all users to have access, then you cannot select users that you do and don't want to give access to. There would be too much activity on that file to check authorization.

Another benefit of PAP is that it acts as an *access firewall* (an access control that is spread out over a system that acts to limit unauthorized access). If a user is being impersonated, the impersonator's access will be limited to precisely what the real user needed access to and no more.

Both CAP and PAP depend on the accountability gained by all users having identification, authentication, and their activity accountable by their identifier.

CIP *Confirmed integrity policy* (*CIP*) is the continuous verification of the integrity of the system software, which is the foundation of the system's security protections. Administrators must regularly run consistency-checking programs on the system files. This prevents the accidental or purposeful undermining of the system protections.

There is a suite of about a dozen excellent consistency programs—such as Crack, Tripwire, and COPs—that are available on Internet sites. There are commercial versions as well.

PUP *Precise usage policy* (*PUP*) is the limitation of the use of system resources, such as terminal ports or memory. It is the key to the prevention of denial-of-service attacks. Tying up resources, such as file space or dial-up ports, is a way to bring down a system and deny it to its legitimate users.

PUP means both placing limits on user and system resource usage with systems such as quotas and monitoring usage and responsiveness to overuse.

Policy statements

CAP, PAP, CIP, and PUP are policy guidelines. They are the goals to guide the detailed choices that organizations make when they write their security policies. Every organization must write its own customized security policies that precisely describe its information-processing environments. I'll mention some of the typical information that is included.

Users Large organizations need a central tracking system for user account authorizations. Users can have accounts on multiple systems, even if their credentials are established elsewhere during sign on.

The basis of a user policy is deciding:

- Which specific users are allowed access to systems by logging in or networking.
- How strongly they must be authenticated.
- When and where they can enter.
- Service and networking use.
- On MAC clearances, physical access, smart cards, host names, addresses, etc.
- Who has access to files, devices, printers, networks, etc.

Audit Auditing requirements are described. Events such as system entry (login or network access), network service connections, access of databases, privilege use, and access of system files are specified. The availability of audit facilities are considered, and maximum coverage is defined.

Alarm limits and how to respond to alarms, the disposition and archiving of log data, and the auditors responsible for its analysis also are spelled out.

The responsibilities of the auditor role are stated. The reconciliation methods are described for the privileged activity and the administrators that it must be reconciled with.

Firewalls and routers Internet firewalls and screening routers determine what networking services will be provided and what packets will be permitted to internal networks.

Firewalls.

Firewalls provide a controlled entry point to internal networks from the Internet by:

- Enhanced authentication and auditing that augments the standard TCP networking services, allowing configuration of service levels by user or user address.
- Hiding internal information (such as users and addresses) by filtering, specifying aliases that present a single address to the external world and not all the internal addresses, selectively mapping the external to internal addresses without directly routing, etc.
- Security-centric system configuration: no IP routing, restricted shells, no extra services, etc.

For each user, policies must specify the services that the user gets, whether they are incoming or outgoing, and with what authentication and logging requirements, address limitations, hosts, and internal addresses.

Routers.

Routers work with firewalls. They are good at eliminating packets from the outside with unwanted incoming connection (service) attempts, address spoofs, port or address source or destinations, etc.

Router policies define the packet-level traffic: allowed source and destination ports (services), directionality (whether packets are from the internal or external interface) allowed, and whether connections or protocols are acceptable.

ACLs ACLs are the Secure UNIX access permission systems. They are on system objects, such as files, devices, executables, and X Window.

ACL policy must specify what users can change their default ACLs or their ACL settings, what file ACL can be changed, default file ACLs, and how auditors should respond to ACL changes.

Pre-Secure Problems and TIB Solutions

In the following section, I'll describe some of the major weaknesses of pre-Secure environments, the functionality of Secure UNIX that corrected them, and how it is employed in a Trusted Information Base (TIB) where Secure UNIX is used according to the policies described in this book.

Excessive privileges of root

Pre-Secure systems gave too much power to superusers and root-privileged programs. Root privileges were hijacked by Trojan horses and other deceptive, malicious programs.

Secure UNIX eliminated the superuser and replaced it with privileges. The privileges govern how processes access resources and make privileged system calls. They are organized into administrative roles with precisely allocated privileges and can act in power-sharing, checks-and-balances systems.

A glaring security problem of pre-Secure environments was that root could make system-rocking changes and nobody would know.

In a TIB, use of administrative privilege is detected by the auditor, and the administrators can't prevent that. Auditors and administrators must reconcile privilege activity, chiefly by programs that match profiles and immediately alarm if its unexpected. Other reconciliations can be by phone, checking off a log report, etc.

Roles In a TIB, use of privilege would be subject to the Confirmed Authorization Policy (CAP), stating that privilege use must be confirmed to be authorized. The administrators and auditors have separate privilege set-based roles to enable CAP.

Auditors would detect all privilege use by administrators via the Secure UNIX Audit system, which only they have the privileges to configure. They confirm that the privilege use was authorized, either through direct reconciliation with the administrators or use of normative profiles.

The checks and balances are that users of privilege cannot disable the auditing of its use to disguise their acts. Auditors cannot use privileges that system administrators use. They would have to engage in a conspiracy to escape detection. By breaking up the superuser's powers, you can trust multiple people whom you hold responsible for the actions of each other.

This is a far safer plan than putting all trust in one unobserved person. Roles can be spread over bigger teams or tripartite checks and balances.

Privileged programs Privilege use by programs is governed by CAP. It is detected by the Audit system and reconciled immediately against a profile set. This detects unauthorized use of privileges by a deceptive program.

Administrators assign privileges to imported applications. They can be tested in a controlled environment to ensure that the applications are behaving as alleged and not asserting excessive privileges.

Lack of accountability

A major security weakness in pre-Secure UNIX was the lack of accountability. Too much was able to happen that couldn't be attributed to someone, be it remote mounts by a host, unauthenticated users or programs, or ordinary file access by legitimate users.

Much of pre-Secure UNIX that was made to be open and easy, and also is an accountability problem, has become embedded into architectures that organizations are dependent on. For example, NIS, NFS, X Window, etc. have to be security enhanced by upgrading inside existing architectures, which Secure UNIX does.

Accountability in a TIB Secure UNIX TIB has as first principle that 100% of user activity is tied to a uniquely identified human being and that the activity can be accounted for. TIBs relate identification, authentication, and audit to provide the accountability.

Activity that isn't accountable can be allowed in a public directory that has a low label and restricted shells similar to anonymous type services. This activity typically would be restricted from entering the internal networks by screening routers and the low label.

Even with strong authentication at the application level, such as by privacy-enhanced mail, anonymity inside the TIB will never be a good idea.

Identification and authentication It is mandatory for users that have system access into a TIB to establish an identity in it by authenticating themselves. That goes for all users who use any networking services, such as NFS or TCP.

Authentication methods are enhanced. Passwords are managed conscientiously and are kept secreted. One-time passwords and challenge-response methods replace transmitting passwords in clear text.

Secure UNIX uses digital authentication for all system entry and embeds it into its applications, central infrastructures, and networking protocols. This allows it to enhance its client/server computing with full accountability.

The basis of this vast improvement is:

- The establishment of a user credential at the system-entry point.
- The transmission of the credential by the networking protocol.
- The presentation of the credential to all system-resource servers.
- The credentials verification by all resource servers.

The effect is that even the pre-Secure networking that had been so problematic (NFS, NIS, Internet, trusted hosts, Berkeley r*, etc.) but were so essential are no longer unthinkable security-wise. Certainly the basic client/server operations attain accountability.

The credentials can consist of a user identifier, MAC label, audit identifier, privileges, and cryptographic certificates, such as public key. Credentials are created at the system-entry point, which can include Internet firewalls, local logins, PC network gateways, dial-up, etc.

Even if applications, such as file servers or networking daemons, lack accountability support, the underlying networking protocols carry enough credential data for systems integrators to capture with wrapper-type systems and provide accountability.

However, applications will provide accountability, most likely by interfacing with a system-wide credential server for identification and authentication of client requests. Kerberos or public-key credentials are used with TCP networking servers and the applications that are built on them.

As a result, accountability is available on a global basis in a TIB because servers can fully audit activity based on legitimate identifiers.

Lack of trust-based access firewalling

Pre-Secure UNIX had a binary user trust classification: logged-in users and not-logged-in users. It didn't matter how users got in, how well they were authenticated, whether their communication line was secure, whether they were on an internal subnet address, etc. The servers made no attempt to qualify them besides the binary one.

The protection was solely the reliance on the level of authentication provided by the system-entry program, usually login. There was one firewall surrounding the entire system.

Trust and distributed firewalls in TIB

TIBs distribute access firewalling by use of the credential system. Rather than a single outer wall, the model is compartments of protection within an outer wall. The compartments are MAC labels, packet filters, credentials checks, privileges, and access control.

A function of an Internet firewall in a TIB is to relate factors, such as authentication strength, to the MAC label that it designates to a connection. The networking protocols then project the trust level via the label into the rest of the TIB. New Internet protocols, such as IPv6 (IPng) with IP tunneling and SSL, will enable trust to be projected over a wide area. The firewall will consider the protocol basis of the connection when it assigns the label to it.

Because servers are sensitive to the trust level via labels and other credentials, they are a distributed-access firewall. Users must not only login, they must pass a credentials check at each resource server. The firewall thereby is spread out into sites within the TIB, not dependent on a wall outside it.

Its not enough to say "a user is logged in, so he or she must be okay and can have access to almost any of the systems resources." You have to ask yourself:

- How sure am I that this really is him or her?
- How much do I trust him or her?
- Could anyone be eavesdropping on his or her line?
- Could anyone be altering the communications on the line?

Also, there's the threats from the user's (client's) perspective:

- Am I logging into the system that I think I am?
- Are the processes that are logging me in Trojan horses?
- Once I'm in, will the processes and users that I deal with be authentic?

You take these factors into consideration and judge each user's trustedness. The trustedness becomes part of the user's credentials, which are projected at all points throughout the system to determine the access rights of the user.

Credentials are checked or created at login and can be updated during the session as well. Each system keeps user credentials according to its architecture. They might be as simple as the /etc/password file or be composed of complex files and dynamic tables. The credentials might only be user identifiers and passwords checked during login, or they might be dynamically built and have encryption keys, certificates, and session state information such as time schedules.

Part of the projection of credentials throughout the system is a labeled protocol, such as DNSIX or CIPSO. These protocols themselves carry credentials (for example, labels, user identifier, privileges, and audit programing). Look for public-key certificates in future protocols. (See Figure 9.1.)

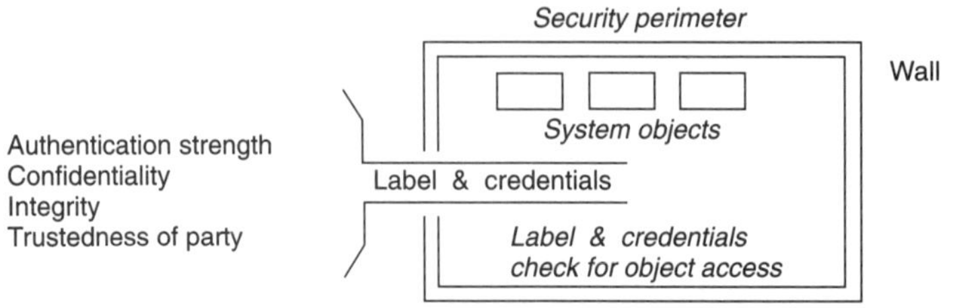

Figure 9.1 Security credentials.

A salient feature of this credential checking is the mandatory access control in place at all critical resource servers. That feature projects the trustedness of the user to where it is considered when access decisions are made.

Credentials need not all be carried by protocols. User environment variables now are frequently used for session management and carry data such as user identifiers and terminal. Otherwise, they can be managed in the typical approach of using the user identifier as the key to data files in the system accounts, such as /etc/password.

A security perimeter has digital authentication and a credential presented to system resources, such as database servers. The DBMS will explicitly do access control based on the user identifiers on its ACLs, as well as the label of the networking connection.

Authentication also can be done on a mutual basis between client and server, which prevents spoofer processes from the client perspective.

This is a major functional chain in place: identification, authentication, access control, and accountability. The user identifier and a label is part of the network protocol. The identifier and its level of trust (by the label and other credentials, such as certificates) are used to determine access control. Access control also relates the identifier to the ACL of the servers. (See Figure 9.2.)

The server is using both mandatory and discretionary access control. The user must be allowed by both the ACL permissions and the MAC labels to have access.

The authentication strength, or other factors that determine the trustedness of the user, is reflected in the user credential. Thus, the security perimeter is maintained because the relative trustedness of the user is considered during access decisions.

Trustedness in public-key architectures is readily distributed over the wide area. Organizations can recognize authorities that maintain certificates, and they can "chain" certificates by using the certificates of other authorities. This is a part of the CCITT X.509 specification.

That is, you are discriminating among users. Users that come in over a PC LAN without smartcards are less trusted that those that came in over an

Internet proxy that checked their public-key certificate, and that trustedness rating is kept with each user's credentials and used during access decisions.

The primary means of projecting trustedness system-wide is through the MAC label that is assigned at the system interface, which roughly is the security perimeter. The MAC-assigning interface is at the Internet, PC LAN, mainframe, dial-up, local login, and all other system entrances and exits. The MAC label will reflect the trustedness of the user and acts as an access firewall that is in place everywhere in the system.

Untrustable connections are labeled with the lowest user label in the TIB. They might be from poorly authenticated users. From the perspective of the TIB, data from a connection with this label is treated with a quarantine. It goes into a directory with that label. Nothing in that directory can be executed (via the ACL settings), nor can any data from quarantine be upgraded to a higher label. Some systems might allow a senior security administrator to do that if the processes are given rigorous attention. Otherwise, upgradings are prohibited by security policies and would generate security alarms.

Users on the UNIX system could access the PC files, possibly at a lower label, depending on the sophistication of the PC gateway and the authentication systems.

There also can be mainframe interfaces. Mainframes can be as secure as Secure UNIX. Connections to them can be at higher labels, but the restrictions on execution of files or upgrading data from it might apply.

Excessive access

Pre-Secure UNIX access control was too imprecise. Groups couldn't be combined and modified flexibly. Networking interfaces accepted packets with little exclusiveness.

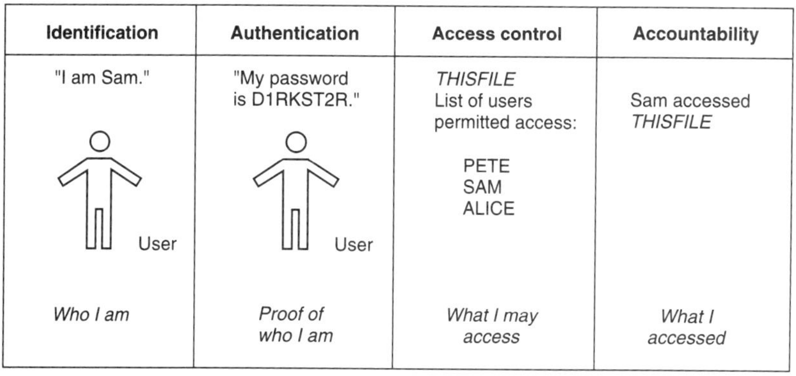

Figure 9.2 ID, authentication, access, and accountability.

Precise access in a TIB Secure UNIX has Access Control Lists (ACLs), packet filtering, privileges, and Mandatory Access Controls (MAC) labels. Programs are assigned access according to the Precise Access Policy. That access is granted on an as-needed basis.

ACLs ACLs allow groups to be combined on an access list. Individuals can be excluded from listed groups, avoiding the unwieldy necessity of creating a special group that lacks the user just for this file. ACLs can be used on all objects, including files, devices, X Window screens, and terminals.

ACLs provide a new level of access control to UNIX, which previously had compensated by the use of setuid and imprecise groups.

TIB policies cover the default settings of ACLs, ACL modifications and verification of ACLs, and policy by audit and consistency checking.

MAC One aspect of MAC labels is that they are like a powerful group mechanism. The users that have the label on their label list or, as is said, are cleared at that label are in a sense like a group—the group of users cleared at that label. Similarly, the label on a file can be looked at as similar to the file's group.

I mention this because one benefit of labeling is that it functions as a powerful means of precise-access specification that works in addition to the files ACLs. Users are related by the MAC label laws to the file (or any object, such as a device).

In TIBs, user clearances and object labels are precisely according to the access requirements that the organization intends. The labels enhance confidentiality by allowing access based on the label laws. Auditing is done by label of objects.

Users are restricted to the use of particular terminals by labeling. Terminals, as all devices, have a label list. In addition, under X Window, keyboards and screens have label lists. User terminal login can be restricted on that basis. Workstations located in secure offices can have higher label, and only those users with a high clearance can login on it.

Privileges Programs are assigned privileges according to the Precise Access Policy. Rather than give privileged programs all powers, they get precisely the subset of the hundreds of specific powers that they need. This also obviates the need for unsafe setuid programs.

ACLs, labels, and privileges To determine access, Secure UNIX first will check the privileges. If they don't allow the suppression of access checks, it will check the MAC label. If access is allowed, it then will check the ACL. A user needs access both by label and ACL.

Packet-level and application access control This type of excessive access is the allowance of uncontrolled network connections and networking services use. On pre-Secure UNIX, network access was done at one or more directly connected interfaces that allowed malevolent individuals to gain a foothold on weakly protected hosts of internal networks.

Use of network firewalls and screening routers is a response to the problem. An Internet screening router blocks unwanted packets as specified in a router rule list. Screening routers also can be used for restricted subnets within an internal network.

Firewalls are security fortified and buffering "bastion" hosts that provide controlled access to networks. They must be the sole interface because also having other less secure access ways would subvert the firewall.

Secure UNIX has firewalls and screening routers strengthened by the advanced security that it offers. The salient new architectural feature is the bastion that makes assignment and designation of a trust level to connections by MAC label and other credentials. This allows the trust level to be carried everywhere inside the TIB.

Firewalls are a primary site for authentication service and credential establishment. Firewalls will consider the networking protocol and authentication services used to establish the connection to assign a MAC label to it. Other factors might include the trustedness of the credentials and certificates presented.

They have extensive logging facilities, based on add-on wrappers to networking protocols and Secure UNIX audit. Audit analysis is best done after dumping the raw audit to a dedicated audit machine where it can be securely archived and analyzed without burdening the firewall.

Lack of organizational control over its confidential information

This is the age of industrial espionage. You need to take action to upgrade the confidentiality of your information systems. Pre-Secure environments had no way to give extra confidentiality protection to resources. They all were protected with limited permissions features, from the garbage files that clog up everyone's home directories to the organization's most sensitive secrets.

Once users gained access to files, they were free to copy or transmit them as they wanted.

Confidentiality in a TIB

Secure UNIX offers MAC labels for enhanced confidentiality control. They impose the organization's confidentiality requirements on resources because they are subject to the label laws and, as such, determine what users can do with files that they have gained access to, such as copying or transmitting.

To gain the confidentiality benefit from labels, organizations have to identify the information that they want to give special protection, which is a process of classifying it. Then, they have to label the environment so that the organization determines what the user who accesses files can do with them.

It is by labeling its TIB that an organization determines what its users can do with its information. The file's owner (in the UNIX owner sense) must comply, too.

Precision is gained by planning the design of TIBs—the relation of users to information access. Organizations classify information by its importance, confidentiality, exclusivity, or monetary or strategic significance. They lay out exactly what users have access to each file and what they will allow users to do with it: transmit it out dial-up lines to their PCs at home, share only among top executives in its department, make tape copies at their workstations or in a monitored facility on a bar coded tape, and printing it.

You decide if you want logins only from Secure X Window terminals in a restricted access office or over public data networks where the identity of the caller is at best iffy, whether you want the secretarial staff to have access to the files of all top managers or just those of their bosses, etc.

To impose this organizational will on your systems, you decide these matters and label your information and your systems accordingly. (See Figure 9.3.)

You can visualize this access relationship of users and information as an information flow. If labels were altitude, you could draw a topographical map, except information never flows down. By the label laws, you can write to an equal label, but never to a lower one, because that would be disclosing information. All those on your hilltop can write to each other. The devices, services, and networks connect you to other hilltops at the same height.

You also get more visibility the higher you are. You can read information at a lower or equal label. Altitude doesn't grant an all-seeing eye. Much information is neither higher, equal, or lower than you, because its labels are incomparable, not subsets or supersets. So even at a high label, or altitude, you look down and only see information that you are higher than or equal to, not incomparable information.

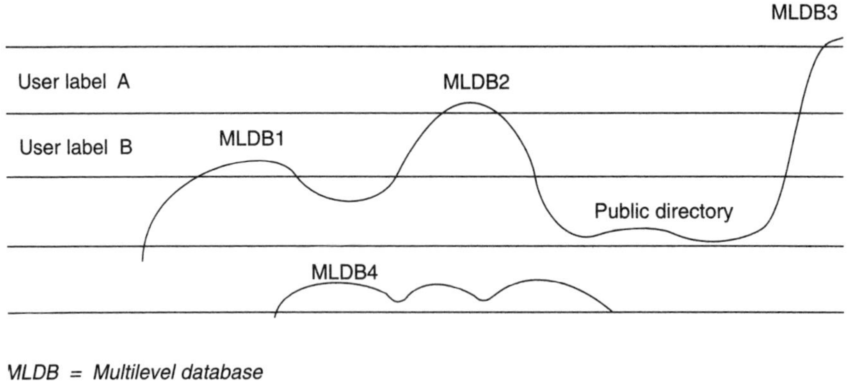

Figure 9.3 Label topography: User label determines systemwide access rights.

The effect of this is that, for example, if you list a directory with files that are higher or incomparable, you won't see it. It simply won't be there. You won't know you're not seeing it; there won't be a message about it.

The label firewall has many other manifestations. Whether they're trying to sell secrets or not, if users have access to important (high-labeled) information and they try to send it out the door, they will hit some walls. That information is labeled, and it's under the control of a system that has everything labeled—users, communications lines, output devices, etc.—and is always checking what user can do what operation on what device to what information. The user might even own the file, but he or she can't tamper with the label on it.

TIB design will determine what the access firewall is. A user with access to high-labeled information, say a client list, and with this high label in their label list probably can at least read the organization's information. They also might have access to many devices, including communications services, that might provide handy file transfer to your competitors.

The TIB labeling can be as protective of this file as you want, and I'll discuss a few scenarios. Communications services are open and publicly available, but only at lower labels. The wide-open public network also is the one that is far less under the scrutiny of the auditor and the alarming program. If this bad user can get the file out, he or she probably won't get caught until the clients have been looted.

However, this is a high-labeled file. The user can access it (if he or she has the right label and is allowed by the file's ACL) or might even own it. However, if the user attempts to send the file out to the low-labeled network, the system won't let them, whether he or she is the owner or not. The user can't change the label of the file to a lower label; that would allow it to be disclosed. Furthermore, if the user attempts either of the these actions, the resulting failure would be audited and picked up by the alarming software.

The reason that the user can't use the low-labeled network to pirate the file is that the system won't let a low-labeled device carry high-labeled data. That's a write down that is prohibited by the labels.

So this user's alternative is to use the communications services that will carry the high-labeled information. To communicate over high-labeled connections, there has to have been a highly extensive agreement among all of the organizations sharing the service to give anything carried on it the protection of exclusivity or monitoring that's appropriate to its label so that they become one TIB.

This would include factors such as which specific users have access to it, what the level of physical access to devices that carry it is, the responses required of alarms, whether it can be copied or printed, etc. This agreement would have to take place by conference among the parties who establish the network by mapping their labels to mutual interpretations or among distributed offices of the same organization with the same label system.

Therefore, crooked users are faced with a network that severely limits their capacity to escape with the high-labeled information. Competitors would never be connected by such a service. The connections that would be available to send the file would be to other organizations that have an appropriately high level of regard for the file's importance and protection requirements.

Only administrators can have the privileges needed to make tape copies of the file, because the label laws can prevent its output to devices that the user can access.

Lack of integrity

Pre-Secure UNIX lacked a persistent system infrastructure-verification facility. The underlying protections provided by the system software mustn't be subverted by malicious plants, accidents by administrators, or hardware problems.

Integrity in a TIB

In a TIB, integrity is checked on a continuous basis. It is handled by an administrator who reviews reports generated by integrity-checking programs.

Consistency checking A major element of the Confirmed Integrity Policy is the consistency alarm-detection program. Unlike audit alarm detection, it doesn't use input from the Secure UNIX audit facility. It is an independent alarm detector from the audit detector, although it might do some of the same checks. It displays its alarm information via an independent interface than that of audit and "reports to" an administrator other than the auditor. It can display some audit alarm information via an audit system interface.

The redundancy and the separateness is deliberate: each system cross-checks the other. If either goes down, the other detects it, and the system won't be without some assurance.

This program always is polling the state of the system and comparing it to its descriptions of what the normal state of the system is. By doing so, it will detect any inconsistency that somehow got by the entire TIB protection systems. The most likely such occurrence would be a mistake made by an administrator, but sometimes "mistakes" aren't so innocent.

Consistency detectors rely on comparison of the current system state to description data of it that it previously compiled. Whenever administrators change the state of the system, they must recompile the system-description data.

Finally, another check in the consistency program will do a basic examination of the system consistency with some basic principles of system ACL and labeling so that any egregious mistake that the administrator made while modifying the system will be detected.

There are five consistency checks that the program makes: security-attributes description, internal, processes, user, and system attribute policy.

The security-attributes check the existing security attributes of the system files against those of an attribute database that includes the ACL, labels, and privileges. Other data also is compiled and checked, such as CRCs and paths. The detector will be continually checking the system for the consistency of these values with those of the database.

Any inconsistencies evoke consistency alarms that are on the same urgency scale as audit alarms. However, they are reported to the security administrator, not the auditor. The auditor also would be notified by the consistency program generating audit events via the audit system.

Another check made by the consistency alarm detector program is an internal consistency check. It uses a list of objects and rules to check that processes are permitted, startup files have correct permissions and default ACL, that attributes conform to policy rules, and setuid privilege is allowed.

Process consistency might use programs that monitor processes called transaction-processing monitors. They use the UNIX batch facility to provide a JCL-type format. They would detect process events such as `exec` and `kill`.

Processes also will exchange credential information that includes integrity checks during system boot and for service sessions.

Administrative interface A major threat to integrity is administrative errors. A powerful, input-checking administrative interface is needed to prevent errors.

There no longer are administrative logins, such as adm or bin. Users will gain administrative privilege if they are entitled to through a special interface. The privilege will allow them to operate on the files owned by these users.

The special administrative interface is available only from the *trusted path*, which is so named because it guarantees that the user is executing the real system executable with its system file path name (thus the trusted path). The trusted path also is used to login, change user passwords, and perform other assorted functions.

When using it, users get a guarantee that, during login or a password change, they're entering their password with confidentiality to the authentic system processes, and not to a spoofing process (Trojan horse) that will steal their password.

When invoking the system administrator's interface with the trusted path, administrators are assured that they are getting the system executable for the administrative and not a fake executable that might inherit the administrative privileges that administrators are entitled to.

Other integrity factors are keeping up with known bugs or security faults by subscribing to the emergency-response services (such as CERT or commercial CERT services such as IBM's), assurances (such as secure distribution from vendors), current and thorough documentation, and hardware diagnostics.

Spoofing

A major threat in pre-Secure environments was spoofing. That was the use of a phony process, such as a server, that would intercept client requests to steal information or provide false information.

To prevent spoofing, Secure UNIX protocols provide mutual authentication between clients and servers.

Another spoof is a *replay*, where a transmission is captured and used to impersonate a user. Another is a man-in-the-middle attack where data is intercepted and forwarded, possibly after being altered.

Secure UNIX digital authentication deters these attacks by using timestamps and random values (nonces) as part of the protocols.

Lack of precise usage

Usage of system resources is necessary for system operation, and blocking its use can be used as attack on a system: a denial-of-service attack. TIBs define per-user limits on resource usage and monitor global resources for depletion. Resources include system memory, processes, file space, communications interfaces, servers, printers, etc.

Some systems provide mechanisms to set per-user or system limits on these resources. In any case, their use must be monitored, and responses (such as shutting down processes) must be made when overuse occurs.

Applications also must be alert to attempts flood them with junk data.

Lack of object reuse

"Junk" on a system is dangerous. Lost or deleted files contain information that a hacker might utilize. Recently, a criminal gang was busted that had created phony credit cards by looking through garbage dumps. Electronic gangs think just like their noncyber ones.

Secure UNIX provides an automatic facility that "scrubs" resources when they are deallocated. Object reuse is done in all circumstances, whether it's reallocating a system memory buffer among processes or reusing file space. In other words, when a Secure UNIX file is deleted, not only is its inode and file spaced reused, but it is cleared of user data by the system.

Feelings of vulnerability

Computer criminals sometimes have not been prosecuted by the victimized organization in order not to publicize that the organization's computer systems are insecure and vulnerable to fraud. Yet courts appreciate the seriousness of these crimes. Secure UNIX Audit trails will make superb legal evidence, especially if collected on write-once media such as a WORM disk drive.

The information established by networking protocols and analyzed by Secure UNIX makes identifying wrongdoers no longer the job of a Sherlock Holmes. A reputation for being tough on hackers now is a competitive advantage for organizations.

The Secure UNIX Organization

Secure UNIX provides the means for a level of computer security that is needed to meet modern demands. With it, and by applying organizational policies, you can survive in a hostile world by becoming The Secure UNIX Organization.

Index

A